ANIMAL MYTHS AND METAPHORS
IN SOUTH AMERICA

CONTRIBUTORS

GARY URTON
Colgate University

J. CHRISTOPHER CROCKER
University of Virginia

TERENCE TURNER
University of Chicago

GERARDO REICHEL-DOLMATOFF
University of California, Los Angeles

JOHANNES WILBERT
University of California, Los Angeles

R. TOM ZUIDEMA
University of Illinois, Urbana-Champaign

BILLIE JEAN ISBELL
Cornell University

ANIMAL MYTHS AND METAPHORS IN SOUTH AMERICA

Edited by

Gary Urton

University of Utah Press
Salt Lake City

Library of Congress Cataloging-in-Publication Data
Main entry under title:

Animal myths and metaphors in South America.

Bibliography: p.
Includes index.
1. Ethnology—South America—Addresses, essays,
lectures. 2. Totemism—South America—Addresses,
essays, lectures. 3. Indians of South America—
Addresses, essays, lectures. 4. Indians of South
America—Ethnozoology—Addresses, essays, lectures.
5. Animals—South America—Folklore—Addresses,
essays, lectures. I. Urton, Gary, 1946-
F2229.A57   1985   398.2 '45 '098   84-26345
ISBN 0-87480—205-9 (soft)

CONTENTS

ACKNOWLEDGMENTS

I would like, first and foremost, to express a debt of gratitude and appreciation I owe to Jill L. Furst, who early on was instrumental in helping to edit some of the studies assembled here. I also express my great appreciation to both Jill and Peter Furst for their support during the crucial, early stages of the publication history of this volume.

Billie Jean Isbell has been a constant adviser and friend throughout the preparation of this book. She was enormously patient in writing her conclusions for the articles, the composition and contents of which changed considerably over the three-year period that the anthology took shape.

I thank Julia Meyerson, my wife, for her advice and support and also for drawing the map. Staff members at the University of Utah Press were exceptionally helpful in bringing this volume to publication and showed, throughout my work and correspondence with them, a prodigious interest in and commitment to the subject of this volume. I also gratefully acknowledge the support of the Humanities Council of Colgate University for a grant for the preparation of this volume for publication.

GARY URTON

ANIMAL MYTHS AND METAPHORS
IN SOUTH AMERICA

1 – Warao
2 – Desana
3 – Bororo
4 – Kayapó
5 – Cuzco (Quechua)
6 – Pacariqtambo (Quechua)

Locations of the societies discussed in this volume.

Introduction

Gary Urton

The contributions to this volume address a set of issues that has been
of central importance to anthropology since the mid-nineteenth century. The issues, stated as broadly as possible, concern the following
kinds of questions: What similarities and differences do humans see
between themselves and animals? Why do people commonly make
metaphorical comparisons between human beings or social groups
and animals? And to what degree are people's attitudes and beliefs
about animals parallel to or contingent upon their attitudes and
beliefs about human beings and human society?

Questions of this nature have been asked of the ethnographic
record since Lewis Henry Morgan brought the matter to the attention of the social scientific community with his description of Iroquois social organization. Among the Iroquois a group of clans, each
going under the name of a particular animal, was found in association with matrilineal descent and clan and moiety exogamy. From
this example and others like it came McLennan's formula: totemism
is fetishism plus exogamy and matrilineal descent (cf. Turner, this
volume). Although it is not the purpose of this introduction to
rehearse the history of theories of totemism (which has been done
with admirable clarity and insight by Lévi-Strauss, 1967), it is
nonetheless important to raise the topic at the beginning because it is
my feeling that this volume addresses issues that are at the root of the
formal and comparative study of "totemism" and the general problem of human and animal relationships as they have been discussed
in the anthropological literature since the time of Morgan. By this I
mean to suggest that, from a comparative and historical perspective,

this volume, with its focus on South America, makes significant contributions not only to the areal study of ideologies of human and animal relationships but also to the theories informing those studies.

From a theoretical perspective, this work represents what might be termed a series of uncoordinated assaults, each laying siege in its own way to the notion that society and its formal divisions (e.g., clans and moieties) are the ultimate, if not the only, sources and objects of metaphorical comparisons between humans and animals. That is, while the articles here all focus to one degree or another on the categories and classifications of human society, in no case are animal metaphors taken to refer *primarily* to comparisons between animals and static social groups; rather, the metaphorical comparisons are predicated on conceived similarities and differences between animals and particular types of human beings living in these societies. For example: kites are like hunters/shamans (Wilbert); tapirs are like fathers-in-law and foreigners (Reichel-Dolmatoff); parrots are like men in a matrilineal society (Crocker); macaw fledglings are like adolescents (Turner); pumas are like fully initiated men (Zuidema); and foxes are like young married men (Urton). Only the Bororo, who uttered the now famous dictum, "We are red macaws!" (Crocker), seem to possess anything like a classically "totemic" system of naming clans after particular animals. Crocker is clearly hesitant to label the Bororo system totemic; he concludes instead that at least in the case of the red macaw statement men are expressing the irony of the masculine condition in a matrilineal society: the condition of being like "pets."

The importance of the shift in focus of human-animal metaphors from the categories of social organization to the various types of human beings in society that are produced by specialization and life-cycle transformations cannot be overemphasized; the shift allows us to adopt a fundamentally different and more dynamic perspective on the problem. As long as social groups and their interrelations are considered to be the primary motivation in human-animal metaphors, the metaphors will ultimately be intelligible only in relation to the patterns of interaction which obtain at formal levels of organization, such as systems of alliance, descent, residence, and so on; that is, they will concern the formal, idealized institutions, structures, and practices by which society as a whole reproduces and validates itself within the public domain. The question then becomes: how does this relate to the formation of human social identity and the human (individual) construction of metaphors? One suggestion from the studies in this volume is that it is perhaps more relevant to look to the formations and transformations of people living in society for the initial motivation of metaphors, rather than at the static categories of social classification. If we adopt this perspective, a different but related set of concerns emerges in the strategies and motivations of metaphor making, concerns such as birth, death, life-cycle changes, and the dynamic formation of relations within the household and the community.

To give an example of how a shift of emphasis of the kind described above can produce a significantly different analytic focus in the study of human-animal relations, we can consider briefly the case of the Iroquois. In the traditional system of interclan and inter-moiety relations, the members of the four matrilineal clans of each moiety referred to each other as "brother" and "sister"; between the moieties, the clans were considered to be related as "cousins" (MBc, FZc). In the traditional system of marriage, the rule of exogamy applied both at the level of the moiety and the clan, although in Morgan's time the rule had been relaxed to apply only to the clan (Morgan 1975, 79–83). If we then add to this system the information that each clan went by the name of a different animal or bird and if we address the question of what this system of nomenclature indicates about Iroquois notions of the relationship between humans and animals, we have available two apparent but not mutually exclusive social "complexes" from which to begin the analysis: one centers on clanship, moiety interactions, and ideal patterns of alliance and descent; the other centers on social processes such as the constitutive and transformational nature of siblingship and the structure and dynamics of the formation of the nuclear and extended family. It is clear from a reading of the history of theories of totemism that the complex of formal social structures and relationships has most often been the analytic focus for these studies. Only within relatively recent times has the other complex of principles and processes been emphasized in studies of human-animal comparisons (e.g., Beidelman 1975; Bulmer 1967; Douglas 1975; Sapir 1977a, 1977b; Tambiah 1969; and Willis 1974). This volume makes a significant contribution to the second type of analysis.

To clarify further the potential importance of the second type of analysis, I want to discuss a rather remarkable change of emphasis that has taken place in studies of human-animal relations as they are evoked in metaphors and myths. In order to set the issue in its most relevant context, I will turn briefly to Lévi-Strauss's study of totemism (1967). One might say that, but for the last chapter (which I will discuss in a moment), the "drama" of *Totemism* builds to and culminates in what Lévi-Strauss refers to as Radcliffe-Brown's second theory of totemism (Lévi-Strauss 1967, 82–83). The wrinkle in Radcliffe-Brown's second theory was to ask the question of Australian (totemic) moiety systems: why are the moieties associated with *particular* species of birds or animals? This question prompted Radcliffe-Brown to study the behavior of certain species of birds and to note similarities and differences in the relations between pairs of birds that might be like the similarities and differences between the moieties that went under the names of these particular birds. This new perspective, focusing on the behavioral characteristics of "real" birds in nature, allowed the problem of totemism to be resolved in native beliefs in homologies between two systems of differences, one in nature (birds), the other in culture (moieties) (Lévi-Strauss 1963, 4–5; 1967, 86–89).

What is most remarkable about this pair of episodes (Radcliffe-Brown's second theory and Lévi-Strauss's discussion of it) is that the recognition of the significance to totemic studies of the question "Why these particular species of birds?" was not followed by the question "Why these particular 'species' of human beings?" That is, in one example, Radcliffe-Brown showed that two moieties went by the names of Eaglehawk and Crow and that in mythology, Eaglehawk was often portrayed as the uncle (MB) of Crow. Therefore, when the problem of this particular totemic system was partially resolved by noting the importance of species similarities and differences between this pair of birds, the implications might have been not only that the groups of people (moieties) are similar and different as the pair of birds is similar and different but also that this gives us a clue as to how the Australians think about related but different classes of human beings (i.e., uncles and nephews). The latter conclusion gives access to questions of maturation and the dynamics of the extended family, while the former resolves itself on the formal level of the dual organization of the moiety system. The two domains (family and moiety) are *not* dissimilar or unrelated; they simply give access to indigenous notions at different levels (social

persons and social groups) of what constitutes a species and of how
different species are related to each other.

The importance of totemic classifications in providing a perspective on the ideology of social persons (or actors and agents, in modern parlance) did not go unrecognized by Lévi-Strauss, for this is the
theme of the concluding chapter of *Totemism*. Citing Rousseau, Lévi-
Strauss points out that

> it is because man originally felt himself identical to all those like him
> (among which, as Rousseau explicitly says, we must include animals)
> that he came to acquire the capacity to distinguish *himself* as he
> distinguishes *them*, i.e., to use the diversity of species as conceptual sup-
> port for social differentiation. (Lévi-Strauss 1967, 101)

In concluding, Lévi-Strauss suggests that

> there is nothing archaic or remote about it [totemism]. Its image is pro-
> jected, not received; it does not derive its substance from without. If the
> illusion contains a particle of truth, this is not outside us but within us.
> (Lévi-Strauss 1967, 104)

This theme is echoed throughout the studies presented here,
where, for instance, from the point of view of one tribe, the people of
other tribes are considered to be *like* animals; as phrased in the image
of the Tapir, "other" people are also seen to be like fathers-in-law
(Reichel-Dolmatoff). In the case of the Kayapó, a young boy's
change of residence from the natal household to the men's house,
which takes place under the aegis of a "substitute" father, is seen, in
the myth studied by Turner, to be like both the consumption of
fledgling macaws (who are "adolescent" birds) by a jaguar and the
jaguar's subsequent adoption of a young boy who was in the nest
with the fledgling macaws. One characteristic that makes the comparison between the fledgling macaws and the boy appropriate is that
they are at similar stages in their life cycles (Turner). The life cycle,
as expressed often in rituals and myths associated with initiation,
provides one of the unifying themes of the articles collected here
(Wilbert, Turner, Zuidema, and Urton). The importance of this
theme is to provide the work with a focus on the processes (e.g., the
life cycle) and institutions (e.g., initiation) that are commonly
associated with the maturation and, therefore, the diversification of
individuals in society. This and other topics are discussed by Isbell in
the concluding chapter.

Another major contribution of this volume is its focus on South

America, one of the final remaining bastions of wildlife—although even the short-term survival of the rich flora and fauna of the continent is very much in doubt. In the literature on human-animal relationships, there have been many important contributions by scholars working in different areas and within different theoretical and disciplinary perspectives in South America (e.g., Cadogan 1973; Lathrap 1977; Reichel-Dolmatoff 1975, 1978; Roe 1983; Roth 1908–1909; Seeger 1981; and Tastevin 1925). However, without any doubt, the body of work that has generated the most interest and controversy within the discipline of anthropology is Lévi-Strauss's four-volume study, *Introduction to a Science of Mythology* (1969, 1974, 1979, 1981). Lévi-Strauss's study of the mythological systems of the Tropical Forest Indians is perhaps the single most important modern document in the comparative study of South American Indians. In the "poststructuralist" fervor of the present day, it is perhaps all too easy to forget that regardless of the legitimate questions concerning structuralist methodology and theory that were brought more sharply into focus by *Introduction to a Science of Mythology*, the volumes, nonetheless, have made at least two lasting, monumental contributions to American Indian studies: first, the collection, into a single set of volumes, of over 800 myths, the majority of which are from South America; and second, Lévi-Strauss has firmly placed animals in the foreground of American Indian studies. The articles presented here expand these topics toward a deeper investigation of animal myths and metaphors within particular South American societies.

A remarkable, although perhaps not altogether unexpected, feature of this volume is that certain animals appear and reappear in the various studies until, by the end, the volume fairly resonates with animal images and dialogue. The lumbering father-in-law tapir of southeastern Colombia helps steal the fire of the jaguar in Kayapó territory; the fledgling macaws of the Kayapó grow up to become adult pets among the Bororo; the powerful, transforming jaguar of the Kayapó becomes the savage, jungle "outsider" to the Incas, who had their own feline, the puma; and finally, the puma and fox of Inca mythology and ritual reappear in a modern-day Andean community as, respectively, the grandfather and father of a newly born baby.

It should be mentioned here that Zuidema's article, with its use of ethnohistorical rather than modern ethnographic data, is an especially important contribution to this volume because it provides links among the others in two dimensions. On the one hand, it provides horizontal connections between the highland and lowland areas, especially with regard to feline metaphors used to characterize—and therefore to distinguish between—peoples living within the two regions. On the other hand, Zuidema also provides a vertical, historical perspective on the study of human-animal metaphors in South America. This is critical in terms of assessing specific forms of continuity and change in symbolic systems and metaphoric processes within the Andes, as well as in establishing a comparative and historical perspective on the myth, ritual, and social organization of those complex lowland societies for which we have generally fewer and less detailed ethnohistorical sources.

The principal themes of this volume, then, are contained within two similar "environments" that characterize the social and physical settings of the groups discussed within the various articles. One environment is characterized by the universal processes of human transformations brought about by the life cycle in combination with constitutive social practices leading to ordered living in groups. The second major environment is provided by the fauna of the South American continent. As we find repeated in virtually all of the articles here, people are intensely interested in the animals that live around them, and along with that interest and fascination comes the desire to make these other living things participants in what humans are doing; this is accomplished through the dynamic of metaphoric processes—as Isbell points out in the conclusions—in which the social relations and transformations that are central to the reproduction of society are "found," through asserted similarities to animals, to be, in the end, wholly natural relations and transformations.

Finally, it is of more than passing interest to note that the human-animal metaphors discussed in this volume refer overwhelmingly to asserted similarities between *men* and animals. Although the male focus is apparent throughout the volume, we do not gain a clear understanding from any of the articles of why this should be so (Crocker is most explicit on this point: men in a matrilineal society are like pets); neither, with the exception of the article by Reichel-Dolmatoff, are there suggestions that the societies in question maintain equally rich traditions of female-animal metaphors. Perhaps the male focus is partially a product of the fact that the ethnographic materials in the volume were for the most part collected by male anthropologists or, in the case of the ethnohistorical article by Zuidema, by male administrators and chroniclers. On the other hand, the emphasis on men in the human-animal metaphors in this volume may reflect a common characteristic of men themselves, which is that ambiguities of identity, such as the role of men in matrilineal societies or the inability to reproduce, call for these naturalizing embellishments of the human male.

REFERENCES

Beidelman, T. O.
    1975   Ambiguous animals: Two theriomorphic metaphors in Kaguru folklore. *Africa* 45(2):183-200.

Bulmer, Ralph
    1967   Why is the cassowary not a bird? A problem of zoological taxonomy among the Karam of the New Guinea highlands. *Man* (n.s.) 2:5-25.

Cadogan, Leon
    1973   Some plants and animals in Guaraní and Guayakí mythology. In *Paraguay: Ecological essays*, ed. J. R. Gorham, 97-104. Miami: Academy of the Arts and Sciences of the Americas.

Douglas, Mary
    1975   *Implicit meanings: A cross-cultural approach to body symbolism.* London and Boston: Routledge and Kegan Paul.

Lathrap, D. W.
    1977   Gifts of the cayman: Some thoughts on the subsistence basis of Chavin. In *Pre-Columbian art history*, ed. A. Cordy-Collins and J. Stern, 333-52. Palo Alto: Peek Publications.

Lévi-Strauss, Claude
    1963   The bear and the barber. *Man* 93:1-11.
    1967   *Totemism* (1962). Boston: Beacon Press.
    1969   *The raw and the cooked* (1964). New York: Harper and Row.
    1974   *From honey to ashes* (1966). New York: Harper and Row.
    1979   *The origin of table manners* (1968). New York: Harper and Row.
    1981   *The naked man* (1971). New York: Harper and Row.

Morgan, Lewis H.
    1975   *League of the Iroquois* (1851). Secaucus, N.J.: Citadel Press.

Murphy, Yolanda, and Robert F. Murphy
    1974   *Women of the forest.* New York: Columbia University Press.

Reichel-Dolmatoff, Gerardo
    1975   *The shaman and the jaguar: A study of narcotic drugs among the Indians of Colombia.* Philadelphia: Temple University Press.
    1978   Desana animal categories, food restrictions, and the concept of color energies. *Journal of Latin American Lore* 4(2):243-91.

Roe, Peter
    1982   *The cosmic zygote: Cosmology in the Amazon Basin.* New Brunswick: Rutgers University Press.

Roth, Walter E.
    1908–   An inquiry into the animism and folklore of the Guiana Indians. In
    1909   *The Thirtieth Annual Report of the Bureau of American Ethnology,* 103–387. Washington, D.C.: United States Government Printing Office.

Sapir, J. David
    1977a   Fecal animals: An example of complementary totemism. *Man* (n.s.) 12(1):1–21.

    1977b   The fabricated child. In *The social use of metaphor,* ed. J. D. Sapir and J. C. Crocker, 193–223. Philadelphia: University of Pennsylvania Press.

Seeger, Anthony
    1981   *Nature and society in central Brazil.* Cambridge: Harvard University Press.

Tambiah, S. J.
    1969   Animals are good to think and good to prohibit. *Ethnology* 8:423–59.

Tastevin, P. C.
    1925   La légende de Bóyusú en Amazonie. *Revue d'Ethnographie et des Traditions Populaires* 6:172–206.

Willis, Roy
    1974   *Man and beast.* New York: Basic Books, Inc.

My Brother the Parrot

J. Christopher Crocker

This essay* investigates the social nature of cosmological metaphor through an extended discussion of a single ethnographic case. The problem, which has been the subject of academic debate for over sixty years, is just what the Bororo of Central Brazil mean when they say, "We are red macaws." I intend to discuss first the classic analysis offered by Levy-Bruhl when he originally brought the issue to general attention, and then to argue that the aphorism is not so much an example of "totemic participation" implying identity, but rather must be interpreted as a metaphor of similarity. To substantiate this view, it will be necessary to explore various Bororo concepts and practices concerning macaws, as well as their several definitions of "we." My conclusion shall be that neither a totemic framework nor one reflecting metaphysical beliefs nor yet one based on Bororo taxonomic classificatory principles is sufficient grounds for understanding the postulated identity between a certain animal species and human kind. Rather, it is an example of paradigmatic association in terms of the structural equivalence of men and macaws in several distinct relational contexts. Its meaning and logical character cannot be understood without an appreciation of the particular social situation in which it is utilized, as a strategy for expressing the ambiguous character of the actors in that context. Through this analysis

---

*This article has profited from the analytical systems of T. O. Beidelman, James Fernandez, and Claude Lévi-Strauss. For their careful editing and many valuable insights I wish to thank David Sapir, Marc Schloss, Peter Stone, and Joseph R. Crocker, Jr. Reprinted by permission, J. David Sapir and J. Christopher Crocker, eds., *The Social Use of Metaphor*, University of Pennsylvania Press, 1977, 164–92.

I also hope to show that an understanding of the distinguishing characters of various tropes in figurative language is essential to any analysis of a society's cosmological system.

In his first work addressed to the nature of mystical participation (*Les fonctions mentales dans les sociétés inférieures*, 1910), Levy-Bruhl utilizes a Bororo datum to document some of his most crucial points about the characteristics of this phenomenon. While the importance of a single illustrative example to his total argument should not be overemphasized, its early and recurrent appearance in that book raises it above the level of the casual, anecdotal aside. Further, the apparent lack of ambiguity in the statement, as Levy-Bruhl reports it, is likely to impress even the sophisticated reader (Van der Leeuw 1928, 8; Lowie 1937, 218; Percy 1961; Vygotsky 1962, 71–72; Geertz 1966, 37–38). He took this and other Bororo material from Steinen, whose work on the Indians of Central Brazil had appeared in 1894.[1] The critical passages in Levy-Bruhl are the following:

> "The Bororo . . . boast that they are red araras (parakeets)." This does not merely signify that after their death they become araras, nor that araras are metamorphosed Bororos, and must be treated as such. It is something entirely different. "The Bororos," says Von den Steinen, whose affirmations, "give one rigidly to understand that they are araras *at the present time*, just as if a catepillar declared itself to be a butterfly." It is not a name they give themselves, nor a relationship [parenté] that they claim. What they desire to express by it is actual identity. That they can be both the human beings they are and the birds of scarlet plumage at the same time, Von den Steinen regards as inconceivable, but to the mentality that is governed by the law of participation there is no difficulty in the matter. All communities which are totemic in form admit of collective representations of this kind, implying similar identity of the individual members of a totemic group and their totem. (1966, 62)

> Primitive mentality sees no difficulty in the belief that such life and properties exist in the original and in its reproduction at one and the same time. By virtue of the mystic bond between them a bond represented by the law of participation, the reproduction *is* the original, as the Bororo *are* the araras. (1966, 64)

> [He goes on to specify that this bond is above all a totemic one]. The very existence of the social groups . . . is most frequently represented . . . as a participation, a communion, or rather a number of participations and communions. . . . The collective representation in this case is exactly like that which so astonished Von den Steinen when the Bororos "rigidly" maintained that they were araras. . . . Every individual is

both such and such a man or woman, alive at present, a certain ancestral individual, who may be human or semi-human . . . and at the same time he *is* his totem, that is, he partakes in some mystic fashion of the essence of the animal or vegetable species whose name he bears. (1966, 75)

It is worth examining these statements, and other aspects of Levy-Bruhl's argument, in some detail.[2] He quite explicitly raises some of the most vexing issues in the analysis of figurative language and belief systems, and the various interpretations which he rejects form the ethnographic substance of this essay. First, Levy-Bruhl says that the Bororo claim to be macaws does not reflect any belief in particular transformations of the individual soul. Actually, this was the conclusion Steinen reached, in spite of the ultimate acceptance of the "literal" truth of the native's own position with which Levy-Bruhl credits him. Steinen finally decides that the declaration "We are macaws" is to be understood, neither as reflecting the supposed metamorphoses of the soul after death, nor as deriving from totemic aspects of the clan system, but strictly in reference to the physical appearance of the soul when it leaves the body at any time (Steinen 1894, 512–13). He reports that the Bororo believe the soul assumes the form of a bird, usually a red macaw, when it departs the corporeal self, regardless of whether this occurs during dreams or at death (1894, 510–11). Steinen's own evidence on this point is internally contradictory, and I found no confirmation of such a belief during fieldwork seventy years after his. But Levy-Bruhl rejects it out of hand in favor of his dominant totemic emphasis.

Just what was Levy-Bruhl after here? It should be made clear that the Bororo do indeed compare themselves to macaws, although only in certain social contexts that shall be described below. While there are some problems with Steinen's description of the native exegesis, in comparison to the ones I obtained, the basic facts are as he reported them. Given that Levy-Bruhl had apprehended a true ethnographic problem, what significance does his interpretation have for the general topic of this volume, and for the recent work on animal symbolism (Firth 1966; Leach 1964; Tambiah 1969; Bulmer 1967; Douglas 1972)? More particularly, what are we to make out of his contention that the Bororo statement, and others like it, reflects the "actual identity" between clansmen and their totems which is the logical essence of any totemic system, in view of Lévi-Strauss's analysis of such systems in terms of symbolic, figurative meanings

(1963a)? For Levy-Bruhl makes it very clear that in his view the Indians mean literally what they say. He explicitly denounces the view that a Bororo = macaw equation might be a label or emblem, a "name." This we would now understand as a case of synecdoche, a part-whole relationship. No more, he says, is a historical relationship of descent from some original macaw involved; in our terms, such an association would be an instance of metonymy, in that cause (ancestor) would stand for effect (descendents). Likewise, Levy-Bruhl denies Steinen's synecdochic interpretation that the soul (part) appears as a macaw when it leaves the body (whole). The "law of mystical participation" does not rest either on syntagmatic contiguity or on paradigmatic association, for both imply a logical distinction of some type between the conjoined entities. Levy-Bruhl claims that totemic systems make no distinctions of any type between clan members and their totems; consequently such analytical niceties as symbols and tropes are simply irrelevant to the understanding of these systems.

In sharp contrast, Lévi-Strauss's conception of totemism emphasizes the conceptual separateness of the animal-human domains. Comparisons between these domains can therefore only be metaphorical in logical nature. Metaphor, by definition, involves intuitive leaps which connect aspects of two distinct semantic realms. But metaphor can occur only where these realms overlap in some fashion. "The metaphor in a word lives when the word brings to mind more than a single reference and the several references are seen to have something in common . . . the name of one subordinate is extended to the other and this, as we shall see, has the effect of calling both references to mind with their differences as well as their similarities" (Brown 1958, 140). This feature—the way metaphor establishes connotative similarities through a recognition of denotative contrast—is crucial to Lévi-Strauss's approach. But if "a metaphor is a device of representation by which a new *meaning* is learned" (Van Steenburgh 1965, 678), Levy-Bruhl would argue that, as Bororo dogma, "we are parrots" is a self-evident truth and far from anything "new"; as readers will attest, Lévi-Strauss's treatment of such dictums involves novel revelations indeed.

Clearly the issue cannot be resolved on a priori grounds and must rest on a complete ethnographic account of the logical connections between man and animal, culture and nature, perceived by the society. It is necessary to examine all the various connotations and denotations of the Bororo senses of "man" and "macaw" to determine which of the meanings are actually operative in the statement "we are macaws." For other situations are theoretically possible here beyond the two envisaged by Lévi-Strauss and Levy-Bruhl. We might discover that red macaws and the Bororo are characterized by the same set of criterial dimensions, that the two species are identified as one or another aspect of a single whole (e.g., the clan or some "universal spiritual substance"). As long as some kind of indigenous distinction is made between such aspects, such that a macaw totem might represent the clan but is as partial an expression of that whole as any single member, then synecdoche rather than "mystical participation" would be operative.

Indeed, there are general difficulties with Lévi-Strauss's absolute division between the natural and cultural realms. As Tambiah points out, his categorical rejection of the Radcliffe-Brownian notion that rules of ethical conduct toward animals reflect man's sense of affinity and even identity with them renders his answer to the problem of why societies have a "ritual attitude" toward animals much less than satisfactory (Tambiah 1969, 453–54). Lévi-Strauss stresses that such normative considerations as dietary regulations, sacrifices, and clan names demonstrate that the totemic system is much more than a linguistic code, and is far from being an abstract metaphorical series having the most distant intellectual relation with the concerns of daily life. But his analyses beg the issue of why this should be so (1963a, 15–32).[3] I contend that certain Bororo ritual attitudes toward macaws involve synecdoche, in that various attributes of macaws are considered aspects of clanship, and vice versa; other Bororo comparisons between men and macaws will be held to rest on more purely syntagmatic contiguities, and reflect metynomy. In these totemic and cosmological terms per se, the conclusion must be that Levy-Bruhl is more correct than Lévi-Strauss even though the former's argument rests on a faulty premise. But I also argue that neither the totemic nor the related cosmological realms of discourse are at all relevant to the case in question, which instead deals with the problem of man's nature rather than the clan's culture.

THE CASE FOR TOTEMS: CLANS AND SPECIES

The contemporary villages of the Eastern Bororo[4] are scattered along the São Lourenço River and its tributaries in north central Mato Grosso, Brazil, to the east and southeast of Cuiaba. The

language may be distantly related to Ĝe (Kietzman 1967, 34), and
certainly the Bororo manifest such Ĝe characteristics as a hunting-
gathering ecology, dyadic social structure,[5] uxorilocal residence, and
great complexity of ritual and cosmology. Although the society has
suffered severe population loss in recent years and been intensively
exposed to Brazilian influences, certain communities manage to
preserve much of their traditional organization and ceremonial practices.[6] Normatively, all Bororo villages are divided into exogamous
moieties in which postmarital residence tends to be uxorilocal. Each
moiety is composed of four clans, and membership in these corporate
groups derives from possession of personal names taken from a stock
of such names owned by the mother's social unit. Each clan is divided into two "sub-clans"[7] which are in turn differentiated into
three to six matrilineages each.

Although the characteristics of these last units are somewhat ambiguous, even in the orthodox Bororo view, they are here assumed to
be the locus of rights over the usage and disposal of a variety of
cultural "goods," or scarce values. These include the personal
names mentioned above, without which a person is not a member of
Bororo society; various decorative styles used for utilitarian objects
(baskets, pots, clubs, sleeping mats, and so forth) and for ceremonial
objects (ornamental bows, headdresses, rattles, armbands, musical
instruments, necklaces, and somatic paintings); and specific ceremonies which purport to represent various species of animals, fish,
birds, and marvelous spirits. These last are part of an extensive
though supposedly fixed set of natural and supernatural entities intimately associated with the clan.

I frankly hesitate to label these entities "totems." Although their
relationship to the corporate group is characterized by many elements which an earlier generation of ethnographers would have
deemed properly totemic, Lévi-Strauss (1963a) has thoroughly
demonstrated the logical and empirical fallacies of their criteria. He
himself, I think, would label the Bororo case "totemic" since it
seems to reflect that postulation of a homology between two systems
of differences, the one natural and the other cultural, that he has
cited as basic to "totemism" (Lévi-Strauss 1963a; 1966, 152,
153–55). It is true, for example, that in certain contexts, the entities
associated with the clans serve to differentiate them and appear to be
utilized as a metaphorical code for human relationships. Yet thus far

I have not been able to demonstrate to my own satisfaction any consistent, systematic, logical homology between the systems that must, in Lévi-Strauss's theory, exist in any totemic system. Further, as the next section of this chapter will describe, certain aspects of the clan members' relationship with their totems have a logical and social character that can hardly be described as purely metaphorical. For the sake of convenience, and until a separate publication can examine the problem in detail, I shall provisionally refer to the species linked to each Bororo clan as its totem, and let the reader draw his own conclusions as to the appropriateness of Lévi-Strauss's definition of the term for this case.

It might be mentioned here that all modern Bororo communities generally agree on the details of the "totemic" system, including which of the more than three hundred entities is associated with what clan; such consensus also obtains for nearly all of the other distinctive rights of each social unit. That is, the Bororo share the same complex and systematic structural, ritual, and cosmological systems wherever they are found. This is perhaps all the more remarkable since the Bororo have apparently never had a supra-village political organization. While maintaining a strong sense of its tribal identity, the community is the largest autonomous unit. This is relevant to the present issue because, for the Bororo, dogmas such as "we are macaws" are something more than local poetic intuitions; they are political manifestoes of the cosmological implications of tribal membership.

Now, as to Levy-Bruhl's hypothesis: is it the case that the man = macaw equation derives from the totemic system? The matter is very complex, and involves Bororo conceptions of the totemic entities themselves, of the relation between them and the clan, and of the connection between individuals and totems in various contexts. The Bororo say that all totems are *aroe*, which I translate as "spirit." This category is also applied to a number of other mystical beings and conditions, and the logical connections between the synonymous types of *aroe* are crucial to a comprehension of the principles linking Bororo cosmology with their social organization. One of the most important referents of *aroe* is to the immortal, incorporeal, and individuated spirit possessed by all creatures, especially man. It is this personal spirit which leaves the body at night during dreams and which departs permanently at death. Consistently *aroe* is also applied to the collectivity of souls of deceased Bororo, that is, to the ancestors. These spirits are thought to follow traditional Bororo customs in an afterlife very much like that of the living, although with certain differences, some of which, by no means coincidentally, involve parrots and other birds. The ancestors are irrelevant to nearly all daily concerns of modern Bororo, and with some exceptions, ritual does not involve them to any notable extent. Informants often give the Portuguese *alma* ("soul") as a gloss for *aroe* used in reference to individual spirit or to the ancestors.

Another use of the term *aroe* initially seems quite distinct from this first set of meanings. The Bororo speak of a class of spiritual being in a manner that appears to express a concept of an animated form unique to certain natural species, somewhat in the manner of a Platonic ideal. Thus they refer to *Bokodori Aroe*, "Armadillo Spirit"; *Adugo Aroe*, "Jaguar Spirit"; and *Nabure Aroe*, "Red Macaw Spirit." Each of these is said to consist of a single male and female which have the general form and attributes of the species, but with transcendental differences. They are described as much larger than normal, with odd bands of color, unique growths around the head, and other unusual morphological features which make them at once very beautiful and "awful," in the archaic sense. Normally these *aroe* forms dwell in the other world inhabited by the souls of the ancestors, but they sometimes venture into this life where they may be seen by mortals, usually with dire results.

It is this pure being rather than the species itself which the Bororo say are associated with the clans in that variety of manners I have characterized as "totemic." The relation is cosmological. Thus, just as each clan occupies a specific segment of the compass in the east-west oriented village, so too in the other world the *aroe* totems of each clan are said to live together in the corresponding region. The Bokodori Exerae clan is localized, for example, in the northeast segment of the village. The *aroe* totems of that clan, including Bokodori Aroe, live in the homologous geographical area in the world of the dead. In the Bororo view, all living beings, things, and space itself are ordered through the same eightfold division.

Now, particular members of the species and the clan itself stand to the spirit version much as, in Platonic philosophy, a given chair stands to the Ideal Chair. In this sense the spirit form can be said to be at once the very essence of the species, its ideal form and the emblem of the clan's uniqueness and perpetuity. Moreover, all the clan's property—ceremonial artifacts, decorative styles for utilitarian objects, songs, and ceremonial representations—stand in the same logical relationship to the totemic spirit as members of the species do. Six of the eight Bororo clans are eponymous in being called after one of their totemic *aroe*, and the stock of personal names from which an individual's title is taken again derives from the same source. Therefore the totem *Bokodori Aroe*, Armadillo Spirit, can be expressed through the proper name *Bokodori Paradu* ("the armadillo which balances"), a somatic painting consisting of red and black patterns, by a bow with such markings, by a ceremonial rattle decorated in the same way, by a necklace made from its claws, and by the total ensemble of these aspects of the Bokodori Exerae clan as well as by individual armadillos of the species *Priodontes giganteus*. But I believe the point made by Evans-Pritchard concerning the nature of Nuer totems (1956, 77–79) also applies here. The Armadillo Spirit itself transcends these concrete reflections of its being, which are only the modes through which man apprehends its reality.

THE CASE FOR TOTEMS: RELATIONSHIPS

The Bororo characterize their individual and corporate relationship to the *aroe* totems of their own clan by calling them "*aroe i-edaga, aroe i-maruga*," relationship terms which are otherwise applied respectively to senior men of the clan (e.g., the mother's brother) and to senior women of the father's clan. This usage does not reflect any belief in the derivation of the individual soul from maternal and/or paternal sources, but is instead a very literal consequence of contemporary ritual practice. Bororo infants are given names by a senior matrilineally related male, preferably the mother's uterine brother or *i-edaga*, and by the woman who assisted the mother at birth, whom the child terms *i-maruga* regardless of whatever genealogical bond might exist between them.[8] As mentioned above, it is this naming which endows the child with corporate membership and with all the rights and obligations encumbent upon it. It should be stressed that all the clan's *aroe* totems, from twenty to fifty of them, are *i-edaga* and *i-maruga* to the clan member, not just the one from which his or her personal name is taken. Now the clan property, also derived from the totems, is usually given to persons and segments of other groups through a complex system of ritual presentations which symbolize all facets of intergroup transactions. The *aroe* totems thus provide the material content as well as the categorical form of all interclan relationships, and are not without their relevance to behavior within the clan. In providing names they are the ground of every Bororo's social personality, and through their refractions in property and ritual permit him to express vital elements of that social being.

But the closeness of this relation to the totems should not be exaggerated. The Bororo do not believe themselves to be even mystical descendents of their clan *aroe* totems, nor do they claim that what happens to the species they represent has any impact on them. With one or two exceptions, there are no normative injunctions to particular behavior with respect to any species qua totem; members of the Bokodori Exerae ("the Armadillos") kill and eat armadillos with as much relish as any other Bororo. Does any of this material demonstrate Levy-Bruhl's contention that clan members mystically identify with their totemic *aroe*? The situation with macaws may be utilized to resolve this issue.

The Bororo distinguish three kinds of macaw, contrasting them on the explicit basis of color and habitat: *xibae* ("blue" macaw, *araracanga* or *Ara cholroptera*); *kuido* (yellow-breasted macaw, *arara* or *Psittace caerulea*); and *nabure* (red-breasted macaw, *ararapiranga* or *Psittace cholroptera*). They claim that *kuido* inhabit gallery forests while *nabure* and *xibae* nest only in the cliffs and rock pillars found along the upper São Lourenço. The *kuido* is one of the totemic *aroe* of the Paiwoe clan, while the *nabure* is associated with the Arore clan and the *xibae* with the Bokodori Exerae (the last in a less systematic way than the first two). Thus an Aroredu can and does refer to a particular *nabure* as *i-edaga aroe* and it is possible, although I have never heard such a usage, that he might say to an outsider, "I am a *nabure*," or "*ipie*" (otter) or "*bakorororeu*" (coral snake), or similarly identify himself with any of the other totemic *aroe* of the Arore clan. The sense of any such utterance might be phrased as "I, my mother's brother, my sister's sons, and all other members of the Arore clan share a unique cosmological and social status which is reflected in the uniqueness of the *nabure*'s pure form" (or otter's or coral snake's). The Paiwoe, of course, stand in an analogous manner to the *kuido*, and members of the two clans are thus potentially able to express various nuances of their clan's relationship through a

"parrot code." Lévi-Strauss would phrase this as Paiwoe:Arore::
kuido aroe:nabure aroe. But the aptness of this formula does not in itself
demonstrate that the parrot-clan connection is necessarily a metaphorical one. Surely the analogy rich:poor::satin:rags rests on
synecdoche, on contiguity. Some kind of contiguous part-whole relation between man and totem, or even Levy-Bruhl's postulation of
"total identity" could underlie the Bororo case just as well as Lévi-
Strauss's insistence on semantically equivalent paradigmatic resemblance. It is necessary to examine another aspect of the relation between *aroe* totem and Bororo clan to arrive at a conclusion as to
whether this relation is one of metaphor, metonymy, synecdoche, or
mystical participation.

One of the most esteemed components of the clan's jural
character is its rights over the symbolic representations of certain of
the clan's totemic spirits. The representations themselves involve
body paintings, ornaments, dance steps, and songs through which
aspects of the spirit entity, the "Ideal Form" of Jaguar, Armadillo,
or whatever, can be embodied by men. By far the greatest part of
Bororo collective ritual involves the performance of such representations. The members of the clan owning the costumes and other
paraphernalia seldom perform as representatives of their *aroe.* Instead, they apply the appropriate paintings and ornaments to the
personnel of specified lineages or clans in the other moiety. These
persons then dance and otherwise perform as the *aroe* entity, while
the actual owners watch and sing. Thus, one of the representations of
the Arore clan is that of "Nabure Aroe." Two members of the Kie
clan are selected to perform this representation of red macaw
"essence." The Arore clansmen decorate them with a certain facial
painting, coat their bodies with red juice from the urucu bush, and
provide them with specific types of headdresses, armbands, and
other ornaments owned by the Arore clan, all of which are made
with feathers from all three types of macaws. The two Kie then imitate the movements of macaws in a short dance.

Performing as *aroe* representatives is regarded as conferring great
honor on the performers.[9] The paintings, ornaments, and the act of
representation are indeed considered a gift from the owning clan to
the performing clan. As with all prestations of scarce values, it entails
considerable obligations on the latter group, and the owners of the
representations must be compensated with various ritual services, in-

cluding the counter-prestation of performing as representatives of
one of the debtor clan's *aroe*, and with certain goods, including
women. That is, the *aroe* representations are expressions and instruments of the prescriptive alliance between the moieties. Thus
persons can and do address those members of the other moiety who
perform as their totem as husband (*i-toredu*) or wife (*i-torududje*), even
though there may be no current marriages between the groups involved. One reason for such extreme importance of the representations is that, in Bororo opinion, the performers actually *become* the
aroe entity represented. The address terminology sometimes embodies reference to this belief. For example, on this general normative and categorical level, an Aroredu might correctly term a
Kiedu as either "my wife the red macaw," or "my brother-in-law
the parrot."

In point of fact I never heard Arore use these or comparable
statements as far as *nabure* were concerned. The representation of red
macaw essence is considered a very minor prestation, and *nabure aroe*
a rather trivial totem; only two of my informants remembered its actual performance. The Arore, though, have a number of highly regarded entities among their totemic *aroe* such as the *aije* (loosely,
water spirits). These are represented in major ceremonies which
bring great honor both to the sponsoring Arore clan and to the performers' group. Indeed, on formal occasions I have heard an
Aroredu address the members of the other moiety who represent specific *aije* with the titles of those spirits, coupled with the appropriate
sex-and-age alliance category. As minor as macaws might be in this
system, then, we might conclude that there are more epistemological
grounds for a given Kiedu in the midst of the ceremony in which he
performs as *nabure aroe* to state in an entirely literal way, in Levy-
Bruhl's sense, "I am a red macaw," than there ever is for any
Aroredu to make the same claim, even though his clan "owns" the
totemic essence of *nabure*. The direct Arore relationship to *nabure* is
bound up with quite specific refractions of the "Idea of Red Parrot,"
such as certain personal names and particular artifacts. But this is
far from claiming identity or even affinity with the species as a whole.
Just as the Arore are not equivalent to or substitutable for red
macaws, neither are the Paiwoe for *kuido*, nor the Bokodori Exerae
for *xibae*. The latter two clans even lack complete representations of
the *aroe* version of the parrot species associated with them.[10]

The Case for Totems: Names

At this point we might recall that the Bororo characterized the *aroe* totems as "name-givers," and this would seem to imply that they realize the distinction between definer and thing defined. In terms of the material already examined, it can be said that along with all the other entities singled out as totemic, macaws might be utilized in certain ritual contexts as an extended synecdoche to express the relations among corporate groups, of belonging and not belonging. This does not exclude the possibility that in other contexts the relationship with the totem might have metonymic elements. A limited number of each clan's totems, usually those regarded as its principal ones, can be differentiated into levels of specificity in an hierarchic order that corresponds to varying levels of inclusiveness within the clan. As a unique, idealized form-of-being, the totemic entity is associated with the clan; two subforms (male and female, black and red, large and small, and so on) are connected with the two subclans; yet more particularized forms, differentiated on the basis of size again, specific markings, or yet other morphological or behavioral attributes, correspond with the lineages; finally, the precise attributes of the most specific form supply the individual name. I was able to obtain only a few instances of perfect symmetry between all totemic forms and each level of inclusiveness within the clan, but informants were convinced that all totems were capable of such social segmentation, although the details had been "forgotten" in most cases.

It is thus hypothetically possible that an Arore might refer to an older brother in the other subclan as "my brother the red-banded male *nabure*," contrasting him to a senior brother in his own subclan who was "my brother the black-banded male *nabure*." In fact I have heard this done in quite formal contexts with respect to jaguars, armadillos, *dourados* (a large species of fish, *Salminu cuvieri*), and other important clan totems. In this sense, in the intraclan context an individual's or lineage's relation to the totem might well be characterized as a case of metonymy, since the derivation of proper names follows a syntagmatic rather than paradigmatic pattern.[11] (Cf. Lévi-Strauss on this same point, 1966, 166–90, 200–209, but especially 212–15). As intriguing as these considerations might be, and as important as they are to the comprehension of the semantic logic of Bororo totemism, they have little bearing on the specific issue of macaws. In my experience, at least, proper names derived from any of the macaw species are never utilized to differentiate clan members and segments from one another. Informants gave examples of highly specific personal names derived from macaw attributes, and were confident that these could be arranged hierarchically in terms of clan organization, but they were unable to give any account of this conceptual order.

In short, whether as generative devices for differentiated personal/group statuses, as empirical referents for corporate property, or as the subject of ceremonial representations, macaws are simply not important within the context of the Bororo totemic system. Such creatures as armadillos, crows, monkeys, jaguars, and many others are exceedingly crucial to that system, and the Bororo do use a code based on it to express many aspects of social relationships. The semantics of this code must be analyzed in a later publication, but it is apparent from the preceding information that metonymy, synecdoche, and metaphor are all involved. Even Levy-Bruhl's mystical participation is quite relevant. But obviously the meaning of the particular assertion "we are red macaws" is not to be found in additional consideration of the nature of the totemic system. Such a conclusion is enhanced by two further points. There is absolutely no reason to assume that Steinen's interlocutor was in fact an Aroredu. And even if he were, I trust the material presented above has demonstrated that the variety of subtle associations between an Aroredu and the red macaw species could never be summarized in such a gross overstatement of total identity. Steinen was quite capable of distinguishing between statements about totemic relationships and other assertions concerning the character of man's connections with animals. As we shall see, when Bororo use the phrase they have in mind human kind, not clan kind.

TAXONOMY, ANOMALY, AND THE NATURE OF MACAWS

The task now is to account for the logical connection between the two terms, "man" and "macaw," as it is perceived by the Bororo. This can only be accomplished by examining the total range of meaning of each term, and then determining which portion of that range is actually operative in our key statement. A logical starting point for such examination is avian taxonomy: what criterial attributes do the Bororo use to differentiate macaws from other bird and animal species? But any account of such classificatory activity must include the social contexts in which men interact with macaws, and the ethical rules which govern these transactions. That is, I feel an interpretation of the symbolic importance of macaws in Bororo thought which is based exclusively on their taxonomic status would be woefully incomplete. As Tambiah puts it so well, "Simple intellectual deductions from a society's formalized scheme of animal categories will not take us far unless we can first unravel the core principles according to which people order their world and the valuations they give to the categories (see also Bulmer 1967)" (1969, 452). These "principles" and "valuations" ought to be manifest in the details of Bororo interaction with macaws. In this particular case, we have seen that the "core principles," whatever they might be, have little connection with the totemic system in any of its ramifications. To anticipate, they will be found in the area of male-female relations but only as these transcend the arena of corporate, exogamous social bonds—just those partially expressed in the totemic code. The importance of examining this aspect of the problem does not, of course, deny the equal analytical relevance of the empirical attributes of the species as they are perceived by the society. Clearly it is necessary to investigate how the Bororo view macaws as part of the natural order: the emic interpretation of macaw morphology, habitat, diet, plumage, and so forth is critical. In the following sections I shall try to show first how each of these perspectives, the taxonomic and the transactional, relate to one another, and second how they might express aspects of Bororo identity.

In most contexts, Bororo classify together under the term *kiege akiri* ("white-feathered birds") macaws and other members of *Psitacideos*, most of the other families of the order *Coraciformes* (tucans, kingfishers, mutums, woodpeckers, etc.), and nearly all water birds. This category is contrasted to that of "carnivorous birds" (*kwagere poiwe kiege*, exact meaning obscure) and a somewhat residual category of "birds" (*aribe*).[12] It is perhaps worth noting that the Salesians derive the generic designation for bird, *kiege*, from *kuido*, commenting that the macaw is the very essence of bird (Albisetti and Venturelli 1962, 725–26). Informants specify that nearly all members of the first category share the attribute of beauty (*matureu*), although they admit that a subset (*kiege mori-xe*) in the second group (birds of prey such as hawks and owls) also has this qual-

ity. There is some aversion to eating the majority of birds in the first
two categories, and in the case of certain species (hawks, flamingos,
cormorants, and tucans) this almost amounts to a specific prohibi-
tion. But in no case are they regarded as inconceivable as food, nor
are they included among those species regarded as highly polluted
and dangerous (*bope ure*). Rather, they are held in low repute as
foodstuffs; the crippled, maladroit, or very young demonstrate their
inability to secure better food by consuming water fowl and parrots
publicly. These views may reflect the somewhat liminal attributes
perceived as common to both classes. Within the first category
distinctions are made between birds of running water, birds of still
water, and land birds. Each of these classes is further broken down
on the basis of contrasts in diet, habitat, and plumage. These considerations are mentioned here only to demonstrate that macaws are
hardly anomalous in terms of Bororo taxonomic principles.

Together with beauty, perhaps the most emphasized common
element in the first category, is that all species included in it are said
to be manifestations of spirit (*aroe*) in the generic sense. The empirical elements cited as evidence of this association have a somewhat
ad hoc quality. In the case of most water birds, their habitat itself,
white plumage (*akiri*) and fish diet are perceived as isomorphic with
eminent characteristics of the spirits. (Perhaps one might regard this
as a case of metonymous association, since water birds and spirits
are different semantic domains of a single natural zone.) The bones
of deceased Bororo are immersed in lakes, although in some parts of
Bororoland they are usually deposited in caves. All nonhuman types
of spirit are said to live in rivers and lakes. The most terrible of this
kind of spirit, the *aije*, are ceremonially represented by somatic
paintings done with a special kind of white mud (*noa*) which is found
only on the banks of a few streams and lakes. The bullroarers which
imitate the *aije*'s roar are made from certain species of soft wood
trees which grow only near water. The spirits of the dead themselves
are usually pale or actually white, according to the shamans who
alone among mortals may actually see the spirits. Indeed the
spiritual element in all living men, that same soul (*aroe*) which survives after life, is compared to smoke or fog, and the Bororo do
recognize the "wetness" of fog. Finally, all types of spirit are very
fond of eating small fish.

But while indigenous explanations for the association between water birds and spirit are numerous, the situation in the case of parrots and related species is a bit more obscure. Informants give essentially five kinds of justification for linking parrots with spirit.

Macaws and Spirits: Categories and Conditions

1. Although *aroe* (here, spirits generically) enjoy eating fish, the major component of their diet is thought to be vegetable products such as nuts, fruits, palm shoots, corn, and the postcontact domesticants rice and beans. These substances are contrasted to all kinds of meat, above all those which have a strong "gamey" taste; these are considered the regular diet of the other variety of supernatural entity, the *bope*. The type of shaman who dealt with the *aroe* traditionally limited his diet to vegetable products, fish, and the immature young of mammals in order not to offend the *aroe*. Parrots are strongly associated with a vegetable diet, especially one featuring nuts and fruits.

2. The Bororo seem to infer that the strongly variegated and dramatic coloring of parrots in general, and macaws most of all, is clearly a manifestation of spirit. Although whiteness, or absence of color, is treated as the most usual condition of spirit, it is also expressed through presence of all colors. I have heard it said that such creatures as the harpy eagle and the jaguar reveal spirit in their mottled coloring; although the observation came from an unusually perceptive and learned informant, it could not be termed a conscious element in the collective representation of these species. Of more general validity is the frequent metaphorical comparison of the extended chants describing the elements and activities of spirits to a multicolored cloth which stretches "just as a trail" along which the singers and the song progress. Soon after contact, the shaman of the souls (*aroe etaware are*) forbade the indiscriminate use of variegated cloth on the grounds that such color combinations, especially red and black, were restricted to matters connected with spirit (Albisetti and Venturelli 1962, 174). Finally, rainbows are regarded as a direct manifestation of one particular category of *aroe*.

This identification of spirit with mottled hues should not be that exotic to us, for it is not unknown in our own cultural tradition. Hopkins in "Pied Beauty" proclaims, "Glory be to God for dappled things—/For skies of couple-color as a brindled cow;/ For rose-moles all in stipple upon trout that swim;/ Fresh-firecoal chestnut-falls;

finches' wings; . . ." (Hopkins 1956, 30). One might even suppose
that such iridescence is often found characteristic of liminal conditions or entities, a possibility which finds confirmation in at least one
other culture (Kaguru; cf. Beidelman 1968, 119–23) besides the
Bororo and our own Catholic one.

3. Macaws are connected with spirit in the dogmatic context of
the soul's metamorphoses after death. During the rites that accompany the final interment of the body, the soul (*aroe*) is instructed to
enter in turn jaguar, macaw, otter, and hawk. (Ocelot is sometimes
given as the terminal species in the sequence.) The diet of this
species is thought to include those particular types of mammals, fish,
and plants which are considered polluted, and which Bororo cannot
eat before shamanistic intervention has made them pure and safe.
Such polluted species (*bope ure*) include deer, tapir, rhea, capybara,
corn, wild honey, and some others. In the indigenous view, that
class of mystical beings dialectically opposed to the *aroe*, the *bope*, has
certain rights over these species which are manifested in their dangerous quality for men (Crocker 1975). The improper consumption
of these restricted foods and related polluting acts are usually considered by the Bororo to be the effective cause of death. Through the
sequence of metamorphoses, in the emic view, the deceased's soul is
able to secure revenge on those things and powers (i.e., the *bope*)
which destroyed his corporeal self. That is, as a macaw or jaguar the
soul may consume at will and in perfect safety those substances
which previously were restricted, and thus commit with impunity
those same transgressions which led to the death of his body.

With the exception of Van Baaren, earlier analyses of the
macaw = self metaphor have considered but finally rejected this
aspect of Bororo cosmology as underlying the metaphor. Van
Baaren argues that the caterpillar-butterfly analogy Steinen used to
clarify the belief probably came from the Bororo themselves, and
therefore, "The comparison of caterpillar and butterfly leads us to
conclude that the arara is a form in which man manifests himself
after a transformation, after death" (1969, 12). But Steinen himself
states at one point that the belief in metamorphoses has nothing to
do with the declaration of identity with red macaws since he understood the informant to mean that the identification obtained now, at
the present moment. Not only did my informants agree with this,
they also asserted that caterpillars and butterflies were two entirely

different species. Finally, the macaw is only one of the forms tem-
porarily assumed by the soul, and the Bororo deny they are jaguars
or otters or hawks in the same sense they are macaws. It might be
added that they do not believe in reincarnation; there is no presumed "cycling" of souls back into this life. Nor, for that matter,
did I ever hear any Bororo aver that the soul during dreams often or
ever assumed the form of a macaw.

4. Macaws are associated with the *aroe* on the basis of purely syntagmatic contiguity. As mentioned above, *nabure* are said to live in
rocks and cliffs, and *kuido* in buriti palms (*marido*). The leaves of this
palm are staple items in the construction of Bororo ritual paraphernalia; the tender shoots of the buriti are one of the souls' and the
Bororo's most preferred foods. Indeed, one might say that in terms
of providing raw material for the representation of spirit, buriti
palms are in the plant domain what macaws and jaguars are in the
bird and mammalian domains. Moreover, these palms are often
found in low, marshy places, such as the borders of those small lakes
in which the decorated baskets of ornamented bones are deposited in
the secondary interment. Traditionally these baskets were also
placed in caves in the same rocky prominences where *nabure* nest.[13]
Furthermore, those same caves are regarded as leading directly to
the other world where dwell *aroe* in all their variety.

These associations between *aroe* and macaw provide the ground
for many varieties of tropes, which are employed in songs, myths,
and other traditional lore. The shared attributes of diet, habitat, and
variegated coloring are the bases for synecdoches and for metaphors
derived from these, while the macaw as agent for the soul's revenge
after death is itself metonymy. However, none of these rhetorical
figures provides any clues as to possible connections between
macaws and man. For these it is necessary to turn to the last of the
modes in which macaws are linked with spirit.

5. The last aspect of this connection involves exactly that dimension of interaction between macaws and human society which I
maintained earlier was basic to any investigation of the collective
representation of natural entities. The entire argument of this essay
hinges on the fact that macaws, and to a lesser degree other parrots,
are the only kind of domestic pet now found among the Bororo. Recent analyses of various cases of this topic (Leach 1964; Lévi-Strauss
1966; Beidelman 1966; Tambiah 1969) have stressed that domesti-

cated animals, and especially those living in intimate commensality
with man, are likely to be the vehicles of a complex symbolism. They
are structurally anomalous in occupying a position neither wholly
animal nor completely human, and hence they may be utilized with
great rhetorical effect to affirm, deny, modify, or otherwise express
various nuances of man's nature. It seems crucial to me to make a
sharp distinction between commensal association per se and those
fosterings of creatures which have a marked nonutilitarian character, such as that expressed in our category "pet." Thus, the
Bororo indigenously had domesticated dogs and still continue to
raise them; and since contact they have adopted chickens and pigs
from the Brazilians. Although these animals live in conditions of
great intimacy with their masters and other members of the nurturing household, they are practically never the object of any affec-
tionate regard. The last two species are raised as cash crops for sale
to Brazilians and other Indians, and the dogs for their utility in
hunting. Dogs do have certain qualities of pets in that they are given
names and are never eaten. But their names compare with human
nicknames, and even are marginal to these in that most are derived
from Brazilian language and usages. For example, one dog was
called "Preguicoso," the Portuguese term for "lazy." Their owners
take minimal interest in them, so that they are nearly all emaciated,
half-wild, and vicious. A good hunting dog is sometimes given more
care than is usual, but even these are so unimportant as not to be included in the disposal of property following the owner's death. Most
often only the owner knows or cares which of the dozens of dogs
lying about the general precincts of the village are actually his.

   In contrast, everyone from the very young to the aged knows
who owns which tame macaw. These birds are one of the few items
of personal property aside from certain ritual items (e.g., jaguar
teeth necklaces) which an heir receives. Inquiries into the possibility
of eating domesticated macaws (and other parrots) occasioned expressions of intense repugnance, whereas the same suggestion concerning dogs was regarded as bizarre but not unconsiderable. Many
pet macaws receive proper names, or dimunitives thereof, taken
from the owner's matrilineage. To be sure, practically no one outside the family and not even all its members know a particular
macaw's proper name, but everyone is aware it might have one.
Further, a macaw, and to a lesser extent other parrots, is included

among the property and persons which are considered to be exten-
sions of the owner's social personality. Infractions of the rights over
such property are considered a serious matter indeed. If a pet macaw
is stolen or accidentally injured or killed its owner may legitimately
demand compensation over and above simple restitution. In the
single case of this in my field experience a dog severely mauled a
macaw. The dog was immediately killed by its owner, who then
made a number of minor ceremonial prestations to the damaged
party. For these reasons macaws and other varieties of parrot
wander around the community with as much impunity, and with the
same effect, as a cow in a Hindu village.

In one village in which I worked, about one hut in every three
had pet macaws, smaller parrots, or parakeets as co-residents.[14]
These pets receive excellent care; they are given food at least once a
day, their flight feathers are trimmed regularly, and shelter is given
them in inclement weather. Women and especially children play
with them by the hour. The birds are taken from the nest as fledglings and fed premasticated food directly from the mouths of their
owners, with the result that they become extremely tame. Unlike
dogs and other domestic animals, macaws always accompany their
owners on journeys away from the village, riding on top of the
women's loads (Albisetti and Venturelli 1962, 809).

Indeed, ownership of macaws is almost entirely limited to
women. The stereotyped Bororo explanation of why certain households maintained domestic parrots to the extent of invariably replacing ones which died was, "Women who have lost many children
now have *kagere*."[15] While very few Bororo are reluctant to sell items
of traditional property, no matter how great its symbolic value, adult
macaws, parrots, or even parakeets are practically never willingly
sold by their owners. Finally, and I hope this clinches my argument,
the death of such a pet is sometimes formally mourned (*oragudu*) by
its female owner, admittedly briefly and cursorily. Only humans are
otherwise mourned, and Bororo men regard such behavior for a
defunct macaw as perhaps a little ridiculous but by no means illegiti-
mate.

In response to the query "Why do you keep pet macaws?" Bororo usually say that they are convenient sources for the raw materials used in ritual, and because the spirits like them to do so. (The
Salesians, who often cite verbatim glosses of informants' comments,

give the same two reasons [Albisetti and Venturelli 1962, 809].) The first of these motives involves the fact that nearly all the highly diverse items in the Bororo ritual catalogue must utilize macaw feathers to conform to traditional standards, which are taken very seriously. The blue, yellow, and red macaw breast feathers, for example, are painstakingly glued together to form mosaics which are applied to gourd whistles, rattles, and dolls, and to the head or skull of those undergoing such rites of passage as name-giving and funerals. The long tail feathers are used to make the spectacular headdresses (*pariko*) of which every clan owns four or five distinctive forms. Hence macaw feathers are essential to Bororo ritual, and the social relationships it mediates, and yet are quite scarce, especially those of red macaw (*nabure*). These figure in virtually all ornaments perhaps because, as noted in an earlier note (13), red is the medial color.

While tame red macaws are prized above all other varieties of parrot, all domesticated macaws are living banks of rare and critical ritual material. Following a major ceremonial cycle nearly all the birds in the village are pathetic denuded bundles of flesh and bone. A frequent excuse for delaying a ritual is that the individuals responsible for making the ornaments have not been able to acquire the requisite feathers. Wild macaws are killed whenever possible and *all* their feathers carefully removed. The long tail feathers are so rare that after a headdress or similar item becomes ruined through long usage, the less bedraggled feathers are removed, cleaned with oil, and stored against employment in a new ornament. Nearly every adult male and some females have cylindrical boxes (*maregwa*) made from the trunk sections of the buriti palm (once again, cf. item 4 above, the Bororo being fairly systematic in their symbolism) which are used exclusively for the storage of macaw feathers.

Although the items made from these feathers are never sold but given away in formal exchange for ritual services, the feathers themselves are sometimes sold to nonkinsmen. However, even this action is fairly rare since a stock of feathers whether boxed or alive virtually guarantees ability to carry out ritual obligations, and such ability is a potent factor in political prestige. It is almost axiomatic that every man of status has either a full box of macaw feathers, or is related by consanguinity or alliance to a woman with a tame macaw, or both. I would not argue that macaw feathers are the

equivalent of noncommercial money for the Bororo, for they participate only in a very limited cycle of transactions in which the other
equivalent items are animal skins, teeth, and claws, and certain
ritual services (Bohannan 1955, 1959; Dalton 1967, 276–77). But
they are perhaps the most important instance of a scarce noncon-
sumable resource in the Bororo system.

The other indigenous justification for domesticating macaws,
that the spirits approve of the practice, rests on somewhat obscure
grounds. Entirely aside from the momentary and singular transformations of the soul during the post mortem cycle of metamorphoses,
aroe generally are believed to enter or to transform themselves into
both wild and tame macaws rather frequently. The Bororo postulate
three motives for this habit. First, "the *aroe* wish to be beautiful
(*matureu*) like the macaw." Second, the *aroe* are wont to eat the nuts
and other plant substances which are the staple in both macaw and
spirit diet. (Both these reasons draw on the syntagmatic or synecdochic association between these forms of being.) Informants said
these facts were part of the justification for providing plentiful food
for pet macaws, since a deceased relative might benefit from such
largesse. I find this rationalization of dubious worth for the analysis.
There is absolutely no way to distinguish those moments when a pet
macaw is actually harboring the soul of a dead parent or child or
other Bororo, nor are there, as far as I could discover, any other
"empirical" consequences to this belief. In any case the souls of the
ancestors, as well as other forms of spirit, are only marginally involved in Bororo social life. They are rarely credited with causing illness, accident, or misfortune either to individuals or to groups; they
are never propitiated and their assistance in crisis situations is
seldom implored. To be sure, the *aroe* are invited to participate in
communal rituals, and most Bororo appear to believe that they do
so; yet even in those circumstances they are characterized as having
the manner of aloof and distinguished visitors. It is, one might say,
the deceaseds' absence rather than their presence which is the focus
of Bororo ritual concern.[16] The pet macaw, then, can in no way be
interpreted as any sort of "domestic shrine." It is not in itself a
direct mode of communication between this world and that of the
spirits. To employ an illustrative metaphor, it is a window rather
than a door between these worlds and a somewhat clouded window
at that.

The belief in the *aroe*'s frequent assumption of macaw form might be regarded as simply a logical deduction from the whole set of associations between *aroe* and macaw, rather than significant in itself.[17] But there is the third factor mentioned above but yet unconsidered, another attraction besides preferred food and desirable appearance that motivates *aroe* to become macaws. The Bororo believe that the ancestral souls and most other forms of spirit never copulate in their "natural" condition, supposing them indifferent to all such bodily appetites. On the rare occasions when desire overcomes them, they instead enter or transform themselves into living entities for intercourse, and prefer the vehicle of macaws to any other creature. Informants cited as evidence of this practice the shamanistically revealed fact that the legs of spirits bend backward rather than forward at the knee, "so that they must copulate from behind, like macaws." They also specified that the spirits have intercourse in this manner only with other spirits, never with actual macaws. It is very tempting to speculate on the possible symbolic status of the offspring of such hypothetical spirit-macaw unions; the Bororo regarded my queries on this topic as too obscene to warrant a response.

But these points are crucial. Red macaws are clearly thought distinct from the *aroe*, for otherwise the *aroe* would not have to become macaws for the unspiritlike activities of eating and fornicating. The Bororo regard other bird species, such as the heron, as much "purer" total refractions of the essence of spirit. Their attitude toward the raucous flocks of parrots and macaws, for all the birds' utility as the source of ritual material and frequent vehicle of spirit, is one of indulgent respect rather than reverence. At the same time, for all the intimacy of their domestic association with human beings, macaws are far from being the objects of anthropomorphic sentiments. The men typically regard the women's occasional demonstrations of feeling toward their pets with tolerant amusement for such inability to discriminate between radically different states of being. They still scorn any of their fellows so shameless as to eat a wild parrot, and sharply reprimand a child who teases a domesticated macaw rather than a sibling. In short, the Bororo view macaws as thoroughly bird, albeit as having natural attributes which render them attractive to the profoundly different spirits and valuable to man. Therefore we have answered one of the initial problems, in that the distinction between the domains of spirit, man and macaw, has been established. I must conclude that macaws can be treated as liminal mediators precisely because they are neither pure spirit nor totally human, while sharing both some esteemed and some gross qualities of each. The postulation that "we are macaws" is thus not founded on metonymy nor on synecdoche; it remains to be seen how it is metaphorical.

THE HUMAN CONDITION: BIRDS AND MEN

The important point now is just how the macaw's status as domestic pet and as the vehicle of spirit connotes adornment when mankind is compared to it. A response to this requires an examination of the other term of the equation, the cosmological and social characteristics of man within the Bororo system. I can only sketch in the rough outline of these dimensions here. They are typically perceived as ambiguously dyadic, in that human beings are often said to be a compound of "spirit" (*aroe*) and "force" (*bope*). The *bope* are an inclusive category of spiritual being dialectically and dramatically opposed to the *aroe*. In their most typical, or most essential manifestations, the *bope* are associated with all processes of growth and decay, specifically with fertility and death. They are the dynamic force which manifests itself in day and night, and in the oscillation between rainy season and dry; the sun and moon, and rain itself, are actually specific ramifications of *bope*. *Bope* cause all living things to reproduce, and to die.[18] That dimension of man which is represented through the *bope* is precisely his "natural" self, including his appetites for food, sexuality, and deviance from normatively enjoined conduct. An individual's personal idiosyncrasies and particularly those physical transformations through time which we would characterize as aging (white hair, wrinkles, feebleness, and the like) are ascribed to this particular history of interaction with the *bope*. Since these spirits control all transformations, they respond to human infractions of their rights over the natural order by causing various types of anomalous disasters, such as eclipses, epidemics, floods, and early deaths.

It is important to stress that, in the Bororo view, not only men but the entire natural world in its varied aspects is a compound reflection of both principles, *bope* and *aroe*. Therefore the dichotomy between two forms of spirit, and the logical principles they represent, cannot be expressed in terms of a simple opposition between

nature and culture, since all things have characteristics of both principles. For example, the Bororo are not so consistent as to maintain
that an infant derives his *aroe* from his mother and his *bope* from his
father, as a cursory examination of their social organization might
lead one to expect. They believe each parent contributes the same
physical and mystical substances to the fetus, and differentiate the
sexual roles on a nonsociological basis. In arguing the appropriateness of this view to the logic of Bororo collective life, informants
point out that a child, as a member of the opposite moiety, can embody the *aroe* totems of his father's clan, and is otherwise intimately
connected with them.[19] At the same time, they stress, the uxorilocal
household is the locus of consumption both of food and of women,
and the site of all death and birth, all of which are very much matters
connected with the *bope*.

As I shall now try to demonstrate, the metaphor "we are red
macaws" attempts to express through a single convincing image the
inchoate sense in which Bororo find themselves to be the fusion of
antithetical cosmological principles.

These principles have their correlates in manifold aspects of
Bororo social life, but the ones most relevant to the present issue involve the dichotomous relations between men and women both
within and outside the context of the domestic group. This is
because informants strongly implied that it is only Bororo *males* who
are said to be macaws. This opinion emerged only during direct inquiry into the assertion. Although when the formula was mentioned
informants recognized it as a traditional expression, I have never
heard it uttered spontaneously.[20] Typically, I believe, it is perceived
as characterizing various situations in which Bororo men have direct
contact with the *aroe*, such as the sacred hunts (*aroe e-meru* or *aroe
e-kodu*), funerals (*itaga*), or any totemic representation (*aroe etawuje*).
During such moments there is a sharp symbolic antithesis between
men and women: the latter are not allowed to witness various por-
tions of the rituals, under pain of angering the spirits, while the men
(excluding noninitiated boys) are secluded in the men's house or off
in the jungle. During a few rituals, notably the *aije aroe etawuje* (intrinsic to funerals and initiations), this ritual separation develops
into formalized aggression against the cloistered women. The actors
portraying the *aije* spirits throw balls of white mud against the houses
and boast among themselves how terrified the women are of these

supernatural entities. They maintain with some glee that if a female should chance to see one of these actors or the bull-roarers they manipulate, the *aroe* spirits would cause her belly to swell up until she dies (Albisetti and Venturelli 1962, 19). Many discrete beliefs reflect a view of femininity as inherently dangerous to men. Since during the sexual act a woman robs her partner of his vigor (*rakare*), men should avoid intercourse as much as possible; a menstruating woman contaminates food and masculine weapons; women are inherently dissentious and lacking in a sense of shame; and so forth.

All these attitudes reflect the more general social fact that Bororo males are in a sense caught between matrilineal origins and uxorilocal residences. Each man is an intruder into the female-dominated households of the other moiety, in which he resides, ingests food and enjoys sexuality, procreates, and exists on a daily basis. This residence is not without its more sublime attractions. The Bororo prize conjugal happiness even while admitting it is all too rare. They emphasize the unique value and joys of patrifilial bonds, and the genuine solidarity of the father-son bond is given considerable jural and ritual weight (Crocker 1969a). On the other hand, a man is responsible for the affairs of his mother, his sisters, their children, and all others living within that house, which is his legal domicile. He possesses status and controls scarce resources, such as rights over spirit representations, only to the extent that he fulfills his matrilineal obligations. Caught between the demands of his uterine and affinal bonds,[21] he spends a great deal of time in the men's house, where the *aroe* also congregate during rituals. There he may share his existential dilemma with all other Bororo men. These are, to be sure, categorically divided into "brothers" and "brothers-in-law" (*i-mana* and *in-odowu*), "fathers" and "sons" (*i-ogwa* and *i-medu*), or "mothers' brothers" and "sisters' sons" (*i-edaga* and *i-wagedu*). Yet they all share the status of ambiguous creatures whose obligations of uterine domicile are in some ways opposed to their affinal residential duties. As Lévi-Strauss noted so perceptively a number of years ago (1963b), the concentric dualism of the village is one concrete expression of this masculine solidarity gathered together at the center in the face of the female-derived conflicts of the periphery. The opposition, though, transcends even the village structure, since the men frequently go off together on ritualized collective hunting and fishing expeditions. These are under the aegis of the spirits, and therefore are rigidly interdicted to women, just as is the men's house (except under certain conditions, Crocker 1969b). When in ritual, the *aije* "attack" the women in their huts, the spirits come from the river, through the forest and to the men's house, and then back again; the "exterior" is as much opposed to the periphery as the "interior."

The men's society, wherever it might be found, is generally tranquil and relaxed. Yet ties through women order relationships within it and disturb its harmony. Uterine brotherhood is one of the most basic models for masculine solidarity, yet in the Bororo view brothers are notorious for their inability to get along with one another. The shared jural status of common matrilineal descent that binds them normatively also entails their bitter competition for the scarce resources to which they share title. A "zero-sum" situation is assumed to hold in that one brother's loss is taken to be another's gain. This is obviously true for wives, and since jural authority in the clan is ordered hierarchically, brothers can only be "superior" or "inferior" to one another. (Much the same is true for sisters, of course.) The arbitrators in intraclan disputes between siblings are supposed to be their affines, especially the fathers of those quarreling. I sometimes feel that the Bororo ritual and normative emphasis on patrifiliation represents one vast convulsive effort to escape the almost total dominion of women. But, as in all thoroughly matrilineal societies, agnatic bonds cannot endure through time. Although relations through males and through the *aroe* may order transactions within the men's society, no one can live permanently in the men's house. Thus, all enduring social relationships among the Bororo are initiated and defined by reference to women. Through their procreation and nourishment of men, they bind masculine loyalties and check their freedom of action just as surely as they domesticate macaws. Male symbolic protest in ritual notwithstanding, there is ample justification for the feminine view that it is they who are exchanging men, rather than the reverse.

These considerations, aside from the odd and uniquely Bororo twist of the "inverted" representation of totemic spirits, are obviously common to many matrilineal societies. I believe it would falsify and impoverish the Bororo case to let the matter rest on this sociological level, without consideration of the more idiosyncratic cosmological elements. Certainly the Bororo appear to realize that it is in the social nature of things for wives to draw men away from their clans, and divide brothers. Some may even apprehend that the clan itself is internally differentiated by contrasting uterine descent. Yet none of this is the crux of the matter for the men themselves. Rather, they appear to respond to the way in which, on the conceptual level, the matrilineal totemic system is a "terministic screen," in Burke's sense (1966, 45–47). This "system-screen" exhaustively defines reality through a single terminology and thus, due to its very nature as a classificatory system, is a deflection of reality. The Bororo, I think, share with other men some resentment of such arbitrary constraints. Even death itself does not transcend the limits of matrilineal self, for even after dying a man's identity continues to be defined by his corporate group's categorical attributes, through their projection into the domain of spirit. In a very real sense, a Bororo can never leave home. Like a macaw, he is perpetually a child of collective mothers.[22]

The single mode through which a Bororo can escape the female dominion of definition is within the context of the ceremonial representations of the totemic spirits and the souls of opposite moiety persons. It is then that a man can become not-self, and moreover, the very essence of pure being and form, as he performs as the representation of a totemic being or as the personification of another's soul. Yet even here there are limitations, which are summarized quite neatly in the comparison of men to macaws. Both transmutations of defined form occur only for limited periods during specific rituals. Both entities, men and macaws, are only partially and temporary vehicles for the *aroe*. The spirits utilize these means for quite utilitarian ends of their own, manifesting little concern in the process for the consequences to either birds or humanity. To put it another way, the feathers of macaws and the bodies of men are the raw material for social transactions. The feathers are the common material element in all the clan's ceremonial wealth which men exchange, as well as the vital portion of the costumes with which men enable other men to represent the *aroe*. But even in the midst of the ceremony a man is just as limited an aspect of spirit and of transcendence as a macaw. For all these transactions under the feathered aegis of the *aroe* involve prestations of food and of sexuality, and do not the *aroe* eat and copulate in the form of macaws? In metaphorically identifying themselves with red macaws, then, the Bororo do not seek either to disparage or to adorn themselves; but to express the irony of their masculine condition.[23]

NOTES

1. I am indebted to Van Baaren's perceptive article on this same topic (1969, 9) for the references to Van der Leeuw, and to James Fox for drawing my attention to this material. I also wish to thank Rodney Needham for the Vygotsky reference.

2. As Van Baaren notes, Levy-Bruhl probably used the second edition (1897) of *Unter den Naturvolken Zentralbrasiliens.* He cites one critical passage as occurring between pages 305 and 306, whereas in the 1894 edition the same passage is found on pp. 352–53 (Van Baaren 1969, 10). Unfortunately I have not been able to secure a copy of the second edition to confirm this point.

3. This issue is most obscure and slippery; Lévi-Strauss does certainly not affirm that the four logical types of totemism he distinguishes (1963a, 16–18), of which the last three may well involve our connections of metonymy and synecdoche, are logically water-tight compartments.

4. The Western Bororo are extinct and have been so for at least two generations. However, I shall follow current usage in referring only to the Eastern Bororo (Albisetti and Venturelli 1962.)

5. I understand this phrase in Maybury-Lewis's sense, "A theoretical society in which every aspect of the social life of its members is ordered according to a single antithetical formula" (1967, 298).

6. I have worked mainly in two of the four or five such self-preserving communities, during 1964–65 and again in 1967. By "preserve" I mean that a quite self-conscious and thorough effort was made to maintain ancient customs, so that, for example, communal rituals occurred nearly every week.

7. In earlier publications both I and the Salesians have described the clan as divided into three sub-clans. While these statements reflect the views of the most traditionally learned informants, it must be admitted that neither they nor other Bororo place much importance on the "middle" (Boedadawu) subclan. It seems to be utilized as a residual category when it is mentioned at all. I am obliged to Zarko Levak, who has recently done extensive field work with the Bororo, for sufficiently emphasizing the importance of this point.

8. Generally, informants state that the prototypical *i-maruga* is a female member of the father's clan (e.g., a FZ). But in this case, the midwife

should normatively be a female member of the infant's father's father's clan (i.e., a member of ego's own moiety). She is regarded as a putative patrilineal relative even though she usually is the MM or MZ.

9. Such a situation should not strike American readers as particularly strange, since the Hopi appear to have had a strikingly analogous custom (Titiev 1944, 109–16).

10. I assume Lévi-Strauss had in mind comparable situations when he insisted on a sharp distinction between the totem species and the attributes of the clan members. However, at least for the Bororo case, this logical breach between category of nature and social category exists only at the most abstracted level of relationship. As far as individuals and clan elements are concerned, their bond with totem involves extremely personalized aspects of totem, which is to say, cases of synecdoche and metonymy.

11. This is a bit more than a formal argument, since the named statuses are loosely associated with the right to various artifacts and to occupy ceremonial roles (all of which are seen as deriving from the totem). Such privileges are an important aspect of the Bororo political process.

12. As far as my data go, Bororo animal taxonomies do not have many inclusive generalizing categories; they utilize descriptive phrases rather than distinct lexemes to differentiate large sets. Such taxonomies are not uncommon and are said to rely on "covert categories" (Berlin, Breedlove, and Raven 1968, 296–97). However, my material on these points is unclear; certainly the terms used here are not mutually exclusive or exhaustive of Bororo terms for this topic. For example, certain species of hawks are included in the category *kiege akiri* as well as that of *kwagere poiwe kiege* and *kiege mori-xe*.

13. Red macaws (*nabure*) are perhaps more intimately associated with the essence of liminal force precisely due to their coloring. Although white is the color of the *aroe* under most conditions, just as the *bope* are consistently associated with black, red is always utilized in ritual contexts stressing vitality and transcendent beauty.

14. As a general rule, all the considerations involving domesticated macaws apply to lesser parrots and parakeets, but with much less symbolic and social force. Just as it would be a desperate man indeed who resorted to parakeet feathers for his clan's ornamentation, so too few Bororo would deign to bestow a name on such a pet or to bequeath one.

15. Although the Bororo clearly recognize the implied psychological identification between children and pets, they also have in mind the symbolic consequences of such associations. Such women have certain ritual items (such as gourd whistles by which the "soul's breath" is reproduced), heavily decorated with macaw feathers and kept in special baskets filled with white down. The lost child's soul enters these items for short periods, as it may possess the birds kept by the grieving mother.

16. Much of Bororo ceremonial hinges on the institution of the *aroe maiwu*, the "new soul." Every Bororo decedent, except for infants who die before receiving a name, has a ritual replacement drawn from the members

of its father's clan, in the opposite moiety. To a limited degree, this replacement, the *aroe maiwu*, assumes the deceased's social status, including certain obligations to matrilineal kinsmen (Crocker 1975). Without such a custom, informants claim, dead persons would be very quickly forgotten.

17. It may be appropriate to note, at this point, that the Bororo do not attribute any symbolic or other importance to the parrot's ability to replicate human speech. While they are aware of this potential, they very seldom act upon it and never cite it as a reason for the intimate connection between macaws and human beings.

18. With the crucial exception of fish and certain other water creatures, which are controlled by the *aroe*.

19. Thus, a decedent's ritual replacement (*aroe maiwu*) should be a member of his father's clan. In payment for his various services undertaken in discharge of this role's duties, the replacement may utilize certain of the ceremonial privileges of the dead person's clan. This is the only way other than matrilineal descent that such categorical rights may be legitimately gained.

20. The usual phrase such explicit questioning elicited was "*pa-edo nabure.*" *Edo* designates present conditions of existence rather than permanent states of being. This, of course, does nothing in itself to resolve the problem of meaning since it could apply to presumed metamorphoses of the soul, or, indeed, to all the previous hypotheses.

21. I should stress most emphatically that the Bororo version of this typically matrilineal problem has various dimensions which render it somewhat less acute than the thoroughgoing classifier might suspect. The most general ameliorating factor is that obligations toward uterine and affinal kin are quite different and involve nonoverlapping sets of scarce resources. Thus, one is obliged to instruct one's sister's son in the niceties of clan lore, while one's son deserves material assistance in the form of weapons and instruction in the arts of hunting.

22. Thus, every Bororo decedent's soul, save for those of the newly born, is assigned to the responsibility of some woman of his or her clan. This woman, preferably the mother, is obliged to nourish the soul, and its representative, who is, as noted earlier, invariably a member of the opposite moiety.

23. Sapir's initial response to this conclusion was the perceptive inquiry: "If men are macaws, what does that make women?" He was asking, in other words, if it was possible to discover a metaphor for the feminine conditions that paralleled the masculine one, thus moving from an internal (men = macaws) to an external metaphor (cf. Sapir 1977, 25–27). My response had to be no, not to my knowledge. The Bororo utilize a great many tropes, including several complex analogic systems to express aspects of sexuality, but of the figures utilized to describe women none has the same logic and the same quality of dogma as the macaw = men metaphor. One possible figure would be "women are buriti," since this plant is intimately

associated with macaws, the *aroe*, social transactions, etc. But men do not "own" buriti palms nor are there the ambiguous associations linking them with the *bope*. And, besides, I never heard the Bororo use such an expression.

REFERENCES

Albisetti, C., and A. J. Venturelli
    1962   *Encyclopedia Bororo*. Vol. 1. Campo Grande, Brazil: Museu Regional Dom Bosco.

Beidelman, T. O.
    1966   The ox and Nuer sacrifice: Some Freudian hypotheses about Nuer symbolism. *Man* (n.s.) 1:453–67.
    1968   Some Nuer notions of nakedness, nudity and sexuality. *Africa* 38:113–32.

Berlin, B., D. E. Breedlove, and R. H. Raven
    1968   Covert categories and folk taxonomies. *American Anthropologist* 70:290–99.

Bohannan, Paul
    1955   Some principles of exchange and investment among the Tiv. *American Anthropologist* 57:60–69.
    1959   The impact of money on an African subsistence economy. *The Journal of Economic History* 19:491–503.

Brown, Roger
    1958   *Words and things*. Glencoe, Ill.: The Free Press.

Bulmer, Ralph
    1967   Why is the cassowary not a bird? A problem of zoological taxonomy among the Karam of the New Guinea highlands. *Man* (n.s.) 2:5–25.

Burke, Kenneth
    1945   *A grammar of motives*. New York: Prentice-Hall.
    1966   *Language as symbolic action*. Berkeley: University of California Press.

Crocker, J. Christopher
    1969a   Reciprocity and hierarchy among the Eastern Bororo. *Man* (n.s.) 4:44–58.
    1969b   Men's house associates among the Eastern Bororo. *Southwestern Journal of Anthropology* 25:236–60.
    1975   *The stench of death: Structure and process in Bororo shamanism*. MS.

Dalton, George
    1967   Primitive money. In *Tribal and peasant economies*, ed. George Dalton, 254–81. New York: The Natural History Press.

Douglas, Mary
    1972   Deciphering a meal. *Daedalus: Journal of the American Academy of Arts and Sciences* 101(1):61–81.

Evans-Pritchard, E. E.
    1956   *Nuer religion*. Oxford. Oxford University Press.

Firth, Raymond
    1966   Twins, birds and vegetables: Problems of identification in primitive religious thought. *Man* (n.s.) 1:1–17.
Geertz, Clifford
    1966   Religion as a cultural system. In *Anthropological approaches to the study of religion*, ed. M. Banton. Association of Social Anthropologists, Monograph no. 3. London: Tavistock.
Hopkins, G. M.
    1956   *The collected works of Gerard Manley Hopkins*. New York: Penguin Books.
Kietzman, D.
    1967   Indians and culture areas of twentieth century Brazil. In *Indians of Brazil in the twentieth century*, ed. J. Hopper. ICR Studies no. 2. Washington, D.C.
Leach, Edmund R.
    1964   Anthropological aspects of language: Animal categories and verbal abuse. In *New directions in the study of language*, ed. Eric H. Lenneberg, 23–63. Cambridge: MIT Press.
Lévi-Strauss, Claude
    1963a   *Totemism*. Trans. Rodney Needham. Boston: Beacon Press.
    1963b   Do dual organizations exist? In *Structural Anthropology*, vol. 1, 132–66 (1956). New York: Basic Books.
    1966   *The Savage mind* (1962). Chicago: University of Chicago Press.
Levy-Bruhl, Lucien
    1910   *Les fonctions mentales dans les sociétés inférieures*. Paris: Libraries Alcan et Guillaumin.
    1966   *How natives think*. New York: Washington Square Press.
Lowie, Robert H.
    1937   *The history of ethnological theory*. New York: Farrar and Rinehart.
Maybury-Lewis, David
    1967   *Akwe-Shavante society*. Oxford: Clarendon Press.
Percy, W.
    1961   The symbolic structure of interpersonal process. *Psychiatry* 24:39–52.
Sapir, J. David
    1977   The anatomy of metaphor. In *The social use of metaphor*, ed. J. D. Sapir and J. C. Crocker, 3–32. Philadelphia: University of Pennsylvania Press.
Steinen, K. von den
    1894   *Unter den Naturvölkern Zentral-Brasiliens*. Berlin: Verlagsbucklandlub Dietrich Reimer.
Tambiah, S. J.
    1969   Animals are good to think and good to prohibit. *Ethnology* 8:423–59.
Titiev, M.
    1944   *Old Oraibi*. Papers of the Peabody Museum of American Archaeology and Ethnology 22, no. 1. Cambridge: Harvard University Press.
Van Baaren, Th. P.
    1969   Are the Bororo parrots or are we? In *Liber Amicorum: Studies in honour of Professor Dr. C. J. Bleeker*, 8–13. Leiden.
Van der Leeuw, G.
    1928   *La structure de la mentalité primitive*. Paris.

Van Steenburgh, E. W.
    1965   Metaphor. *The Journal of Philosophy* 62:678–88.
Vygotsky, L.
    1962   *Thought and language*. Cambridge: MIT Press.

Animal Symbolism, Totemism, and the Structure of Myth

Terence Turner

Animal Symbolism, Totemism, and Fetishism

Among simple societies such as those of lowland South America, social relations and other cultural phenomena are commonly believed to be derived from animals and are symbolically represented in animal form in ritual, myth, iconography, and such various systems of belief as shamanism, magic, curing practices, notions of death, and cosmology. That human (cultural) beings should find it congenial and appropriate to represent social and cultural phenomena to themselves through the symbolic medium of animals and even to account for such phenomena as the products or gifts of such beings, raises a number of questions that have a long history in anthropological theory.

Foremost among these questions is the problem of totemism. Originally conceived as a form of religious cult—in which social groups (matrilineal clans, in McLennan's original formulation) worshipped; respected; participated in the being of; descended from; either did not eat or ritually devoured the totemic animal, plant, or other natural phonemenon—the concept languished because it was realized that the original claims made for it, to wit, that it was the archaic form of all religion and that it constituted a regularly associated complex of beliefs and social institutions, were contradicted by ethnographic experience. After a half century of neglect, the concept was taken up again by Lévi-Strauss (1962), only to be dissolved into the broader question of the use of relations among natural species to encode patterns of relations among social groups or categories.

Among the parts of the complex of ideas constituting the original notion of totemism discarded by Lévi-Strauss in his recension was the notion that the use of animal symbols to denote social phenomena entails not merely the employment of a convenient metaphorical idiom but an element of "fetishism." McLennan (1869-70), the originator of the concept of totemism, defined it as "fetishism plus exogamy plus matrilineal descent," or in more general terms, "the worship of plants and animals." The notion that totemism constitutes a definite form of religion associated with specific forms of marriage and descent is of course unfounded, as a host of critics from Tylor (1958) to Lévi-Strauss have recognized. It is one thing to reject the unviable form of McLennan's idea, however, and quite another to disregard the kernel of his insight: the representation of social or cultural phenomena in animal form involves an element of *mis*representation, which specifically consists in the belief that the social phenomena in question are nonsocial or "natural" in origin or essence.

Approaches to the understanding of symbolism can be divided into two broad types. The first, represented by structuralism and the various forms of what has come to be known as Symbolic Anthropology, treats the symbol (or structure of symbols) as a representation of a meaning or message on the basis of features culturally deemed appropriate to the coding of the particular message in question. The understanding of symbolic forms by either an analyst or a native, from this point of view, comes down to an operation of decoding. That the message should be encoded in a form that is often opaque and in some respects actively mystifying, as in the representation of a social relationship in the form of a relationship among natural beings, is not in itself taken as problematic.

The other main line of approach to symbolism is represented by Marx and Freud, who both emphasize the idea that the symbol is in some crucial respect a *mis*representation of social reality. This misrepresentation has, for both thinkers, a double aspect: on the one hand the symbol is seen as a disguise that obscures some aspect of reality; on the other, the symbol is seen as a fetish that represents the human relations it encodes as attributes of itself rather than of the human actors who created or are otherwise responsible for them. There is no space here to discuss Freud's views (1918), but the obvious connection between Marx's and McLennan's uses of the concept of fetishism may be briefly noted. For McLennan as well as Marx, fetishism is the generic notion, of which totemism is only one manifestation. For both, the totem, or other "natural" symbol for a social relation or product, is merely a fetish on the hoof.

Marx developed his notion of fetishism in the context of his analysis of commodities in capitalist society. He treated commodities not only as material objects but as symbolic representations, which through their form of value and their role as objects of exchange accurately represent some aspects of capitalist society and misrepresent others (Marx 1972, 71–83). The essence of the misrepresentation consists in the way that the role of commodities as objects of exchange, in defining the social relations among their human producers, becomes reflexively interpreted as an expression of the fact that this state of affairs is objectively, or naturally, determined and as such is independent of human agency or social history. The products of social activity thus ironically become the symbolic vehicles of a representation of the social order as a "natural" order. Commodities are, in short, the "totems" of capitalist society.

One of the principal effects of the structuralist conception of totemism in particular, and the relation of nature to culture in general, as one of direct metaphorical correspondence at a purely formal level has been to define the fetishistic aspect of such phenomena out of existence. My argument, on the contrary, is that animals are so heavily used as symbols, not merely because of their formal appropriateness as metaphors for aspects of social structure which they accurately represent, but because, as natural beings with humanlike properties, they are the most suitable symbolic vehicles for the alienation of human (social) consciousness of the social nature of social phenomena through the *mis*representation of those phenomena as "natural."

In this presentation, I attempt to instantiate this proposition in the course of an analysis of perhaps the most important myth of a Ĝe speaking tribe of central Brazil, the Kayapó. Animal symbols play a key role in this myth (as they do in most other Kayapó myths); it thus provides an excellent framework within which to examine the meanings and functions of two of the most important animal symbols in Kayapó culture, the jaguar and the red macaw (*arara*), as well as several other animal symbols that, as I shall argue, are equally germane to the points that have been raised.

Symbols, Context, and Structure

Symbols as Operators and as Structures

As Munn has noted in a review of anthropological writings on ritual, there is a widespread tendency in analyses of cultural symbolic forms to abstract the notional meanings of the symbolic elements of, for instance, a ritual text or performance and then to discuss the abstracted meanings without regard for the specific relations of their symbolic vehicles in the ritual as if these constituted the "symbolic meanings" of the latter (Munn 1973, 580–81, 606). The result of much anthropological analysis of symbolic forms has thus ironically been to reduce symbolic meaning to other, more abstract kinds or levels of meaning such as "classifications in the cultural code" (Munn 1973, 606).

A symbol, specifically as used here, is a sign (in the Saussurean sense of a signifier attached to a signified [de Saussure 1959]) that is employed as the signifier of another signified: a metasign, as it were, in which the first-order signified is related through metaphor, metonymy, or typically a combination of both to the second-order signified. Culturally defined symbols in this sense rarely occur in isolation. Rather, they tend to be combined with other elements of a symbolic character in complex compositions or forms, such as rituals or myths. Within such contexts, the symbols act as operators, serving, through their relations with one another, to polarize, recombine, and otherwise transform the relations among the constituent features of their second-order meanings.

The relations among the symbolic elements of such composite forms, as this formulation implies, are typically of a dynamic or transformational character. Symbols, as elements of such dynamic transformational structures, are themselves internally constituted as systems of transformations of the relations among their constituent features of meaning. These transformations are themselves integral aspects of the meaning of the symbols. They are, in fact, the most specific and characteristic component of symbolic meaning as such —that aspect of meaning acquired by elements of the cultural code through becoming incorporated as symbols into composite symbolic forms.

A general point of the analysis presented here then, is that symbols have an internal structure, not only of static oppositions but of coordinated transformations of the relations among their constituent meaningful features. This structure is homologous with the relations between the symbols in question and the other symbolic elements of the compositions to which they belong. The meaning and structure of a symbol is thus radically inseparable from the structure of the composite form in which it is embedded. The analysis of the Kayapó myth about the origin of cooking fire presented in this chapter is intended as a demonstration of these points.

Context and Narrative Form in the Structure of Myth

My approach here to the structure of mythical narrative differs fundamentally from that of structuralism. These differences are both theoretical and methodological, and on both levels serve to distinguish my approach from recent literary, semiotic, and poststructuralist conceptions of narrative (for a more extended discussion of some of the theoretical points see Turner 1980).

The two primary and interrelated shortcomings of the structuralist approach, in my view, are its failure to take account of the contextual associations among elements of the narrative text and its general lack of recognition of the syntagmatic dimension of the structures it attempts to describe. These points are related. Contextual relations—I define the term more precisely below—are syntagmatic, but not all syntagmatic relations are based on "context-sensitive" rules governing the covariation of elements of the syntagmatic chain within the same textual contexts. The relation between the two points can be thought of as levels of structure. At the highest level, the syntagmatic order of a myth takes the form of its plot line—in other words, the character of the myth as a narrative. The inability of structuralism to account for the narrative form of myths (the macrocosmic aspect of their syntagmatic structure) has, as its equally important microcosmic counterpart, the failure of not taking into account the contextual juxtaposition of symbolic elements (individual symbols, relations, or events) at each successive point in the story. I use the term *context* to denote such a point of juxtaposition of two or more meaningful elements in the text.

The theoretical and methodological approach to the structure of myth that Lévi-Strauss formulated in his first paper on the subject, and has since maintained without significant modification, could be described as a "context-free" approach—by understanding the term *context* as defined above and employing the expression as a whole in its technical linguistic sense. "Context-free" formulations are contrasted in linguistic theory to "context-sensitive" ones. A context-sensitive rule is one that accounts for a regularity in language structure in terms of the constraints exercised by the juxtaposition of structural elements in the same context in the spoken or written chain. The context is defined by the juxtaposition, which can take the form either of contiguous succession or simultaneous superposition. Lévi-Strauss's context-free approach to the structure of myth assumes that the complex web of contextual associations among the elements of mythical narrative, including the sequential order of the story or plot of the myth as a whole, is irrelevant to the structure of the myth or the essential message it carries.

Lévi-Strauss's choice of a context-free method of analysis has had profound consequences for both the formal and substantive aspects of his conception of the nature of myth structure. In the simplest and most concrete terms, it has led him to deny any structural significance to the narrative dimension of myth, in spite of the evident fact that myths are invariably told and understood as stories, with a beginning, a middle, and an end, rather than as arbitrary jumbles of relations to which temporal ordering is irrelevant. I contend that in this respect, as well as in its failure to take into account the microcontextual determination of symbolic structure discussed above, structuralism and its context-free analytical method have produced a fundamentally deformed conception of the structure of myth. This deformed concept of structure has led to corresponding distortions in the interpretation of the meanings or messages encoded in and communicated by myths. Structuralism's context-free methodology has, at the same time, rendered impossible the correction of these errors by cutting off access to the ordering of contextual relations in the text.

In contrast to the structuralist conception of myth and the fundamental assumptions underlying its context-free approach, I propose that an adequate model of the structure of myth, and of complex symbolic forms in general, must be based on an integration of the paradigmatic and syntagmatic aspects of the ordering of relations in the text, giving due weight to the contextual covariation of symbolic elements as well as to the sequential form of the text as a whole. In terms of this formulation, the problem of the nature of the narrative dimension of myth is no longer distinct from that of the structure of myth, but is seen to be identical with it.

THE KAYAPÓ MYTH OF THE BIRD-NESTER AND THE ORIGIN OF COOKING FIRE

Let us now consider the Kayapó myth. The text of the myth as given here is a composite of a number of variants recorded by me in the field and collected by other investigators. It consists of what seem to be the essential features of the story. I have divided it into segments, or "episodes," for purposes that will become clear in the following analysis.

Initial Situation

Long ago, humans did not possess cooking fire. They ate rotten wood, fungus, caterpillars, honey, and palmito (heart of palm). They would cut their meat in small pieces and put it out on rocks to be warmed in the sun.

Episode 1

A man was hunting in the forest. He saw two red macaws fly into a hole high in a cliff. He inferred that the hole was the site of a macaw nest. He resolved to return to his house and get his wife's brother, who also lived there, to come back with him and help him get the fledglings from the nest.

Episode 2

The next day, the man took his young wife's brother (WB) and set out through the forest for the cliff with the macaw nest. When they got there, the man notched a tree trunk as a ladder and leaned it against the cliff so that his WB could climb up. WB did so, secretly carrying with him a round white stone resembling an egg.

Episode 3

Upon reaching the nest (which was full of fledglings), WB called down to his sister's husband (ZH), "There are only eggs in the nest!" "Throw them down, then," replied ZH, and cupped his hands so as to catch the fragile "eggs." WB threw down the stone that he had carried up with him. It broke ZH's hand. ZH rolled on the ground, crying with pain. Then, in a rage, he got up and threw down the ladder, marooning WB in the nest.

Episode 4

ZH returned home, leaving WB to his fate. As he left the foot of the cliff, the terrified WB cried after him, "Sister's husband! Wait! There are fledglings in the nest! I will throw them down to you!"; but ZH ignored his appeals.

Days passed. WB began to die of thirst and starvation. He was reduced to drinking his own urine and eating his own feces.

Episode 5

A jaguar passed by the foot of the cliff beneath the hole with the macaws' nest. He was hunting and carried a bow and arrow, which was not known to humans at that time. He also had a wild pig, which he had shot, slung over his back. The boy leaned out from the nest to get a better look at him, thus casting his shadow on the ground. The jaguar, seeing the shadow appear on the ground before him, pounced upon it as if it were prey. Coming up with nothing in his claws, he realized it was a shadow cast by a boy above him on the cliff. Politely retracting his claws and covering his fangs with his paw, he looked up at the boy and asked him, "What are you doing up there?" The boy told him how he had climbed up to the macaws' nest to look for fledglings to throw down to his ZH, but had tricked him by throwing the stone instead, and how this had led to ZH's abandonment of him in the next. "Are there fledglings in the nest, then?" asked the jaguar. "Yes," said the boy. "Throw them down, then" commanded the jaguar. The boy did so, and the jaguar gobbled them up with bestial grunts and growls, which terrified the boy. "Where did your ZH throw the ladder?," the jaguar asked the boy. "Over there," said the boy, pointing. The jaguar fetched the ladder and set it up against the cliff. "Climb down," he told the boy. "No!" cried the boy, "You will eat me up!" "No, I won't," replied the jaguar, "I like you! You are my son! Come home with me so that you can eat and grow big and strong! I need a hunting companion!" Thus encouraged, the boy overcame his fear and climbed down to the jaguar.

Episode 6

The jaguar took the boy on his back, along with the dead wild pig, and returned through the forest to his house.

Episode 7

They were met by the jaguar's wife (also a jaguar; cf. Lévi-Strauss 1964, 75), who was standing in the doorway spinning cotton string on her spindle. She reproached her husband when she saw the boy, "Why have you brought home this child of someone else? Throw him away!" "Don't talk that way about your son!" answered the male jaguar. "We will keep him and feed him, so that he can grow big and strong and become my hunting companion." Thus overruled by her husband, the female jaguar acceded, and the boy was carried into the house and put down, along with the game, on the floor. On the floor beside the boy lay a great log of *moytch* wood (Portuguese, *jatoba*; *Hymenea* sp.) burning at one end. It was the first time the boy (or any other human being) had seen a cooking fire.

Episode 8

After a while, the male jaguar again went out hunting. Before he left, he told his wife to give the boy anything he wanted to eat. Along about midday the boy felt hungry and asked his jaguar mother to give him some of the roasted tapir meat she was taking out of an earth oven. "No," she cried, "you may have only venison!" The boy, however, snatched some tapir meat and began to eat. At this, the jaguar mother called to him in a menacing voice, "Look here!" Holding up her paws, she extended her claws toward him and bared her fangs, all the while whispering softly, "Don't be afraid!" The boy, terrified, fled from the house and climbed a tree. The male jaguar, returning in the afternoon from his hunting, found him still there. "What are you doing up there?" he asked the boy. The boy told him what had happened. The jaguar coaxed him down from the tree, put him on his back, and carried him back to the house. He scolded his wife and told her not to repeat her behavior.

The same episode, however, was repeated every time the male jaguar went hunting.

Episode 9

After yet another repetition of the same behavior by his wife (and son), the male jaguar lost patience. "Come with me to the river bank," he said to the boy. "Let us bathe together." They walked together to the river. After they had bathed, the male jaguar broke off a few of the arrow-canes that grew by the bank and made them into arrows. Then he broke off a sapling and made a bow, twining some inner bark for the string. He showed the boy how to use the weapon. "If my wife acts toward you in the same way again, shoot her through the nipple of her breast!" he commanded the boy. "If you do this, we two will separate; you go that way, and I will go this way." They returned together to the house, each carrying his bow and arrows. The boy hid his in the thatch of the house.

Episode 10

Soon the male jaguar went hunting again. Before he left, he told his wife to give the boy any sort of meat he desired to eat. When the boy asked for a certain type of meat, however, she again refused, demanding that he substitute another kind. The boy, as before, took the meat he had asked for. The female jaguar, infuriated, came at him with claws extended and fangs bared, as if to kill him, still whispering her comforting maternal formula, "Don't be afraid!" When she was standing directly over him and appeared to be about to do him in, the boy took his bow and arrows from the thatch where he had hidden them, and put an arrow to the bowstring. "Wait! Wait!" cried the jaguar mother, but to no avail. The boy let fly his arrow, which pierced her nipple and killed her. As she lay dead on the floor, he shot his other arrow through her other nipple.

Episode 11

The young man gathered some of the roast meat and some of the cotton string the female jaguar had been spinning and broke off a piece of the burning log with fire on it. Taking these items together with his bow and arrows, he left the jaguars' house. Outside he met the male jaguar, who made no objection when informed of what had transpired. He told the boy, however, that they should separate, that the boy was to follow a creek back to his former home and that he himself would go into the forest in the opposite direction.

Episode 12

The young man went in the direction of his house. Just outside it he met his sister. She at first did not believe it was he, but when he convinced her she wailed passionately over him (a formal Kayapó manner of greeting, appropriate in such a context). The young man, however, barely reciprocated her gesture. The sister next brought their mother to meet the boy. The mother was even more reluctant to believe that the young man was really her son; but, when convinced, she broke into even more passionate wailing than the sister had done. The young man, however, was even more reserved in his response. They went together to the house. When they were inside, the young man showed the women the things he had brought from the jaguars' house: the fire, the bow, the string, and the roast meat. The women exclaimed over these wondrous things, none of which had ever been seen before by human beings.

At this point, the men of the village, who were assembled in the men's house in the center of the village plaza, sent a messenger to summon the young man to come to them, tell of his adventures, and show them what he had brought. As he walked from his mother's house to the men's house, the chief cried, "The newly grown man has come!" He was thus recognized by the adult men as one of them.

Episode 13

The men decided to go together to the jaguars' house to take the fire, roast meat, cotton string, and bow and arrows. For this purpose, they all assumed animal form. One man became a tapir; it was he who carried the fire log. Another became a wild pig; he carried the roast meat. Another became the larger savannah deer; he carried the cotton string. Others became the toad and *jaho* (tinamou), both red-throated species, who got their red throats on this occasion by hopping along behind the log as it was being carried along and gobbling up the sparks that fell from it so that none of the fire was left in the forest for the jaguars.

The expedition was a complete success. The men raced back with the log and threw it down in the center of the plaza, whereupon they all reassumed human form. At this time all the women came from their houses and broke off bits of the fire (or were given them by the men; versions differ on this point). They took the pieces back to their houses and started their own cooking fires from them.

Final Situation

Since then, humans have had cooking fire and have cooked their food. They no longer eat fungus, rotten wood, caterpillars, or meat barely warmed in the sun.

ASPECTS OF CULTURAL CODE EMBODIED IN THE SYMBOLIC ELEMENTS OF THE MYTH

Social Relations: Sister's Husband (ZH)
and Wife's Brother (WB); Father and Son

The fundamental segmentary unit of Kayapó society is the extended family household, founded on a rule of matri-uxorilocal residence. As in other Ĝe societies, this rule is regularly observed; and there is a uniform pattern of differential emphasis or weighting of the categories of relations constituting the structure of the family and the domestic group. This pattern is inculcated by a collectively standardized ritual process of recruitment into various collective institutions: moieties, age classes, men's houses, etc. The system of collective institutions thus constituted forms a generalized projection and prototype of the weighted pattern of relations comprising the structure of the extended family household segment (Turner 1979).

This pattern may be briefly summarized insofar as it concerns the relations that play a role in the myth. Marriage is strongly accentuated. A man's attachment as husband to his wife's domestic group is emphasized at the expense of his continuing ties as son, brother, or maternal uncle to his household of origin. At about the age of eight, boys leave their natal households to live in a men's house at the center of the village. This change of residence is carried out under the aegis of a figure called a "substitute" father who adopts the boy but can have no real genealogical ties to him. This man's wife becomes formally defined as the boy's "substitute" mother. The ritual adoption in effect transfers the filial relationship of the boy as son from his real parents in his natal family household to his relation with his "substitute" parents focused in his new residence (the men's house). The break with the boy's real parents and household

is thus carried out without discontinuing the social form of the tutelary parent-child relationship itself, which is only transferred to the
new venue of the men's house. The boy, in other words, remains a
minor in social terms, the "son" of his "substitute" father.

The "substitute" father ceases to be considered the boy's guardian when the boy consummates his own marriage in the Kayapó
sense by becoming himself a father. At this point, he transfers his
residence to his wife's household. The effect of the sequence of somewhat abrupt changes in residence is to emphasize the status of the
father-husband as the dominant position in the nuclear family unit.
It is, in other words, the father-husband who is the dominant adult
male figure in a boy's natal family, and who, at the same time in his
displaced symbolic form as a "substitute" father, serves as the pivotal status to which a boy relates in making his transition from natal
family to initiation into the collective groups that constitute the
structure of the community as a whole. It is thus essentially through
his relation to the father (biological or substitute), and his own even-
tual accession to that status, that the youth's passage from childhood
(defined by his status as son in his nuclear family of origin) through
adolescence (defined by induction into the men's house) to adulthood (defined in terms of his becoming a father in his own right) is
achieved. The jaguar's adoption of the relationship of father to the
hero of the myth is thus socially appropriate to the role he plays
toward the boy in the story.

The arrival of the hero's ZH in his family household means that
the dispersion of his natal family is at hand. This process, as we have
seen, requires the separation of the hero, as WB, from his natal domestic group. The relationship between ZH and WB at the beginning of the story as co-residents of the same household is therefore
unstable, contradictory, and above all, temporary. The relationship
of ZH to his domestic group is by its very nature an adult relationship, whereas that of WB is intrinsically childish, defined in terms of
his relationship as a child to his natal family in his maternal household. The arrival of ZH signifies, in effect, that WB must leave, thus
setting into motion his passage from childhood to adulthood. This
explains why the ZH in the story is represented as an adult and the
WB as a child. The structural opposition between the two has an intrinsically temporal reference.

The Macaw Fledglings and the Object of the Hunt

Like the Bororo, whom Lévi-Strauss describes at the beginning of *Le cru et le cuit* (*The Raw and the Cooked*), the Kayapó and the other Ĝe tribes capture and raise macaws as sources of feathers for use in the manufacture of ritual headdresses and other ornaments. The only way to acquire macaws is as fledglings after they hatch but before they are fully plumed adult birds able to fly. This is the object of the hunt upon which the two brothers-in-law set out. Though Lévi-Strauss gives a correct account of the purpose of the hunt in presenting the story in *The Raw and the Cooked*, he does not appear to realize its metaphorical significance for the central protagonist, the boy, which is fundamental to the myth. This metaphorical meaning is clear when we consider that the macaw fledglings and the wife's brother (WB) are at the same stage of their respective life cycles (they are both about to "leave the nest") and that the boy and the fledglings are confronted with analogous destinies if the hunt by ZH and WB is successful (namely, an artificially and indefinitely prolonged childhood). The birds would become "permanent fledglings" constantly plucked and therefore never able to fly as adult birds, confined for the rest of their lives to their adoptive "nest" or natal family. The boy would return with his ZH to his natal household, where he is structurally defined as a child.

When the wife's brother climbs into the macaw nest, in other words, he is identified both situationally and structurally with the birds in relation to his ZH on the ground below. Throwing the fledglings down to his brother-in-law would mean sharing their fate, that is, returning to his own "nest" of origin and to the associated status of child. At this pivotal point in his own life cycle, this is precisely what he cannot do. He *cannot* obey the order given by his sister's husband to throw down the fledglings.

Stone, Egg, and Hand

The Ĝe and Bororo variants offer several reasons for the failure of WB to obey the impossible order given to him. In the Kayapó variant, as related above, the failure is a result of the boy's apparently unmotivated trick of throwing a stone "egg" which breaks the hand of ZH. The egg, I suggest, represents the tie between parent and child: it is neither one nor the other, but the incarnation of the relationship between the two. While an egg is fragile and breakable, a stone is hard, making it both unbreakable and capable of breaking other things. The word for "hand" in Kayapó (-*ikra*) is a homonym of the kinship term, "my child" (*i-kra*).

These considerations, along with the sociological correlates of WB's failure to throw down the fledglings as previously noted, permit an interpretation of this scene. The throwing of a stone instead of the fledglings represents the displacement of the parent-child connection outside the natal family household through the *substitution* of a new but "false" relationship *of the same form*. It is significant that while the real egg would have broken, the substituted stone "egg" remains intact and, instead of breaking, breaks ZH's hand. This corresponds to the Kayapó situation in which the father-son link, although displaced, remains socially intact at the expense of breaking the son's ties as a child to his natal household. ZH, in effect, is attempting to substitute himself for the boy's father, that is, the male head of his natal domestic group. This preferred relationship is incarnated in the hands of the sister's husband—held out to catch the fledglings—which are symbolic of the boy's childish status within his natal domestic group. Catching the fledglings in his hands ("my child") would have reaffirmed the boy's relation as a child to ZH as the adult male representative of the domestic group in its next developmental stage. By breaking ZH's hand, the boy repudiates the bid for his sociological infantilization.

The Jaguar

The Kayapó do not kill large carnivores (such as the jaguar, caiman, anaconda, or giant otter) for food. Their attitude toward this category of animals is ambivalent, and it is most intense in relation to the jaguar. As a potential predator of humans, the jaguar is a threat and is considered dangerous, an incarnation of the uncontrollable, antisocial forces of nature. At the same time, the Kayapó admire these animals for their strength, aggressiveness, and courage, qualities that are equally admired in the adult male. From this point of view, large predators, and the jaguar in particular, are considered models for the most highly esteemed social qualities of the male members of human society.

This ambivalent attitude toward the jaguar makes it suitable for the double role it plays in the myth. On the one hand, the jaguar mediates between the boy and his means of transformation from child to adult (the cooked meat that he eats, and thereby grows into a man of jaguarlike powers as a hunter); on the other hand, the jaguar is the mediator of the general form and source of transformation itself (fire) to society as a whole. The jaguar's role as mediator is inherently highly ambivalent, and consists as much in attacking and destroying the hero's outmoded form of social identity as a child as it does in fostering his acquisition of the positive social attributes of adulthood.

The jaguar's role as mediator is quintessentially expressed in his assumption of the role of "father" to the boy. It may be recalled that the jaguar's adoption of the boy as his son is the crucial factor that convinces the boy of his good intentions and thus gives him courage to make the developmentally "progressive" move of coming *down* from the nest. The significance of the jaguar's assuming the pivotal role of father may be appreciated in light of the preceding analysis of the significance of the father-son relationship in Kayapó society. This relationship, as indicated, is the principal structural channel between the social domains of boyhood and manhood.

A STRUCTURAL ANALYSIS OF THE MYTH

The Episode (Minimal Unit of Contextual Association) as the Element of Narrative Structure

A single cluster of contextually juxtaposed interactions among interdependent symbolic elements constitutes what I have called an "episode." The interdependence of the cluster takes the form of an invariant relationship between the transformations of the relations among the features juxtaposed in the episode. Invariance in this sense implies the conservation of the unity of a group of relationships—as a logical "totality." This unity is manifested at the most fundamental level of narrative structure as an inverse correlation of the transformations of the relations in question, which has the effect of conserving a constant proportion of polarization and integration among the elements constituting an episode. The minimal set of inversely coordinated transformations of the relations among contextually juxtaposed symbolic elements that conserves an invariant balance of separation and integration—or in formal terms, contrast and identity—constitutes an episode.

Narrative Space-Time: The Dimensions of Contextual Relations

The action of the story takes place upon two dimensions of spatial contrast, which may be called horizontal and vertical space. The former is essentially concentric in form, being defined in terms of the contrast between the relational space constituted by the social group that serves as the context of the relationship between the actors of the episode and those relations that lie outside that space. In the first part of the myth, where the social group in question is a single household associated with a single nuclear family, the horizontal dimension takes the form of the opposition between the *inside* of this house and forest *outside* the house. The forest represents the extrasocial domain of nature, characterized by relations of mutual exclusion, typified by the mutual destructiveness of the relations between human hunters and their animal quarry.

The second dimension, vertical space, is defined by the contrast between earth and sky or between ground and macaw nest (located high in a cliff-face or treetop). Vertical space is essentially a metaphor for developmental time, the time of growth and of passage from stage to stage or cycle to cycle of repetitive social processes. Vertical removal from the lower (ground) level is invariably associated with childhood, either on the part of the hero or of the macaw fledglings with whom he becomes identified at the beginning of the myth. The ground, as the lower extremity of vertical space, is conversely identified with adults, the only beings capable of moving about on the ground under their own power outside of the house. The opposition of up-down is thus a contrast in space-time, between earlier and later generations or stages of a process that is, on one level, the human life cycle and, on another, the family cycle. The childhood of the myth's hero is associated with his natal nuclear family; his transition to adulthood, which forms the matter of the story, is associated with the dispersion of that family and its replacement within the household by the family of procreation formed by his sister and her husband.

The two dimensions are correlated in such a way as to generate a two-dimensional product—space, or more accurately, space-time. This correlation is metonymic rather than metaphoric, and it is manifested by the correlation of the movements of symbolic elements with respect to the two dimensions. The "movements" in question take the form of successive and functionally interdependent actions juxtaposed within a single context in the text. The dimensions themselves thus assume the character of contextually juxtaposed, metonymically interdependent aspects of the coordination of the interaction of the symbolic elements of the narrative.

In the course of the myth the nature of the two dimensions becomes transformed, as a corollary of the transformation of the symbolic elements whose interaction is regulated and defined by space-time. *Contrast* between hero and jaguar on the vertical dimension is replaced by their *identity*. Vertical space-time, as a result, is transformed from a dimension of asymmetrical polarity between unique and heterogeneous elements to that of the relation between general class (type) and homogeneous instances (tokens), formulated in dynamic terms as a process of replication. The simple horizontal opposition between a domain of reciprocal social solidarity or inclusion ("inside") and a domain of reciprocal exclusion or incompatibility ("outside") becomes transformed into a dynamic process of "pivoting" in which each of these values ("inside" and "outside") becomes transformed into the other in the context of the recursive replication of movements from one pole to the other.

The same form of invariant correlation continues to govern the relations between contextually interrelated moves defined in reference to the two dimensions after their transformations. The achievement of replication on the vertical dimension, in the form of the transformation of the originally contrasted elements into identical tokens of the same type, turns out to entail the inverse form of replication on the horizontal dimensions—to wit, the transformation of each of the originally contrasted elements into its opposite, with the result that, while the form of the transformation itself is replicated as a recursively self-reproducing process, the opposite poles of the original contrastive relation remain contrasted.

The Patterning of Contextual Relations: The Episodes of the Story

We now examine each successive contextually juxtaposed set of operations composing the narrative order of the myth. As we shall see, the segmentation of the myth into episodes along the lines of these minimal contextual frames leads to two intriguing discoveries: first, that all of the episodes replicate the same basic structure; and second, that they constitute an orderly series of transformations of the form of that structure.

Episode 1. The opening event of the story proper takes the form of an association of displacements (i.e., operations) on the two complementary dimensions of symbolic space-time (the horizontal and the vertical). This association is defined from the standpoint of the main protagonist, the hero's sister's husband (ZH), who, as an incoming affine of the hero's maternal household, is located outside the household in the forest, but, as an adult man, is situated at the lower extremity of vertical space with his feet planted firmly on the ground. The set of displacements in question takes the form of ZH's plan to move his young brother-in-law (WB) out of his house into the forest (i.e., from *inside* to *outside* in horizontal space) and make him climb to the macaws' nest to capture the fledglings (thereby displacing him from *down* to *up* on the vertical dimension).

The two displacements in WB's location relative to ZH are interconsistent and inversely correlated from the point of view of the transformed structure of WB's family and household brought about by the arrival of ZH. WB is to be *separated* from his natal household on the horizontal dimension and *integrated* into a substitute "natal household" (or nest) on the vertical dimension. ZH's marriage to the hero's sister (Z) and their formation of a new family of procreation within the same household, as noted, implies the dispersion of WB's natal family, which amounts to its exclusion from the household, in what might be called the "structural present" defined by the formation of ZH's new family, and its consequent relegation to the "structural past," which is the previous stage of the developmental cycle of the household considered as an extended family. Relative structural exclusion is marked by displacement from *inside* to *outside* on the horizontal dimension, while relative priority in developmental time is coded by displacement upward on the vertical dimension.

ZH's project, however, contains a hidden contradiction, encoded in the macaw fledglings and his intentions with regard to them. As has already been made clear, the fledglings symbolically embody the position of the hero as a boy on the verge of leaving his natal family household to begin his social transformation into an adult. We are now in a position to see that they also represent, in their capacity as natural beings (i.e., creatures of the forest, excluded in horizontal space from human society) and as birds (i.e., denizens of the upper level of vertical space), the aspects of the boy's situation precipitated by the advent of ZH himself.

The basis of ZH's plan and the part that directly manifests the social form of his relation to WB is the association of the boy's displacement from the household with the displacement of the macaw fledglings from their nest. These displacements, taken by themselves, are irreversible, as indeed are the social transformations they represent. ZH's scheme, however, envisages their encapsulation within a structure of reversible movements: WB is to climb down from the nest and return "home" with ZH upon casting down the fledglings, who, for their part, are to be carried back and incorporated in the new developmental stage of the household, which would represent the previous (and structurally incompatible) stage. This reversible part of ZH's plan is plainly incompatible with the irreversible character of the structural displacements of which his scheme is the symbolic vehicle. In the narrative context, the contradiction takes the form of irony: ZH and WB both act as if unconscious of the structural impossibility of their continued solidarity as members of the same family.

The next three episodes develop the contradictory implications of ZH's reversible scheme, through which the ironic appearance of solidarity and cooperation between ZH and WB gives way to a break marked by physical agony, rage, terror, extreme regression (the hero's ingestion of his own excrement), misery, and despair.

Episode 2.   The second episode enacts the first pair of correlated displacements in horizontal and vertical space envisaged in ZH's plan. The two brothers-in-law proceed together from their mutual household to the site of the macaw nest in the forest (i.e., from *inside* to *outside* in horizontal space). Upon arrival, ZH remains below while WB ascends to the nest. The two affines are now polarized in vertical space in terms corresponding to their relative structural positions in the household.

Episode 3.   The dramatic focus of this episode is the explosion of the contradiction hitherto latent in ZH's scheme, in the form of WB's failure to throw down the fledglings and ZH's prevention of his escape from the nest. Once again, displacement on the horizontal dimension is inversely correlated with displacement on the vertical: the inability of either WB or the fledglings to move or be moved out of the nest from their place inside it is correlated with the inability of either to pass from their elevated perch down to ZH waiting below on the ground. The prevention of separation on the one dimension, in other words, entails the prevention of integration on the other.

The specific form of WB's failure to carry out ZH's instruction to throw down the fledglings (namely, his trick of casting down a stone under the pretense it is an egg, which results in ZH's broken hand) has been analyzed above. It is only necessary to recall here that these concrete details symbolically encode the precise pattern of weighting and transformation of relations involved in the normative pattern of transformation of Kayapó family relations.

Episode 4.   When ZH abandons WB in the nest, throwing down the ladder and returning home, WB's vertical isolation from the ground is complete. The circumstances of his juxtaposition with the fledgling macaws in their nest, by the same token, negate any possibility of differentiation between him and them in horizontal space. All access to the space outside the nest is cut off, so that the horizontal dimension, like the vertical, is effectively neutralized. The corollary of the structural isolation of WB's situation in symbolic space-time is the absence of ZH. ZH's return to his household reverses and thus completes his own pattern of movements as projected in his plan for the macaw hunt, while depriving WB of the means to reverse his. ZH's departure, in sum, signals that he and WB no longer belong to the same structure of interaction space-time. The fourth episode thus represents the realization of the implications of the contradiction of the preceding episode in the form of the disarticulation of narrative space-time into two separate and unintegrable zones.

The gap opened between the reversed pattern of ZH's movements and WB's unreversed pattern now becomes a force in its own right, a drive for the reversing of WB's displacements (and thereby the reintegration of narrative space-time). This is the objective structural counterpart of WB's subjective motivation to escape from the nest, which now reaches the pitch of desperation born of his misery and starvation. WB must find a way to reverse his movements in vertical and horizontal space-time: to get down from the nest and back to human society.

Episode 5. What the jaguar discovers from his ironic efforts to pounce on the boy's shadow is that the boy has become an ambiguous being. He is no longer a simple, homogeneous creature that can be treated like an ordinary animal (i.e., unsocialized being, a child) but a provisionally differentiated entity, the unviable, natural aspect of whose identity (his shadow) has become separated from his potentially viable, social aspect. From the boy's answers to the jaguar's questions that immediately follow this discovery, the jaguar learns that the boy has arrived at the pivotal point of his social development: he has rejected his childhood association with his natal family but has been unable to begin his positive transformation into an adult by himself. The pivotal aspect of the crisis of the boy's relation to society, suspended between the relatively natural, unsocialized phase of childhood and social adulthood, corresponds exactly to the pivotal character of the jaguar figure and the ambiguous combination of social and asocial attributes and role-identities he bears.

The arrival of the jaguar presents WB with an opportunity to escape from his predicament. The role-behaviors and -identities that the jaguar adopts towards the boy and the fledglings are clearly differentiated where those adopted by ZH were ambiguous and contradictory. The jaguar is a real hunter, whose bow and arrow, dead game slung over his back, and predatory pouncing on the boy's shadow leave no doubts about his bona fides as a killer and devourer of his prey. The ambiguity of ZH's relation to the fledglings, as simultaneously a hunter and a prospective co-family member, is replaced by the jaguar's unmistakably predatory behavior of devouring them on the spot. It is significant that the jaguar neither kills the fledglings with his arrows nor carries them home with his other game to be cooked before being eaten. The killing of the fledglings is unambiguously an animal act that marks the act itself, as well as its victims, as outside the space of social relations established by the civility and adoptive kinship of the jaguar's relationship with the boy.

The kinship relation the jaguar adopts towards the boy, that of father, is also free of the contradictory ambiguity of ZH's affinal relationship to him. The status of sister's husband, as noted, is incompatible with the role of co-family member to a wife's brother since the two statuses in question can only be occupied by members of developmentally consecutive families within the same household under the Kayapó uxorilocal regime. The role of father, a consanguineal relationship, is plainly compatible in these terms with co-family membership and thus with the jaguar's proposal to return with the boy to his household.

The jaguar, by first devouring the fledglings on the spot and then adopting the boy as his son, creates a clearly differentiated pattern of relations on the horizontal dimension of inclusion within, or exclusion from, the social space he defines between himself and the boy. As to their part in this polarization of horizontal relations, the boy and the fledglings are mutually displaced (excluded) from the nest, their mutual inclusion in which up to this point has defined their objective social identity. This separation on the horizontal dimension of narrative space-time has as its direct corollary the vertical displacements of both boy and fledglings from the nest to the ground, where each is assimilated with the correspondingly differentiated aspects of the jaguar as father and hunter.

These vertical passages, like the horizontal displacements with which they are associated, are of unambiguously opposed kinds. That of the fledglings is negatively marked (they are thrown down to be killed and eaten), whereas that of the boy is positive (the jaguar replaces the ladder so that he can climb down unhurt, promises to nurture him, and adopts him as his own son). Note that the vertical moves of both fledglings and boy have opposite *temporal* connotations. The jaguar brings the boy down from the nest so that he can begin his transformation from childhood to manhood. The killing and eating of the fledglings, the symbols of the boy's late childhood status, conversely connotes the closing of the developmental stage of which they are the emblems.

There is, however, an important sense in which the father's role, like that of the sister's husband, is structurally ambiguous in its projection in developmental time. As the "pivotal" male relation in Kayapó society—the "once and future" relational link of the boy to his natal family, on the one hand, and to his future role in the structure of the community as a whole, on the other—the father simultaneously represents the boy's dependent relationship as a child to his parent and his future identity as an independent adult. This

"pivotal," developmentally transformative character of the ambiguity of the jaguar's paternal relation to the boy points towards its
"disambiguation" through the practical social process of the boy's
transformation into a man.

The jaguar's assurances and promises to the boy as he coaxes
him down from the fledglings' nest portend the essential ambiguity
of his relation to the boy. The jaguar emphasizes that he is adopting
the boy for the purpose of helping him grow up to be like himself,
equally big and strong and thus able to act as a "hunting companion" (note the ironic reference to ZH's contradictory attempt to
make the boy his "hunting companion" on the quest for the fledglings). At the same time, he promises to bring about this growth by
taking the boy home and giving him food and drink: that is, nurturing him as a parent does a child.

The set of correlated moves constituting this episode does not
merely express the contrast between the opposing aspects of the
boy's and the jaguar's identities on the two dimensions. The fos-
tered, mutually supportive aspects are not only contrasted to the
suppressed, mutually exclusive ones, they are also preserved and re-
inforced whereas the latter are destroyed, so that the opposition
ceases to exist through the very acts that allow it to be expressed.
What is at stake here is not merely the removal of ambiguity from
the structure, but its transformation. The inception of a reflexive,
self-transforming process within the structure of oppositions and
operations in this episode is obviously an important development in
the formal structure of the story. It will be noted that in this and all
succeeding episodes the positive (integrative, reinforcing) and
negative (exclusive, destructive) aspects of this reflexive process
always balance each other as attributes of inversely correlated moves
on the two dimensions. The dynamic, reflexive form of the structure, in other words, conforms to the same invariant constraint that
regulates its simpler, unreflexive form.

Episode 6. The jaguar's first move after coaxing the boy down
from the macaw nest is to take him home with him; the jaguar's
home is now the boy's adoptive natal home as well. The jaguar's act
thus has the form of returning the boy to the parental household he
left behind to set out on the hunt for the macaw fledglings. It is, in

this sense, a symbolic reversal of the boy's initial displacement from the house by ZH.

The "reversal," however, is only tentative, only a rehearsal: the house is, after all, not the house of his social mother and father or even that of his sister and her husband, but a house of jaguars, transitional beings between the natural and social domains. It is, above all, identified as a context of transformation: the transformation of the boy into a mature man, which turns out also to entail the transformation of the family as a whole (i.e., its dispersion and destruction). The boy's "return" with the jaguar to his house is, in one sense, like the return from the macaw hunt projected in ZH's plan (the return of the boy and an adult comember of his family to their joint household); but it is unlike it in the crucial aspect that the boy's stay inside the household in the capacity of a child (as a nurtured dependent) is this time specified as temporary (the time necessary for the boy's transformation into a man).

The ambiguity of the father role that the jaguar adopts toward the boy must be understood vis-à-vis the contrast between that relation as a family role and the hunter's role the jaguar adopts towards the fledglings, which becomes the object of the boy's identification and emulation. At this latter, gross level of contrast, the jaguar, in the preceding episode, plays out the implications of his role as a pivotal figure in stark and simple terms: by first destroying the embodiments of the outgrown, unsocialized, childish aspect of the boy's identity (the fledglings), he clears the way for his adoption of a supportive, fostering relation to the boy's potential aspect as future socialized adult.

The very weakness and the undeveloped character of this aspect of the boy's identity, however, means that this fostering social relation, the role of adoptive father, must assume the ambiguous form of a combination of negation and affirmation that repeats within itself, albeit in a gentler and mediated form, the juxtaposition of destruction and encouragement toward the two aspects of the boy's identity respectively represented by the jaguar's bestial slaughter of the fledglings and his paternal solicitude for the boy. The jaguar must progressively repudiate the developmentally regressive role of nurturing parent as a function of strengthening the boy's growing capacity to identify with him as an adult hunter (in social terms, to act as a man outside of the family context). There is, in other words, a sense in which the ambiguity of the jaguar's paternal relation to the boy replicates the form of the juxtaposition of negative and positive role relations (hunter and father, respectively) that frames it.

These considerations find expression in the spatiotemporal patterning of moves in this and the following episodes of the hero's sojourn with the jaguars. Note that when the jaguar succeeds in coaxing the boy to climb down from the nest, he does not allow him to come all the way down, but places him on his back next to the dead game he is carrying slung across his shoulders. The boy is "down" relative to his previous position in the macaws' nest, but within the lower level of gross vertical space he is still "up" in relation to the jaguar, who walks directly on the ground ("all the way down"). The dead game, which shares the boy's relatively elevated position in relation to the jaguar, now takes the place of the macaw fledglings as the quarry of the hunt in which the boy and the jaguar have become "companions" of a sort. Unlike the fledglings, it has been killed with the proper instruments of the socialized hunter, the bow and arrow; and also unlike them, it has not been devoured raw on the spot, but is being transported back to the hunter's family and household to be properly cooked before it is eaten. Like the boy, in other words, the game is embarked upon a social transformation. Its transformation is to be the opposite of the boy's. Its alteration by cooking leads to its total annihilation and absorption rather than to its survival and development into a fully integrated social being, as in the case of the boy; but its metamorphosis is nevertheless linked to that of the boy as the necessary medium of his transformation into adulthood.

The antithetical directions of the transformations of game and boy notwithstanding, both stand at this point in an identical structural relation to their mutual transformer, the jaguar. Both are utterly dependent upon the jaguar as the agent of their respective transformations; neither can accomplish it under his own power. Equally helpless and dependent beings, they must both be carried by the jaguar in the same way, or, in other words, in the same position relative to the jaguar as defined on the coordinates of narrative space-time. Both are situated in the lower sector of gross vertical space—that is, within the sector proper to beings who have passed out of their primary developmental phase as unsocialized entities (beasts or children, respectively) into the sector proper to socialized beings. Being still at the beginning of their respective "socializations," however, they are situated within the upper level of this lower sector.

A similar situation prevails on the horizontal dimension. The respective transformations upon which the game and the boy are embarked lead, in the one case, toward a destructive form of exclusion from the realm of social relations (being cooked and eaten) and, in the other, to positive integration within this domain. At this initial moment of the process, however, before either transformation has properly begun, the boy and the game are in analogous positions in terms of their relative exclusion/inclusion within the domain of social relations, marked by the contrast between "outside" and "inside" on the horizontal plane of narrative space-time. Neither is more than incipiently integrated within the social domain (the game is not yet cooked, and the boy has not yet eaten of it and begun to grow up); conversely, neither is utterly excluded from it, since both are being carried by the jaguar (now the representative of social space, the agent of social transformation) toward his house to be transformed.

The positions of boy and game are thus undifferentiable on the horizontal dimension. In concrete terms, they are crowded together next to each other in the same spot on the jaguar's back. This undifferentiation has its counterpart in the undifferentiation of the jaguar's roles in relation to the two as kinsman (father) and hunter, respectively. At this point in his hunting expedition, both roles come to the same thing, namely, the obligation to carry both boy and game on his back, the one because he is too weak and unviable to walk on his own (in fact, almost dead), and the other because it is in fact dead and thereby similarly incapacitated.

This entire set of relations between the boy, the game, and the two role-aspects of the jaguar as father and hunter is located within the context of a single ("outside") sector of gross horizontal space (i.e., the forest, at the foot of the cliff with the macaw nest). The situation thus takes the form of the replication of the contrastive structure of horizontal space as a whole within only one of the contrastive sectors of that structure as originally defined. This pattern of embedded contrast on the horizontal dimension is thus analogous with the pattern of embedded contrast on the vertical dimension.

Taking the two dimensions together, it can be seen that the entire structure of symbolic space-time has been reproduced within one quadrant (the lower-outside section) of that space as defined at the higher level of contrast comprising the movements of the first five episodes.

This reflexive embedding of the structure of narrative space-time is the formal expression of a process of reflexive transformation of the structure, which takes the specific form of the juxtaposition of that structure with a transformed version of itself. The relations between boy, game, and jaguar constitute a transformation of the previously existing structure, or rather the beginning of the realization of such a transformation, inasmuch as they are the products of a coordinated set of transformations of the spatiotemporal relations of the boy, the fledglings, and the jaguar on both dimensions of space-time. The representation of this set of relations as an articulated structure of dimensions of narrative space-time, which at the same time constitutes a moving point *within* the previously existing structure defined by the same dimensions, conveys the message that the set of relations defined on those dimensions, which had previously reached an impasse, now exists as a successive moment of itself. The set of relations has, in other words, begun to change.

Episode 7.   The contradictory roles of the jaguar toward the boy are associated with different domains of symbolic space-time. The role of nurturing parent is associated with the intrahousehold space of the boy's natal family, while the role of future hunting companion (that of adult male equal) is associated with the extrahousehold space of the forest. At this stage in the boy's development, however, the two roles, although anchored as it were at opposite ends of the temporal continuum of the boy's maturation process, are structurally contemporaneous. During adolescence, the two role-relations coexist as complementary, opposing but interdependent tendencies. The two roles can be clearly differentiated only in horizontal space, where the contrast between social inclusion and exclusion is still represented by the contrast between the inside of the natal household and the wild space of the forest that begins immediately outside it.

When the jaguar reaches the threshold of his house, at the end of his trek through the forest from the cliff of the macaws, there are suddenly two jaguars. The male jaguar, the hunter and future "companion" of the boy, is still there, standing outside the house, but now there is a female jaguar standing at the door of the house (i.e., at the boundary between outside and inside, guarding the inside space, which is her domain). As the jaguar's wife, she is obviously destined for the role of the boy's adoptive mother and consequently for the task of nurturing the boy within the house while her husband returns to the forest to hunt. She initiates the ensuing interaction by rejecting the boy and any parental relationship to him (calling him "someone else's child"), but she is overruled by the male jaguar, who reiterates that her nurturing the boy as her (their) son is necessary so he can become his (the male jaguar's) hunting companion when he grows big and strong. He then unloads both boy and game from his back onto the floor of the house: the boy to be fed, the game to be cooked.

What has happened? In the context of the division between intrasocial and extrasocial space (the threshold of the house), the contradictory elements of the jaguar's relationship to the boy have become polarized and embodied in two distinct figures. It is important to bear in mind that of the two contradictory role-aspects, that of adult male social equal ("hunting companion") has already been established as predominant over that of nurturing parent in relation to dependent child by the actions in the fifth episode. At that point, the jaguar exercised his powers as hunter to destroy the embodiments of the boy's role as dependent child, opening the way for the appearance in episode six of the mediated and weakened expression of this aspect of the boy's identity as the dead game. The pattern of role-identities and relations that manifests itself in the disambiguated form of the doubled jaguar figure and its complementary relations to the boy thus has three elements: first, a pair of roles, one of which (nurturing parent) is essential to the realization of the other (adult companion); second, a contradictory relationship between these roles, such that the adult companion role must realize itself at the expense of the progressive extinction of the nurturing parent role; and third, an asymmetrical relationship between the two roles, such that the adult companion one predominates over the other one.

The triangular relationship of the two jaguars and the boy embodies these three aspects in a manner that allows the male jaguar, representing the dominant and future-oriented aspect of the boy's developing role-identity, to support both the boy's identification with

him and his own contradictory but necessary nurtural relation with
the female jaguar, while at the same time expressing the contradiction between the two roles in the form of direct conflct with the
female jaguar (a conflict that the male jaguar wins because of his
identification as the dominant role of the pair).

The female jaguar, conversely, is forced to assume the opposite
pattern of behavior toward both the boy and her husband. The dom-
inance of the adult male hunter's role personified by her husband
means that the contradiction between their two roles becomes focused within her relation to the boy. Her own nurtural relation to
him is necessary only in order to create the basis for its rejection, and
the predominance of the male role guarantees that this will be the
form of the resolution of the contradiction. The female jaguar is
therefore forced from the outset to assume a stance of overt rejection
toward the boy. It is she, rather than her husband, who thus directly
expresses the contradictory aspect of their joint relation to the boy.
This makes her appear as "the problem" in the relationship, obscur-
ing the fact that the contradiction is created by the transformation
entailed in the male jaguar's relation with the boy. It also permits
the male jaguar to express the contradictory aspect of his position,
namely its ambivalent requirements for both the performance and
the rejection of her role, in the indirect form of rejecting her rejection
of the boy.

The polarization of the jaguar figure into mutually opposing
manifestations of the contradictory aspects of the parental role provides the necessary context for the differentiation of the boy from the
dead game. Immediately following the exchange between the two
jaguars and their entry into the house, the boy and the game are separated from their common position on the jaguar's back and moved
in opposite directions, the boy toward constructive inclusion within
and the game toward destructive exclusion from the social space of
the jaguar family. This differentiation on the horizontal plane of
symbolic space-time is directly correlated with the displacement on
the vertical dimension of both boy and game from the jaguar's back
to the ground.

The episode has the same self-embedded form of structure as the
preceding one. The structure of the action, however, is analogous to
the pattern of successfully accomplished transformations in episode
five, rather than to the paralysis of movement on both dimensions in

episode three, which is replicated in the preceding episode. As in episode five, the coordinated polarization and integration of complementary aspects of a set of relationships leads to the transformation of the pattern itself. The game is now to be cooked and eaten. This means both that it will become the sustenance of the boy's development from the weakened near-child that he is into a man who is fit to be the hunting companion of the male jaguar and that it will disappear as a separate entity in its own right.

Episode 8.   The framework of the boy's transformation into a man is now complete. As the preceding analysis has attempted to bring out, this transformation entails a pattern of contrasting role relations between the boy and his jaguar "parents" that is contradictory at the level of the structure of the natal family household. This contradiction, however, provides the dynamic for the process of development that is to take place. It is, moreover, implicit in the developmental character of the transformation in question that it must transform itself as it proceeds.

The first overt expression of the contradiction in the preceding episode takes the form of a confrontation between the polarized aspects of the parental jaguar figure. This, however, is prior to the beginning of the transformation itself, which starts when the boy begins to eat the cooked meat of the game. If this transformation entails the boy's acquisition of the ability to act as a man like his father, or, in concrete terms, to take on the character of that archetype of male autonomy and self-sufficiency, the hunter, it must mean that as he eats the roast meat and grows he will become able to take over from his father the task of confronting, defying, and dominating his jaguar mother. His ability to do this should, in fact, become the essential index of his progress towards the completion of his transformation into a man. While the male jaguar is present in the house, however, there is no opportunity for the female jaguar to express her rejection or, therefore, for the growing boy to manifest his resistance to it. This was the situation in episode seven after the jaguar and the boy arrived together at the house upon their return from the macaws' nest.

Episode eight, by contrast, begins when the male jaguar leaves the house to go hunting again. In his absence, the boy demands a certain kind of meat from the female jaguar, who indirectly refuses by demanding that he substitute another kind of meat. It may be noted in passing that the theme of substitution is encountered here for the second time, the first being the boy's substitution of the stone "egg" for the fledglings in his trick on the ZH at the macaws' nest. As in the previous instance, it is germane that "substitution" is the mode in which the Kayapó separate growing boys from their natal families to become adults in the men's house under the aegis of their "substitute" fathers and mothers. The boy, on his own, defies her instructions and seizes and eats the forbidden meat. The mother responds with a menacing hiss and a display of her claws and fangs, all the while intoning the reassuring words, "Don't be afraid!" (a succinct expression of the contradictory character of her relation to the boy—as apt an example as any of Bateson's (1972) notion of the "double bind"). The boy, of course, is very properly afraid and flees from the house.

The pattern of the boy's movements now becomes of the utmost significance in terms of symbolic space-time. First, under his own power, he passes from inside to outside the house; but then he immediately climbs a tree, thus retreating upward in vertical space-time to a point analogous to his position in the macaws' nest. He has, at this point, retraced the pair of opening moves in the disastrous macaw hunt with which the myth began. From his place high in the tree, he is then coaxed down by the male jaguar, who carries him back inside the house, thus retracing the reverse pair of moves in the jaguar's rescue of the boy from the nest. The juxtaposition of the two reversible pairs of moves on the horizontal and vertical dimensions in a single episode signals that the contradictory dynamics of the development of the plot have intensified to the point where a resolution (i.e., the attainment of the reversibility of the opening moves) is near at hand. There is now reversibility, but it is the unstable reversibility of the "vicious circle," which in its progressive intensification portends its increasingly imminent destruction.

The reversible cycle of displacements in symbolic space-time that is produced by the boy's first set of moves resembles the dynamic of a turbine revolving within the field of a dipole magnet. The opposition between the male and female jaguars, "opened up" by the periodic absences of the male jaguar from the house, constitutes the field of force within which the boy moves, and, by moving, generates increasing power for himself. The reversibility of the pattern that has been achieved is not yet definitive; it is, rather, provisional and unstable. The boy's return to the house is only temporary; as soon as the male jaguar leaves again to hunt, the same scene is repeated with the female jaguar. This repetition, however, has an important significance of its own. It defines the pattern as generic and structural rather than unique and circumstantial and, therefore, increasingly as a pattern of expectation rather than merely an event. This means that the action of the boy, in provoking the same scene again and again, acquires an altered dramatic character involving courage, deliberation, and independence rather than simply reactions of surprise and terror. The repetition of the sequence of moves thus implies intensification and with intensification the strengthening of the transformation of the boy's character in the direction of the qualities of manhood.

Episode 9.   The circle is finally broken by the male jaguar after another repetition of the conflict between his wife and son. He bids his son accompany him out of the house to the riverbank, where he suggests that they bathe together. This is the first occasion on which the boy leaves the house on foot without immediately climbing a tree and the first time that he has walked on the ground outside the house in the company of the male jaguar. These two details exemplify a momentous fact: the vertical contrast between the boy and the jaguar has disappeared.

The joint plunge of father and son into the river marks a pivotal point in the symbolic space-time of the narrative. Bathing in flowing river water accompanies many Kayapó rites de passage since it combines the two dimensions of symbolic space-time: the vertical (the water flows from up to down) and the horizontal (the bathers plunge into the water from outside it and then reverse their movements from inside it to outside it again). That the father and son perform this act together in identical fashion exemplifies their identification within the same moment of structural time: adult manhood.

The vertical dimension of narrative space has of course not vanished with the disappearance of the overt vertical contrast between the boy, high in nest or treetop, and the male jaguar on the ground. The relationship of the boy, now grown to young manhood, and the adult male jaguar continues to be defined in terms of vertical space-time; it is only that the nature of this relationship has changed from one of contrast (between child and adult) to one of equivalence (of adult and adult).

The structural identity (as defined on the vertical dimension) between the hero and the jaguar is a relationship of a new kind in terms of the structure of the narrative up to this point, and accordingly entails a transformation of the structure of narrative space-time. As the vertical contrast between hero and jaguar gives way to vertical identity, a contrast of a new kind is born: that between the hero and jaguar, on the one hand, as tokens of the same type and, on the other, the general type that their identification has brought into being. This new relationship takes the concrete form of a *replication of a prototype*, which reflexively confers upon the prototype the new logical status of an instance of the *type* now represented by itself and its replica. The identity of the jaguar as an adult male is primarily marked by his role as hunter, which is in turn marked by his bow and arrows. The act that immediately follows the hero's and the jaguar's joint bath in the river is the jaguar's manufacture of replicas of his bow and arrows and his gift of them to his son, whom they define as a man like his father (in a provisional sense, at least).

The jaguar and the hero then return to the house as they had left it, walking side by side. The young man thus reverses his movement at the beginning of the episode between the inner space of the household and the external space of the forest, the space of hunters and therefore of adult men, under his own power (i.e., walking by himself directly on the ground). Reversibility of movement in horizontal space is thus attained as the corollary of the reversing of the hero's characteristic position and identity as defined on the vertical dimensions.

The transformation of the structure of vertical space-time, however, also implies a cognate transformation of the terms of horizontal space. Now that the hero has exchanged the perspective of a child or even an adolescent for that of a man, identified with the role of hunter and thereby associated primarily with the out of doors, what is "inside" for him and what "outside"? The values (social inclusion/exclusion) associated with the complementary regions of horizontal space (inside and outside the natal family household) have implicitly "pivoted" for the boy as a corollary of the pivoting of the terms of his identity as defined on the dimension of vertical space. This pivoting of the horizontal dimension is still provisional and in-

complete only because the hero has not yet actually used his hunting
weapons, not yet become a hunter in fact, and therefore has not yet
concretized his identification with the male jaguar. To become a
hunter in fact—to become a man in the full sense—he must kill an
animal.

Episode 10.   The killing of an animal by a hunter is the prototypical instance of a relation of exclusion from the same social
space: the game is by definition outside the social space of the
hunter, and the hunter stands in a mutually contradictory relation to
the game within the natural space of the forest. The killing of the one
by the other only realizes the implications of the mutual incompatibility of the two protagonists within the same space. To consum-
mate his identification as a man with the male jaguar, the hero must
not only use his bow and arrows to make a kill, he must at the same
time sever his remaining tie of nurtural dependency on his jaguar
mother. This in turn requires that he become fully able to assume
the role of the male jaguar to the female jaguar in relation to himself:
he must be able to defy her rejection and threats without fleeing and
to overcome her opposition to his demands for food (and, implicitly,
for growth). Until he can do this, he will still be dependent upon
both of his parental figures and not yet an adult in his own right.

There is only one act that can accomplish all of these ends at
once, and that is what the male jaguar has already enjoined the hero
to prepare himself to do. To kill one's mother (albeit a jaguar) by
shooting her through the nipples of both breasts is no doubt a drastic
but nonetheless effective method of severing one's nurtural dependence on her. It also defines the space within which the killing is
done (in this case, the interior of the symbolic natal household) as the
"external" space into which the hunter sallies to slay his infrasocial
quarry. In other words, that single act achieves the "pivoting" of the
structural values of horizontal space and thus parallels the pivoting of
vertical space-time effected in the last episode. It consummates the
transformation of the values of both dimensions of symbolic space-
time. What was "inside" is now "outside" to the hero, and what was
"up" (himself) is now "down."

It is important that the mother jaguar's rejection takes the form,
in this final encounter, of a full relapse into predatory jaguar
behavior, treating the boy as if *he* were a game animal rather than

her own child and thereby forcing him to kill or be killed. By killing his jaguar mother under these circumstances with his bow and arrow, the hero reciprocally reduces her to an animal stripped of all social attributes. His act thus establishes him as a hunter in fact as well as in theory, able to assume the role of his father as a killer of animals and at the same time able to play his father's other role of standing up to and overcoming the rejection of his (jaguar) mother, which terminates his dependence on his father in this final respect.

The hero's reduction of his jaguar mother to the status of a slain animal also establishes her as a replica. She has now become, at his hands, a duplication of the dead animal with which he (or more specifically, the regressive, childish, mother-dependent aspect of his social identity) was identified when he arrived at her house. The replication now in question is obviously in the opposite direction and concerns the opposite aspect of the hero's identity than that observed in the earlier episode. In the present case, it is the parental figure who is reduced to the status of replica of the negative, child-oriented (and above all, dead) aspect of the hero's identity. Her slaughter in this capacity marks the definitive termination of the child-oriented aspect of the hero's identity—just as the opposite form of replication in the relation between the positive aspect of the hero's identity and that of his jaguar father marks the equation of the hero's identity as a whole with the social persona of the male jaguar—in a way that leaves no room for lingering regressive traces such as those represented by the hero's relation to his mother.

The "negative" replication of the hero's own "dead," animalized, unviable aspect in the form of the killing of the figure in relation to whom that aspect is defined constitutes that aspect as a general type as surely and effectively as the gift of a new bow and arrows from the male jaguar to his son constitutes the adult identity symbolized by the weapons as a general type. Just as the latter was embodied in a token object, the bow and arrows, the replication or separation of which from the prototype object embodied the definition of the generalized type in question as a function of the reproduction of its tokens, so also a token object (actually, a pair of objects) is separated by the hero himself as tokens of his control over the negated aspect of himself that his act of symbolic matricide has now constituted as a general category.

These objects are the cotton string and the roast meat. Spinning string from cotton (a domesticated plant among the Kayapó, raised by women in the gardens belonging to them) is a characteristic activity of adult women (i.e., women with families of their own). The string, in other words, is a female counterpart of the bow and arrows as an emblem of adult womanhood. The hero's acquisition of it, not as an implement for his own use like the bow and arrow, but rather simply as a possession under his control, represents the control he has now acquired over his female natal family relations and, by implication, his own former dependence on them.

The same message, only this time focused directly on his own (now suppressed) identity as a dependent rather than on the female nurtural figure who served as its object, is embodied in the hero's seizure of a piece of the roast meat that the female jaguar has been cooking. The symbolism of the roast meat and the dead game animals of which the cooked meat is the transformed aspect, has been discussed at length above. Suffice it to say here that the hero's act represents an assertion of control over his own suppressed and transformed identity as a dependent child in a form that no longer requires the mediation of a parental figure, such as the mother he has just done away with. It may be suggested that this act of symbolic self-possession represents not only the final transformation of the hero's social relations with his natal family but also, at a deeper level, a cultural model of the psychodynamic process of repression in the service of the adult ego.

The final and most important of all the tokens that the hero takes possession of is, of course, the fire. His breaking off a piece of the burning log is the first time that fire has been used to reproduce itself. Up until this moment, fire has only been used to "cook" other things (e.g., meat warmed in the sun); it has never been applied to itself. This differentiates it in a fundamental way from fully socialized (ordinary human) cooking fires. This difference is coded by two aspects of the fire, which are regularly emphasized by Kayapó tellers of the myth. The first is that the jaguars' fire consists of a single piece of wood—an entire log—rather than the plurality of pieces arranged in a radially organized pile that came to be the normal social form. The log is burning only at one end, so that its form as a large round disc recalls the sun, which, prior to the discovery of the jaguar's fire, was the only form of cooking fire known to humans. Second, the species of tree to which the fire log belongs, *Hymenea* sp. (Portuguese, *jatoba*; Kayapó, *moytch*), has a unique symbolic significance for the Kayapó and the other Ĝe peoples. It exudes a bloodred resin that is collected and applied to the shafts of arrows immediately above the point, in imitation of the raw blood it is intended that the arrows should draw. The wood of the tree is the same color—namely, the color of raw meat. The message is patent: consistent with its virginal character as a fire unlit (un"cooked") by another fire, the jaguar's fire is raw.

The cooking fire is the joint possession of both jaguars; it is uniquely associated with neither. It serves, by the same token, to mediate the two opposing aspects of the hero's identity—those respectively associated with each of the jaguar parents. It is the agent through which the game, representing the regressive, dependent aspect of the hero's identity, is transformed into cooked food for the progressive, developing adult aspect, thus making the former disappear through the same process by which the latter is brought into being. It is, in short, the supreme transformational operator of the structure as a whole, which transforms all structural values into their opposites: child (in the developmentally progressive aspect of the status) into adult; child (in the regressive sense of dependency) into cooked and eaten food; inside-the-house into outside; up into down (remember that the fire itself begins the story as the sun, "up" in the sky).

It is only by virtue of having undergone the transformation of his own identity and relations in all of these respects, culminating in the "pivoting" of his relation to both dimensions of space-time and his reflexive redefinition of both aspects of his own identity as replicas of the general types represented by his parental prototypes, that the hero is able to replicate the fire itself. His replication of the fire, in turn, transforms it too into a reflexively self-replicating, potentially generalized entity (the entity in question being the agent and operator of the transformations of all aspects of the structure). The hero's new fire is thus the dynamic counterpart of his own new identity: it embodies the structural transformations of the process through which his own transformation has been achieved, which are reflexively caused by that very transformation. Possessed of this ultimate prize, the hero is ready for his return.

Episode 11.   The eleventh episode consists of the hero's emerging from the jaguar's house (carrying his full array of "tokens," including the fire and the bow and arrows), his meeting with the male jaguar, and their separation (they move off in opposite directions: the hero toward his home, following a creek the jaguar points out to him, the jaguar deeper into the forest). This separation has of course been foreseen by the jaguar, and formed part of the instructions he gave the boy about how to use the bow and arrows on his mother. It occurs in fact as the immediate sequel to and consequence of the hero's leaving the house (now redefined, as a result of the "pivoting" of the values of the horizontal dimension of narrative space-time, as "outside" space from his point of view) for the out-of-doors (which now, because of its association with the hunter's role that he has become identified with, has become "inside" for him). In this context, the hero's separation from the male jaguar takes the form of a "pivoting" or transformation of the structural meaning of the male jaguar himself, together with the spatial domain with which he is identified: the forest. From his briefly occupied role as the focus of the hero's new "inside" domain of horizontal space, the jaguar, along with his forest habitat, is relegated to the status of the excluded, "external" domain that includes his dead wife and house.

The question is: Why does this separation, with its accompanying transformation of the meaning of the jaguar, take place? Why does the male jaguar insist that the hero leave him and return to his own society just at the point when he (the hero) is finally able to assume the role of hunting companion? The answer is that the hero, through the very act of making himself a hunter and thus the potential companion of the male jaguar, has severed the connection between them. The hero has not only destroyed the family in whose terms the male jaguar's relation to him as "father" was defined, he has, with the same stroke, symbolically destroyed that aspect of his own identity which tied him to that family, including *both* of its parental figures. He has, in sum, exploded the common social space within which his relation to the jaguar was defined. They are consequently now "outsiders" in relation to one another.

Episode 12. The hero's act of leaving the house for the out-of-doors, by moving from the "outside" to the "inside" domain of horizontal space, thus recursively entails its own repetition in relation to the male jaguar and his forest domain. The forest, as we have just seen, "pivots" in its structural significance from "inside" to "outside" in relation to the hero's separation from the male jaguar.

This pivoting, by putting off the attainment of the original goal of the move (namely, "inside" space), immediately entails a repetition of the move: the return from the forest as a whole, now homogeneously defined, as at the outset of the story, as "outside" space, to human society ("inside" space, in the form it had at the beginning of narrative time, namely the hero's natal household with its associated family relations).

The final reversal of the pattern of moves comprising the opening sequence of the story thus develops as the consummation of the process through which the embedded subdivisions of narrative space-time, generated by the intervening transformations of the hero's identity and relations, are surmounted and cleared away. The reversal of the original pattern of moves and the restoration of the original structure of space-time in which they were made coincide up to a point.

This coincidence, however, vanishes in the moment of consummation when the hero has finally reversed his original move of leaving his maternal household and is once again in the bosom of his family, showing his mother and sisters the things he has brought from the jaguars. These tokens identify him as no longer the boy who left the house to hunt macaw fledglings but as a young man who has "left the house" in the sociological sense of having severed his ties as a child to it. The fact that he carries with him the piece of fire, as the token of the principle of transformation of all dimensions of social identity and relationships into their opposites, symbolically indexes his transformation. So, in more concrete social terms, does the hero's failure to reciprocate the tears of salutation shed for him by his mother and sister in the traditional Kayapó greeting. By this breach of reciprocity he signifies that he is no longer a member of their family and no longer belongs in their social space. Their house, which since the beginning of the story has embodied the "inside" domain of horizontal space (the space of reciprocal social inclusion), has become "outside" to him.

The recurring pattern of pivoting values of horizontal space, which began in the house of the jaguars, has thus repeated itself once again with the pivoting of the spatial meaning of the hero's "real" household. The hero's maternal house has, up to this point in the story, been synonymous with the field of social relations; it (and its surrogate, the house of the jaguars) has, in other words, been identical with the social ("inside") domain of narrative space-time. As such, it has served both as the point of departure of the hero's movements and the goal of his struggle to return to human society; in short, it has been the criterion of reversal of his opening move, the return to which would mark the synthesis of the hero's entire sequence of moves as a reversible set, that is, as a structure.

The pivoting of the hero's natal household from "inside" to "outside" is anomalous as far as the spatiotemporal framework of the story up to now is concerned. There exists, as yet, no other point in social space outside of or apart from the house that can be defined as "inside" from the point of view of the hero. This fact by itself would appear to render the reversal of the hero's movements impossible since there is now no "inside" point for him to return to.

The contradiction is surmounted by the appearance, at this point, of the village with its collective men's association (which, in Kayapó society, is located in a men's house or houses built in the middle of the central village plaza); or, in other words, the appearance of human society in its full contemporary form. The hero, still in the midst of his show-and-tell session in his mother's and sister's house, is summoned by the men of the village, who are assembled in the plaza, to come to them and tell of his experiences with the jaguars. When he arrives, they welcome him as one of themselves— as a grown man and a member of their society. The hero has finally come home; he is "inside" the social space to which he belongs. Reversibility, as far as he is concerned, has been achieved.

The new context created by the reversal of the hero's movements, however, raises a new problem since its very creation constitutes an unreversed move: the generation of a new point in narrative space-time, the communal men's house, as the terminus of a move out of the hero's natal family household. It is significant that this latest move is presented as motivated, not by the hero himself, but by the tokens he carries, and above all the fire. It is the desire of the men to see and hear about these things that leads them to summon the hero to join them. The hero's final move is thus not only *his* move but also, in a distinctly specified sense, a move of the fire as well.

To recognize this is to realize that the unreversed aspect of the move (the appearance of human society in its new form) is merely the culmination of the unreversed displacement of the fire from its place within the female jaguar's house to the new collective form of human society. The final move of both hero and fire from his natal household to the men's house is, as we have seen, only the last in a recursive series of repetitions of a pattern of movement that began in the house of the jaguars when the hero broke off the piece of fire. This sequence culminates, from the hero's point of view, in a reversal of his earlier moves; but, from the point of view of the fire, the same acts constitute a new and unreversed displacement from family household to communal society.

The contradictory situation constituted by the reversal of the hero's movements and the unreversed movement of the fire has its counterpart in the problem of coordinating the developmental processes of individual and family in Kayapó society.

The society that has been created in response to the individual hero's original feat of bringing his bit of fire from the house of the jaguar is, incongruously, a *communal* society. It therefore presupposes a standardized pattern of relations to which each family segment and each adult male member of the communal men's association must conform.

The hero's act of breaking off and bringing with him the bit of fire from the jaguar's house and the transformations of his own social identity and natal family relations of which this feat is both metaphor and metonym become the basis of his integration into communal society. As the grounds of his recognition by the other men as a member of their communal association, these deeds and transformations implicitly constitute the common pattern of adult male relations and recruitment to the mature men's association for society as a whole. The contradiction thus arises: How can a unique case of individual development—achieved in the context of the transformation of a unique family household, embodied in a unique fire, and all defined as taking place *outside* human society—also turn out to be the received, collectively established pattern of social integration? How, in short, can the hero's feat be both original and unique on the one hand and the common, generalized pattern of a communal social structure on the other?

Posed in these terms, the contradiction is irresolvable. The terms in which it is posed, however, reflect a particular point of view, that of the male individual as he develops from childhood within a single family household toward integration as an adult into the communal life of society. This is the perspective embodied in the plot of the narrative up to this point. There is, however, another point of view, the reverse of this, from which the same process appears in a form that avoids the contradiction. This is the viewpoint of society as a whole. From this perspective, society as a collective entity is the source of the pattern of transformation embodied, in identical terms, by each family household and the developmental processes (individual and familial) of which it is the locus. Only on this lower, individual household level is the transformation experienced as a unique and unprecedented sequence of events by each developing individual.

The sociocentric point of view is not simply an analytical abstraction without counterpart in Kayapó social experience or social ideology. It corresponds, first of all, to the sociological fact that the collective institutions of Kayapó society constitute a generalized representation of the structure of the segmentary family household. It also corresponds to Kayapó ideas of the outlook of the mature man, fully integrated into this communal system of social and ceremonial groupings focused in the men's house. The problem of reconciling the sociocentric and egocentric perspectives on society is thus a central issue for Kayapó culture. This general problem is manifested from the perspective of the male individual as the problem of reconciling the form of human society as it appears to him as an adult (an integral structure, uniformly applying to the village as a whole) with the form of society as it appears from the structural perspective of a child (limited to the undispersed natal family household).

This is, in effect, the problem that is posed by the myth in the concrete form of the need to reverse the movements of the fire. The reversal of the fire's passage from family household to men's house means its return from men's house to family household. What is implied by such a movement? The fire's move from the house of the jaguars to the communal society of men is not a simple displacement of the fire as a whole from one point in space to another; rather, it takes the form of a separation of a token bit of fire from the "prototype" fire. The great "raw" log of *moytch* wood remains behind in the jaguar's house. It is essential to remember, at this point, that the hero's bit of fire is treated in the story as a single replication of fire —limited to its character as an individual token—rather than as identical with fire as a general, infinitely replicable type. The hero's

fire does not, in other words, confer the ability to make more fires or
constitute control over fire in general. His movement of the fire from
jaguar family household to men's house thus serves to separate
token from type. Reversing this move would therefore entail reversing the direction of the type-token relation between the two levels of
social organization, with the men's house (with its fire) now serving
as proto*type* and the female-centered family household (with its cooking fire) assuming the role of token-replica.

Episode 13.   To reverse the movement of the fire *as replicated token*
from female-centered family household to men's house, in other
words, would require the movement of the fire in the same capacity
(as replicated token) from men's house to the female family households of the village. This in turn would imply that the men's association in the center of the plaza had become the locus of the prototype
fire from which the replicas were made. The possession of the prototype fire, representing as it does the pattern of transformation both
of individuals (boys into men) and families, by the central communal institution of the society and the replication of fire from that
source by the segmentary family-household units composing the
village as a whole, would amount to a concrete expression of the sociocentric formulation of the process of individual and family development outlined above. It would also correspond to the role that, as
argued earlier, is actually played by the communal institutions of
Kayapó society, which is to embody and guide the reproduction of
the structure of the family household according to a standardized,
precisely replicated pattern, the prototype of which is provided by
the system of communal institutions.

   This is, of course, exactly what happens. The men, having heard
the hero's story and seen the token objects he has brought with him,
resolve to go to the jaguar's house and take the great fire log for
themselves (along with the bow, the cotton string, and the rest of the
roast meat). They successfully carry out their reversible journey to
and from the jaguar's house, returning with the burning log, which
they throw down in the center of the plaza (the space associated with
their collective institutional identity). From there, bits of the fire are
distributed to the women. For the first time fire is used in a general
way to make fire, and cooking fire thereby becomes a universal
possession of human society. Equally important, from the point of

view of the story, each female-centered family household and its developmental processes is formulated as a replica of the prototype identified with the central communal institution of the village, the men's house with its men's association.

To make the trip to the jaguar's house and return with the fire, each man transforms himself into a different species of animal (but not a jaguar or other carnivore, or an immature form such as a fawn or fledgling). Only thus transformed do the men venture out into the forest to the jaguar's house. They transform themselves back into humans only after they have thrown down the fire log in the center of the village. The reversible transformation into animal form and back again thus frames the men's reversible movement to and from the jaguars' house and, more to the point, the transference of the prototype of the fire from the jaguars' family household to the communal space of the village plaza and men's house.

The men's expedition to and from the jaguars' house to steal the fire constitutes a mediation between two levels of social structure seen from two different points of view, respectively represented by two opposing forms of relationship between themselves and the fire. The first of these is epitomized by the hero's arrival in the men's house with his token of fire. In this form of the relation, the female-centered family household contains the prototype of the process of production (socialization) of the members of the men's house as individuals. The other form of the relation is that which results from the men's collective fire theft. In this version, the men's communal association as a whole is identified with the prototype of the process of (re)producing the female-centered family household.

The connection between these two opposing configurations of the structure of Kayapó society is constituted as a reversible movement between men's house and family household. This movement is itself impossible to classify within either of the two forms of the relationship between which it mediates. These two versions obviously correspond to the two structural points of view defined above: the egocentric (perhaps *family-centered* would be a more appropriate term) and the sociocentric, respectively. The two imply one another and appear to contradict one another, unless they are kept separate as perspectives appropriate to distinct contexts or moments of social relations. Together they constitute the totality of Kayapó social structure. The reversible connection between them, the supreme embodiment of the structure as a whole, however, entails a level of ambiguity or "double focus" since it fits into neither point of view, but, rather, seems to contradict the distinction between them. This ambiguous quality, I suggest, renders it unintegrable into the ordinary level of collective consciousness of social structure, which may be formulated in terms either of one perspective or the other, but never both together. For this reason, the men cannot undertake their theft of the fire, entailing as it does the concrete embodiment of the reversible transformability of the two fundamental perspectives on social reality, as ordinary social men. They became instead extrasocial beings (animals) for the duration of their action.

The animal species with which the men identify, as noted, are neither carnivores like the jaguar nor immature forms like the macaw fledglings; neither do they constitute a single, collectively standardized species "reflecting" the men's collective identity as a corporate social group. There are, rather, a variety of species, each identified with a different function or aspect of the action (e.g., the tapir carries the log, the toad and *jaho* snap up the embers that fall from the log and thereby get their red throats, etc.). The message conveyed by this phase of the animal symbolism of the myth is thus the thorough naturalization (desocialization) of the action that mediates between the domains of the individual family household, as an egocentric or "family-centric" entity represented by its jaguar form, and human society as a collective totality. The point in terms of Kayapó social consciousness is that the agency through which such a transformation is effected cannot itself be part of either domain of collective representations.

The men's transportation of the fire from the jaguars' house to the human village effects a disambiguation of the status of the fire (and, in opposite senses, of human beings and jaguars). From now on, animals will be unambiguously animal, and humans unambiguously human. The animal forms appropriate to the action by which this distinction is accomplished are themselves *animal*, with none of the ambiguities and ambivalences associated with large carnivores —above all jaguars—in Kayapó thought.

It is significant that the hero does not appear as an individual in this final episode. His story is finished when he achieves the final reversal of his earlier moves at the end of the preceding episode. The narrative continues because, in bringing his own story to a conclusion, the hero has precipitated another story: namely, how the collective form of human society arose from the dispersal of an individual domestic family, and how the collective institutions in turn established the pattern for the reproduction of all future families. The subject of this new story is thus not individual but collective; it is not the hero as an individual, but the communal society of men to which he now belongs; and not the individual women of the hero's family, but all the women of all the family households that together constitute the village.

In formal terms, the men's actions of bringing the fire log from the jaguars' house to the center of the village plaza and distributing bits of it to all the women's households of the plaza periphery achieve the final reversal of the remaining unreversed moves of the previous episode. Their first move, the theft of the fire, constitutes a reversed movement complete in itself, which in effect replicates the story of the hero that has occupied the preceding twelve episodes of the myth. This reversed movement of the men, however, is also the vehicle of the unreversed movement of the fire from the jaguars' family household to the men's house. This latter move parallels the unreversed move of the fire from the hero's maternal household to the men's house in the previous episode, with the difference that the fire in question is now the general type of fire rather than a mere token. Both of these phases of the movement of the fire from family household to men's house are then reversed in the final act of the generalized distribution of fire tokens from the men's house to the family households of the village. The final episode of the myth thus presents a concise model of the structure of Kayapó society as a reflexively self-reproducing, hierarchically organized system based on the generalized pattern of the developmental process of the segmentary household unit.

The symbolic significance of the cooking fire is clearly apparent in the context of this sociological vision. Cooking per se, as the use of fire to transform the flesh of animals into food for socialized humans, is a step in the transformation of natural content into social form, but it is not in itself tantamount to human society or culture. The jaguars in their isolated, semisocial family could cook with their fire, but they were only transitional forms between nature and society and not fully socialized beings. This quasi-cultural state is succinctly expressed by the rawness of their fire on its single log of *moytch* wood.

Their fire can cook meat but it cannot "cook," or kindle, itself. Human society as such is born when the fire—and the pattern of socializing transformation it represents—becomes reflexively self-replicating. This entails its embodiment in a generalized and recursive form: the fire-making fire. In the terms of the myth, nature is not to culture as raw is to cooked, but rather as raw is to the making (the reflexive self-cooking) of fire.

Initial and Final States: The parallelism between the hero and the fire.

The contrast between the situation at the beginning of the myth and that at its end can be understood in terms of the above interpretation of the fire and the parallelism between the movements of the fire and those of the hero that together constitute the story as a whole.

At the beginning of the tale, the only form of cooking fire is the sun, high in the sky, a single, round object rather like the end of some distant burning log. Human beings and animals are little differentiated, partly because humans lack direct access to fire and are therefore forced to eat their meat virtually raw (not to mention other raw and, to a modern Kayapó, disgusting foods fit only for animals), but also because human society as such exists only in the form of an individual family with its household, a form matched by the "animal" family and household of the jaguars (with the important exception that the jaguars lack children of their own).

The hero also begins his story qua hero (i.e., as an individual subject who is more than a mere appendage to his brother-in-law's macaw-hunting project) at a point high above the earth, in the company of beings (birds) associated with the sky. At the moment in time and at the point in space that the hero finally touches ground (in the jaguars' house), the fire also appears on earth for the first time. The hero's successful replication of the identity of his paternal jaguar prototype is the context of the parallel replication of the fire as a token of its hitherto unitary parent log. The return of the hero from the jaguars' house to the village becomes the path by which the fire also makes its way to human society. Finally, the constitution of human society in general as a replication of the pattern of the hero's transformation finally becomes the pretext for the general self-replication of the fire. In the final situation at the end of episode thirteen, the fire, like the hero and the collective groups of men and women who constitute the protagonists of this last episode, is securely esconced within human society in its general, collective, self-replicating form, and both (people and fire) are categorically differentiated from the domain of animal nature.

The parallelism between the fire and the hero is defined in terms of the systematic analogy between the transformations of their contextual relations in the course of the story rather than in terms of any metaphorical correspondence between them as symbolic elements. The relation between the two patterns of movement is both metaphoric and metonymic; they not only correspond in form but at the same time motivate each other in a causal sense. The principle embodied in this relation is fundamental to the Kayapó vision of society. The principle is: that control over the power of transformation develops as a corollary of the process of transformation itself. Becoming socialized, in other words, implies acquiring the power to replicate the process one has undergone, which is to socialize others. This point is the complement of the principle embodied in the form of each of the two sequences of moves considered separately, namely that society is a process of reflexive self-replication of the process of (re)producing a socialized individual and the social group within which this occurs.

CONCLUSION

Aspects of Myth Structure: Syntagmatic and Paradigmatic, Form and Content

The structure of myth, like that of any narrative, is a logical form. The logic involved, however, is one of dynamic operations—of movements and transformations that have the form of actions—not of static relations of identity and contrast between elements considered as abstract semantic values. The logical structure of a mythical narrative consists of a dynamic system of functionally interrelated transformations among elements that are themselves transformed as a function of the transformation of the relations between them. The logical form of the process is manifested as an invariant relation between the different operations (transformations) that make up the process as a whole.

Invariance, or conservation, is a diachronic relation; it defines the constant form of a process of transformation, which takes the concrete form of a series of actions related as a set of operations. In-

variance defines the reversible aspect of the functional covariation
among the operations composing the structure of the story. It is the
integration of a contradictory element within this reversible structure of operations, motivated by the need to conserve the invariance
principle that alone gives it coherence, which leads, as we have seen,
to the irreversible transformation of that structure (a diachronic result). Invariance is thus revealed as a fundamental constituent of
diachronic time. Structure, of which invariance constitutes the
essential component, is thus itself essentially diachronic in
character. It must not be confused with "synchrony" in the Saussurean sense of a relation of formal identity or contrast abstracted
from the time of speech (i.e., of concrete social activity). Myths are
stories of action; action constitutes their essential content. Their
structure and their time is the structure and time of activity
("diachrony" in Saussurean terms).

The narrative form of a myth is not identical with the structure
that generates it. This form, the story of which the myth overtly consists, presents itself as a recounting of a unique sequence of actions
and events that result in the transformation of some aspect of the
world—in short, as an intrinsically diachronic phenomenon. This,
however, is the content of the myth and not its form, which is that of
a socially standardized tale, told, or at any rate conceived, in a
stereotyped order by all members of the society. It should be recalled
that Saussure (1959) formulated his notion of the diachrony of
speech (*parole*) not primarily on the basis of its character as temporal
sequence but rather in terms of the variability of its sequential
arrangement as an outcome of socially undetermined individual activity. It is not temporal sequence per se, but structurally (which for
Saussure implied "socially") undetermined sequence that constituted the diachronic time of concrete interaction and historical
change. Saussure recognized a limited number of sequential forms,
idioms such as "hot dog" and established usages such as "to understand is to forgive" as synchronic (i.e., as parts of *langue* as he conceived it). By Saussure's own standard, then, the collectively stereotyped narrative form of a myth ought properly to be recognized as
"synchronic" in his sense from the analogy of idioms and other sequential forms of a culturally fixed (invariant) order.

It is therefore necessary to distinguish between the *form* of myth
as a narrative sequence and its *structure*, even if one takes the position

that the structure of myth is integrally a structure of narrative sequence. Structure is defined as a determinate relation between form and content. The structure of myth, then, is the relation between its form, which is that of a narrative, and its content, in terms of which each (form and content) can be understood as determining the other. This relation has been identified in the foregoing analysis as the invariant relationship conserved among the operations that constitute the content of the story.

The structuralist position, as formulated by Lévi Strauss, is that the overt *form* of myth as a narrative is diachronic, whereas its *structure*, as the paradigm of contrastive relations immanent in its symbolic content, is synchronic. This "structure" has a form of its own but one that is quite unrelated to the form of the myth as a narrative. The structuralist conception of myth structure is thus not really defined as a relation between the form and content *of myth* at all, but between the content of myth and the form of the structuralist model of structure, which is something else again. It in effect conflates form with structure, violating the essential distinction upon which the very concept of structure is founded.

The approach I have taken in the above analysis is thus the reverse of the structuralist position in these two essential and interrelated respects. First, I have argued that the *form* of a myth as a whole—as a complete narrative—is properly understood as "synchronic," whereas its *structure*—as embodied in the invariant principle of dynamic coordination between the paired operations and sets of operations composing the content of the narrative—is intrinsically "diachronic." Second, I have attempted to formulate the concept of structure in terms that genuinely relate the form of myth to its content.

Syntagm

What I have attempted to demonstrate in this presentation is that a rigorous analysis of the relations among the components of a mythical narrative, thus defined, reveals a *syntagmatic* structure of a kind not heretofore detected in structural analyses of myth or other symbolic forms in anthropology. This structure is essentially dynamic and consists of operations and the forms of functional coordination among them. A number of specific properties of this structure of potentially general applicability (in some cases to all, in others to some other cases and genres of mythopoeic narrative) have been identified in the analysis. They may be summarily listed as follows:

1. The binary character of the contrastive relations comprising the basic constituents of the structure of the myth and the definition of binary contrast in terms of interdependent relations of identity and contrast on complementary, contextually juxtaposed dimensions.

2. The inverse correlation of operations defined on these dimensions. (This emerges as the manifestation of a principle of conservation, which maintains an invariant balance between the separation and integration of symbolic elements or their features. This invariant principle is merely a manifestation of the principle governing the balance of identity and contrast at the level of the fundamental binary contrast.)

3. The reversibility of operations as a more powerful level of the same principle of invariant constraint, governing relations between sets of inversely correlated operations.

4. The disruption of the correlation between these two levels of invariance by a contradiction, the essential property of which is the impossibility of integrating the contradictory elements within the existing level of the structure of narrative space-time. ("Integration" is defined as the ability to coordinate the operations involving the elements in question according to both levels of the invariant principle within the framework constituted by the dimensions of narrative space-time.)

5. The reintegration of narrative space-time (instigated by number 4), which takes the correlated forms of the drive to attain reversibility of the inversely correlated pairs of operations comprising the interaction of the contradictory elements, and the drive to transform the dimensions of narrative space-time so as to provide a more ample framework capable of accommodating the more powerful set of reversible operations that this would imply. (These parallel drives become the motivating forces and orienting principles of the actions comprising the narrative.)

6. The diremption of the structure of narrative space-time in conformity with the diremption of the two levels of invariant coordination of operations. (This gives rise to two hierarchically interrelated levels of the structure of the narrative. The lower of these two levels consists of segmentary units, or episodes, which em-

body the weaker of the two levels of invariant constraint—the inverse correlation of pairs of operations. The higher constitutes the order of transformations between segments, which embodies the principle of reversibility, albeit in a provisional and incompletely realized form.)

7. The formal properties of this higher level of intersegmentary relations consist of what I have called "negative projection" on the one hand and "reflexive embedding" on the other, and the progressive and interrelated permutations of these two formal devices. (These permutations comprise, in the simplest terms, the inversion of the initial pattern of embedding, in which a "negatively projected," provisional transformation of the original structure of relations is embedded within a subspace of that structure, by the final pattern, in which the original structure as a whole becomes reflexively embedded within the now fully realized transformation of itself.)

8. The transformation of the original dimensions and elements of narrative space-time, as a corollary of this process. (These transformations constitute a progression from simple forms of static contrast to more complex and dynamic forms of relationship such as token-type differentiation, recursive replication, self-transformation or "pivoting," and the reversibility of the directionality of these transformations—which element appears in the role of token and which in that of type, which in that of prototype and which in that of replica.)

9. The end of the story as the final overcoming of the diremption between the segmentary and intersegmentary levels of narrative space-time. (This takes the form of the attainment of a synthesis of both levels of invariant constraint—inverse correlation and reversibility—within a single episode. The action of this episode recapitulates the structure of the whole sequence of interepisodic transformations making up the body of the story in the form of a set of directly reversible operations within the framework of a set of dimensions transformed in ways consistent with this final set of operations.)

Paradigm

This series of contextually bound, syntagmatic structural features forms an integral and interdependent set. They do not, however, create the structure of the myth in and of themselves. As constituents of that structure, they are the complements of the paradigmatic relations of contrast and identity between the meanings of the symbolic elements of the story (e.g., contrasts such as up:down, inside:outside, human (social):animal (natural), raw:cooked, etc.). These paradigmatic features constitute the content of the relations that are combined and permuted by the syntagmatic forms that have just been reviewed. The foregoing analysis has brought out the interdependence of these paradigmatic and syntagmatic factors. Its departures from structuralist notions of paradigmatic structure are accordingly as marked as those relating to syntagmatic structure which have just been enumerated.

The most fundamental of these departures is perhaps the conception of the nature of the constituent elements of paradigm. The immediate constituents of the paradigmatic aspect of narrative structure are operations: transformations in the relations among elements (actors, objects, settings) that are contextually juxtaposed in the narrative text.

Operations as constituents of narrative structure are embodied in actions or movements that transform structurally significant aspects of the relationships among the actors and objects involved in the action. These actions, and hence the operations they embody, are directionally oriented relative to each other within the contexts in which they occur. These orientations are defined in terms of dimensions of narrative space-time (e.g., the vertical and horizontal axes in the story that has been analyzed). These dimensions are not merely abstract semantic contrasts but forms of dynamic coordination of operations. The relative orientation of the operations is governed by the invariant functional principles of inverse covariation and reversibility applying to operations juxtaposed within the same textual context. The orientation and functional coordination of operations in relation to one another (or in some cases to replicated or reflexively embedded instances of themselves), are essential components of their meanings and hence of their paradigmatic values.

These aspects of paradigm, it must be emphasized, cannot be deduced from the semantic values or contrasts of symbolic elements or relations considered apart from their actual forms of association in the text. They depend intrinsically upon these contextual associations. An approach that fails to take systematic account of such contextually defined features will therefore necessarily produce seriously distorted and impoverished accounts of both symbolic meaning and the paradigmatic dimension of structure.

A second fundamental point about operations as elements of paradigmatic structure which was brought out in the foregoing analysis is that they are self-transforming. They change their forms in the course of the narrative. Paradigm as an aspect of narrative structure is therefore not static but dynamic; its variations of form and content are themselves reflexively integrated as components of paradigm.

This is perhaps most obvious in relation to the internal transformations of the dimensions of meaningful contrast that play such a prominent role in narrative structure. As per the preceding analysis, this is no mere matter of the attenuation (or intensification) of the same semantic meanings, as in the structuralist notion of "mediation," but of transformation in the logical forms of meaning, which become intrinsic parts of the meanings themselves. The transformation of the dimensions of the structure of the myth that has been analyzed exemplify this point. The contrast between the simple forms of vertical and horizontal polarity and the more complex contrasts between general type and specific tokens (prototype and replica, respectively) defined by these transformations become the key paradigmatic oppositions in the structure of the myth as a whole. These two transformations represent complementary aspects of the reflexive self-replication of the structure of society at both the individual and collective levels, which is the fundamental meaning of the myth.

The assumption that a single paradigm of contrastive features of the same level can be constructed that will be valid for a myth as a whole (or that such a simple, homogeneous paradigm can be represented as the "structure" of a myth as a whole) reflects a fundamental misunderstanding of both the structural and meaningful aspects of myth. The essence of the meaning and structure alike of a mythical narrative lies in the progressive transformation of the forms and meanings of the contrasts among the features that constitute its paradigmatic aspect.

Animal Symbols, Totems, and Fetishes

The operational approach to the structure of mythical narrative and its symbolic elements makes possible an insight into the specific nature of the class of animal symbols, which reveals the inner connection between their symbolic value as appropriate metaphors and their character as fetishes in the Marxian sense. The animal symbols of the myth (the macaw fledglings, the jaguar, the dead game animals that the hero eats at the jaguars' house, and the animal forms assumed by the men in their collective theft of the fire) can be identified, within the terms of this analysis, as sharing a common structural property. They invariably represent an aspect of the interaction between the dominant protagonist and the other party that is unintegrable within the framework of social relations currently serving as the context of the interaction (represented by the "inside" domain of the horizontal dimension). For most of the myth, as we have seen, this is a single family, defined as the hero's natal domestic group.

Such an unintegrable element constitutes a structural contradiction within the context of the existing level of social structure and from the point of view of the actors involved. At a higher level of structure, or from the standpoint of different actors, the same actions or attributes of identity would not be contradictory. The narrative business of the myth consists in the construction of higher levels of structure, and the transformation of the identities of the protagonists, in such a way that the contradiction can be surmounted and the contradictory elements reintegrated into the newly created, broader synthetic whole.

When, at the beginning of the myth, ZH treats WB ambiguously as a hunting companion (and thus a presumptive adult) and at the same time as a child (by urging him to return to his natal family as a "permanent fledgling"), the contradiction implicit in their relationship, from the standpoint of the family through which they are linked to the same household, is brought to the fore. At this point, one of the contradictory aspects of the relationship—the unviable one from the implicit structural standpoint of the dominant protagonist (ZH)—namely, WB's continued attachment to the common household, manifests itself in an appropriate animal form (fledglings).

In cases where both aspects of the relationship or actor-identity in question are incompatible or ambiguous within the existing social context, *both* are manifested in animal form. This is the case with the jaguar(s). The jaguar has been shown to embody the contradictory aspects of the parent as a transformational figure, on the one hand nurturing the dependent child and thus encouraging its dependence, while on the other hand urging the child to develop toward future autonomy as an adult. From the perspective of the developing child, the contradiction between these two aspects of his relations with his parents appears as a terrifying threat, worthy of impersonation by such a being as a jaguar with its ambivalent cultural associations as the embodiment both of emulous humanlike qualities and savagely antihuman properties.

The most interesting case of all is presented by the animal forms assumed by the men in the final episode (tapir, wild pig, deer, toad, tinamou). Here the social context is constituted by society as a whole, not merely a single family unit, and the protagonist is the collective body of adult men of the village. Even within this ample setting, however, certain ultimate principles of social structure can appear to present a contradiction from the vantage point of a particular position within the society (such as that of an adult man). The men's act of fire theft has been shown to constitute a mediation between two such fundamental aspects or structural perspectives on the nature of the social order, which appear contradictory from the standpoint of any position within normal (profane) society. The men's position as they mediate these two aspects by seizing the fire cannot be integrated in a noncontradictory way within the normal structure of social consciousness. They therefore appear as animals.

The "nature" incarnated in animal symbols is not simply the biological domain of animal species, adopted as a convenient metaphor for human social patterns. At the most fundamental level (what I have called the second order of symbolic signification) it consists of aspects of human society that are rendered inaccessible to social consciousness as a result of their incompatibility with the dominant framework of social relations, which serves to orient the perspectives of the various categories of actors on the social reality in which they participate. These alienated aspects of the human (social) being, which may include the most fundamental principles of social and personal existence, are therefore mediated by symbols of an ostensibly asocial, or "natural," character. The animal symbols of the Kayapó myth of fire are not merely the transparent natural metaphors of the structuralist theory of totemism but totems in the original sense of McLennan and Marx: namely, "fetishes" on the hoof.

REFERENCES

Bateson, Gregory
  1972   *Steps to an ecology of mind.* New York: Ballantine.
de Saussure, Ferdinand
  1959   *Course in general linguistics.* New York: The Philosophical Library.
Freud, Sigmund
  1918   *Totem and taboo.* Trans. A. A. Brill. New York: Moffat, Yard.
Lévi-Strauss, Claude
  1962   *Le totémisme aujourd'hui.* Paris: Presses Universitaires de France.
  1964   *Le cru et le cuit.* Paris: Plon.
  1967   The structural study of myth. In *Structural Anthropology.* Garden City,
          N.J.: Doubleday.
McLennan, J.
  1869–   The worship of animals and plants. *Fortnightly Review* 6/7.
  1870
Marx, Karl
  1972   *Capital.* Vol. 1. New York: International Publishers.
Munn, Nancy
  1973   Symbolism in a ritual context: Aspects of symbolic action. In *Hand-
          book of social and cultural anthropology,* ed. John J. Honigmann, 579–612.
          Chicago: Rand McNally.
Turner, Terence S.
  1977   Narrative structure and mythopoesis: A critique and reformulation of
          structuralist concepts of myth, narrative, and poetics. *Arethusa* 10(1):
          103–63.
  1979   Kinship, household and community structure among the Kayapó. In
          Dialectical societies, ed. D. Maybury-Lewis, 179–214. Cambridge:
          Harvard University Press.
  1980   Le dénicheur d'oiseaux en contexte. *Anthropologie et Sociétés*
          4(3):85–115.
Tylor, Edward B.
  1958   *Primitive culture* (1871). New York: Harper and Row.

Tapir Avoidance in the Colombian Northwest Amazon

Gerardo Reichel-Dolmatoff

I

The Eastern Tukanoan Indians who inhabit the Vaupés territory in the center of the Colombian Northwest Amazon are divided into some twenty tribes.[1] These tribes are exogamous units based on patrilineal descent and virilocal residence, each one subdivided into a number of named and ranked sibs. The main characteristic of social organization is language group exogamy; in fact, each tribe speaks its own language (Jackson 1976). Ideally—that is, according to shamanic precepts—these eighteen or twenty tribes are grouped into six phratries, each one consisting of at least three tribes that stand in a relationship of sister exchange. In this chapter I shall refer to the phratry constituted by the Desana, Pira-Tapuya, and Tukano proper, who occupy mainly the drainage of the Papurí river, a major western affluent of the Vaupés river.

Although it might appear to the superficial observer that these three tribes or, in fact, all Eastern Tukanoans,[2] share an essentially common culture based upon one single body of traditions, widespread resource homogeneity, and a generalized inventory of material culture, there do exist marked differences owing to a variety of intellectual orientations and also to different local ethnohistorical traditions. The Eastern Tukanoans are not a homogeneous people who would have developed from a common stock, but they rather are congeneries of larger or smaller groups, some of which are remnants of older populations. Others, perhaps most of them, are descended from invaders, newcomers from other regions who, for one reason or another, had penetrated upriver and beyond the rapids and falls into this vast rain-forest region that occupies a somewhat marginal position with reference to the wide floodplain of the Amazon Basin. From their traditions it seems that these different peoples met and mixed, raided each other or formed alliances, creating in the course of generations the kind of generalized culture that, when perceived only at its surface level, appears to be so homogeneous.

There also is an apparent overall similarity in the origin myths of all these tribes. It is told by each group in its own particular version that the ancestors came from the east, from where the sun rises, and that they slowly penetrated the land by traveling upriver. Another cycle of myths tells of a semidivine being who carried a magic staff that he thrust into the riverbank to find a place where it would stand upright and not cast a shadow. He eventually found that spot on the equatorial line, and there he created mankind. Each tribe has a repertoire of hundreds of tales that refer to the deeds of the ancestors, to their courage, their determination, not to speak of their superiority to everything they encountered on their perilous voyage.

However, as one probes deeper into these oral traditions, if one discusses and analyzes the textual records with the help of knowledgeable elders, then quite another image begins to emerge. There exist, it would seem, two parallel traditions: one is that of a glorified mythical conquest; the other is the prosaic memory of hardships and fear. Above all, there are the origin myths of how the First People sprang forth miraculously and of how they settled the land and of how a group of agnatic brothers, already specialized as chiefs, shamans, singers, warriors, and servants, built their huge longhouses, danced and sang, and took possession of the land. This is the glory of the ancestors, the ancient ones, the wise shamans and fierce war chiefs who became the progenitors of distinguished lineages. But then another story emerges: the story of a few desperate, hungry men who penetrated into a strange country full of dangers. Among these dangers were "other beings" that uttered incomprehensible sounds and lived in a strange way; these beings were hostile to all outsiders and were a threat to them. The story is one of a struggle for survival.

I am referring here to the Desana, the Pira-Tapuya, and some others, but their case is far from unique; on the contrary, the Northwest Amazon has always been a region of change and movement. For thousands of years, wandering groups, raiding parties, and small bands of men have moved here and there, lost and expatriate, as the last survivors of some disaster, or for any other reason. On the individual level, survival was not too difficult because the tropical rain forest has many resources, even for people with a very simple tool kit; but on a social level, the level of reproductive sex and family life, the matter was far more difficult. If the wandering groups included some women, then most likely they were close kin and the problem of incest arose. The only choice left was the abduction of women from another tribe, and this, of course, meant violence. And so again, the myths and narratives are replete with episodes that, under the guise of cautionary tales, speak of abducted women, women found and lost, women who ran away, and women who would commit any kind of treachery. There exists, then, a large body of oral traditions that refer to the slow process of finding a mate. At first, there are references to incestuous relationships; then came the search for almost any mate from the outside, generally acquired by abduction and often enough preceded by the murder of the woman's male kinsmen. Until, at long last, alliances began to be formed; groups of different peoples met and exchanged marriageable women and, eventually, elaborated a formalized ritual. There exists another large body of myths and tales that describe this process that leads from incest to exogamy, from chaos to order, from the violent abduction of any mate to ritualized sister exchange. This process is the all-pervading theme of Tukanoan oral literature.

It is here where, from the native point of view, the abstract problem of man-animal relationships arises and where animals are attributed with symbolic values. The point is that, in practically all of the texts I have collected among the Eastern Tukanoans, animals play the roles of people. Not that they turn into people or that people turn into animals; not that they descend from animals or anything like this; but that they are *like* animals. The animal image is used to describe "other" people—not only "other" women but other tribes.

According to traditions preserved in myths, tales, genealogies, spells, songs, descriptions of ritual, and so forth, several groups of people were already established in the Vaupés territory before the arrival of the Desana and other Tukanoan tribes. These people were the *behkára* and the *poyá*. The *behkára* were a large tribe of sedentary agriculturalists who lived in longhouses surrounded by manioc fields; the Desana called them "Tapir People." The *poyá* were nomadic hunter-gatherers who, in small bands, roamed the deep forests of the interfluvial regions, appearing here and there, on river-banks, near a longhouse, or a planted field, only to disappear again into the depths of the forest.

In the course of time the Tukanoans prevailed. They established themselves all over the Vaupés terrirory, and at present they can be found in the vast regions lying between the Vaupés river, the Apaporis, the Tiquié, and parts of the Rio Negro, mainly in Colombia but also in Brazil.

Although the modern Tukanoans derive their basic sustenance from their manioc fields, hunting and fishing are important activities, and fruit gathering in the forest constitutes another major source of food. In fact, emotionally, the hunt is a focus of many expectations and fears, gratifications and anxieties, of basic values and vague aversions that together constitute a very complex system of thoughts and actions. Among the many game animals of the Amazonian fauna, three stand out in nature as well as in the emotional world of the Tukanoan hunter: tapir, deer, and peccary. They are the largest mammals of the tropical rain forest, and they are fairly abundant and not difficult to hunt. Still, the Indians are reluctant to kill them and prefer to hunt paca, agouti, armadillo, tinamou, and guan. One might wonder then why they should deprive themselves of such a plentiful source of proteins and fats as that offered by the three large forest mammals. There exist, of course, certain practical considerations: first of all, tapirs are not very plentiful in the forest, deer are found somewhat more often, and only peccaries can be said to be abundant. Tapirs, it is true, can be called by the hunter, but deer and peccaries must be tracked, often for long distances. To hunt them in the depths of the interfluvial forests is a matter of two or three days at least, and the lesser game animals can be found at short distances from residential compounds and the fields. Tukanoans agree that the large game animals would provide greater quantities of meat, but they add that the quality is poor; the meat is musky and fat, and it is not easily digestible. Many are forbidden to eat it; children, expectant mothers, and women who are still nursing a baby must not eat the meat of such forest animals as tapir, deer, peccary, woolly monkey, curassow, trumpeter bird, or tortoise.

Above all, the tapir must be avoided; it is the "old man" (*bëgë*) of the forest, and only rarely will the more tradition-minded Tukanoans kill and eat it. I shall attempt here to analyze some of the reasons for this restriction, and in doing so I shall approach the question through a body of ethnographic observations backed by original texts collected during a long-term association with Colombian rain forest tribes.[3]

II

In the languages of the Desana and Tukano,[4] the tapir is called *vehkë*; in Pira-Tapuya it is *behkë*, and in all three languages this term also means "father-in-law."[5] The Tapir People the Desana and Pira-Tapuya encountered when they first entered the Vaupés territory were called by them *behkára,* which is the same word; and, at present, *behkára* is the name the Desana give to the Kuripáko, a large group of Arawakan tribes that live north of the Vaupés territory, mainly along the Isana river. In fact, a subgroup of the Kuripáko is called *tapiíra,* and all of the Arawakan tribes living to the north of the Tukanoans are generally referred to as Tapir People. It must be added that in many myths and tales of the Desana and other Tukanoan tribes, the tapir is described either as a respected or as a ridiculed father-in-law figure.

Before going into the details of tapir imagery and symbolism I shall first describe the way in which the Desana view the zoological species. A tapir is seen as a huge and heavy beast, very powerful and fast-moving, but clumsy and quite inoffensive; only when wounded might a tapir bite a hunter, a predator, or a dog. Otherwise, it is a cunning, yet slow-witted brute. Tapirs will open trails in the dense underbrush that lead straight to the river's edge and, when frightened, will blindly rush along these tunnels to plunge into the water. They will not hide or silently scuttle away but will noisily overrun all obstacles on their trail. The tapir's large genitals are frequently commented upon by the Indians, and it is thought that tapirs are sexually very active owing to certain fruits they feed on. Indians often say that there is a close relationship between a person's or an animal's food habits and sexual behavior, and since tapirs feed on acidic forest fruits and oily nuts, such as the fruits of the *mirití* palm (*Mauritia flexuosa*), they are said to be examples of sexual prowess. Tapirs relish sweet-tasting *umarí* (*Poraqueiba paranensis*), a fruit that has a quite definite aphrodisiac connotation. They also eat *meré*, a forest variety of *Inga* sp.; *sëmé*, the large lentil-shaped fruits of *Eperna purpurea* trees; and *pubú*, a large round forest fruit of unknown identity. Other foods that the tapir eats are *vahsú, vahsá, vahsúpë*, all these being the fruits of different, latex-exuding *Hevea* trees, besides *buhtí, niá-dëhka*, and a number of other forest products. The fruits, pods, nuts, and kernels that the tapir finds lying on the forest floor have marked fertility connotations and are said to have a strong flavor (*mukúro*) and a yellowish fatty essence (*ëye*) that might be dangerous to a person's health, not perhaps in terms of mere indigestion but rather in terms of disturbing a delicate balance of odors, flavors, and "color energies" that are so important in Indian nutritional theories (Reichel-Dolmatoff 1978). Since, in Tukanoan ideology, food and sex are equated, the tapir's feeding habits are linked to an image of voracious sexual appetites and great fertility, both being conditions that, from a native point of view, are morally condemnable but privately enviable. However, tapirs are praised for being very clean animals that spend much time in the water. They are said to have a strong, and rather human, body odor but to lack the sexually attractive odor that, according to the Indians, characterizes some other animals.

Sometimes the tapir is jokingly referred to as *vehkë gubutí* (literally, 'foot-blunt' or 'stub-footed'), an expression alluding to its hoofed feet but with the implicit meaning of "used, worn out, senile, impotent." Another common epithet for the tapir is *toró vehkë* (literally, 'package-tapir'). The word *toró* or *to'ó* means "package, bundle, bulk" and refers to the size of a tapir's testicles; the word is related to *toári* (to sting), with the implied meaning that the expression *nomé toári* (woman–to sting) refers to copulation. Another word, *toróri*, means "big-eared one" and is a common insult among men. In fact, tapirs have rather large ears that, in some stories, have a phallic connotation. Although a large penis is a shameful thing according to Tukanoans and all these allusions to the tapir's food habits and anatomy put ridicule and shame upon this animal, they are not devoid of a certain admiration.

Desana-tapir symbolic relationships develop on several different levels and use many different images. In one important image Tapir is Thunder, a powerful being who lives, surrounded by his womenfolk, in a huge longhouse high up in the sky. The Desana word for thunder is *buhpú*[6] and Thunder's wife is *bëhpë* (spider), a common metaphor for vagina; significantly, the Desana term for daughter-in-law is *behpó*. In a group of myths, the first Desana takes a dose of narcotic snuff and goes to visit Thunder by climbing up to the sky on a column of tobacco smoke. Thunder is asleep when he arrives, but the Desana youth talks to his wife; she wakens her husband, and a ritual conversation develops in which the youth and Tapir eventually form an alliance. Younger Brother Desana offers his sister to Elder Brother Tapir in exchange for one of Tapir's women. In this image, then, Tapir is respected and feared; he has the roaring voice of thunder; the visitor has seen that Tapir's longhouse is inhabited by many women; but he is also aware that Tapir distrusts strangers, and so the alliance with Tapir becomes a celebrated feat.

This is a stock situation in which matters are described as fairly simple: an audacious young man, a sleepy oldster, and in the background a bevy of giggling girls. In this type of story there often is an element of rain-forest Boccaccio. But many other tales describe Tapir as a wily and distrustful creature, quite unwilling to make any sort of deal with an outsider and jealously watching over his womenfolk. Tapir is described as a glutton, an egoist loath to share his property. In fact, Tapir People are said to be very hostile to strangers.

In a number of tales connected with this general topic, Tapir is described in quite unmistakable terms as practising cultural norms that are strange and unknown to the Desana. One tale describes how a party of Desana raiders hide near a longhouse, watching in wonder a Tapir initiation ritual. In other stories fun is made of Tapir's incomprehensible language; his dances are described, his boisterous songs, his ornaments, even his hammocks and mats. In fact, from detailed textual analysis of a large body of origin and migration myths, genealogies, and other traditions, it becomes clear that when the Tukanoan tribes first entered the Vaupés territory most of it was inhabited by Arawakan Indians, whose culture, language, and physical type were different from those of the newcomers. The Tukanoan invaders raided the Arawakans for women; and these raids are described in the oral literature either as hunting expeditions in which the prey are the females of a certain species or as chance encounters between men (*mashsá*), the Tukanoans, and beings (*mëra*)—the "others," the animallike inhabitants of the forest.

Among the Eastern Tukanoans, male initiation rites that take place at certain times of the year—called *yuruparí* in the Amazonian vernacular—are centered upon the use of certain large trumpets which are played in pairs, traditionally near palms or other fruit-bearing trees. From the analysis of textual sources it seems rather improbable that this ritual complex is of Tukanoan origin; it seems rather to have been taken over from the Arawakan tribes. According to shamanistic precepts, the uncommonly loud sounds emitted by the trumpets make the pollen "vibrate" and fall down; that is, the sounds make the pollen grains, which transport the male gametes, fall on the static female parts of the palm. Symbolically, shamans link this process directly to human sexual physiology. Whether this *is* a botanical fact or not, I am unable to say; but it quite definitely is a shamanic theory (Reichel-Dolmatoff 1981a). The Desana and their phratry members say that different sound waves will produce different effects upon pollen and that successful pollination can be produced only by a complex orchestration of the sounds from different pairs of trumpets, which, it is said, are associated with certain symbolically significant animals.

There are many tales describing how the Desana, by hook or crook, obtained these instruments, meaning that they acquired this fertilizing power. The gist of the story is that Tapir, that huge creature, formerly had a mighty voice, the force of which resided in the trumpets and in their power of pollination. But Tapir lost his voice; the Desana stole the instruments and left Tapir with the feeble whistling voice he has to this day, which is quite disproportionate to his body size. While Tapir pursued the thief, so the story goes, the other Desana raped his womenfolk; and when Tapir returned, voiceless and empty-handed, he was castrated and killed by the victorious Desana. At any rate, the abduction and rape seem to have met with a certain amount of encouragement from the women, and Tapir is pictured in these tales as a cuckold and a fool.

But eventually the situation began to change; soon the Desana began to acquire some of the cultural traits of the Tapir People. Once they had adopted the *yuruparí* complex, they took over certain ritual ornaments and songs and began to imitate Tapir in many ways. After a period of raids and abductions, more formal relationships were established with the Tapir People, and eventually the highly formalized sister exchange developed, as anticipated in the description of the Desana youth's visit to the house of Thunder Tapir and as it is practised today. Throughout the many interrelated episodes described in the oral traditions one can see how the image of Tapir changes from that of a dumb, uncomprehending beast of the forest, into that of an ignorant cuckold, and, finally, into that of a "person" (*mahsë*), a true human being of equal status, with whom from then on all relationships became subject to strict rules of exogamy and reciprocity.

From oral traditions and the commentaries that were elicited about them, one can deduce that this process of transfiguration was accompanied by a gradual change in descent rules. In the beginning, after the first contacts had been established and raiding had become less frequent, matrilineal descent and uxorilocal residence are mentioned. The highest-ranking Desana sib, for example, is descended from *boréka*, the *aracú* (LG) fish (*Leporinus copelandi*) "caught" by the first Desana, who afterwards went to join her family. In genealogies, generations of Fish Women, Duck Women, and other water-related women are named and described; and the importance of uterine descent is mentioned. In mythical episodes Tukanoan men are described as living with their new in-laws. One cycle of myths tells in detail of the hard work to which Desana and other Tukanoan men were put by their new brothers-in-law, who made them work in their fields. In these contexts, mothers-in-law are often described as helpful and friendly to the foreigner, sometimes in exchange for sexual favors. One myth cycle tells of how, at one time, women actually owned the sacred trumpets and thus had authority over men. The gradual change to patrilineal descent is indicated in other tales, and it is no wonder that sometimes descent lines get badly entangled.

It is at this time that Tapir becomes incorporated into the Tukanoan genealogy. At present, practically all tribes consider Tapir as one of their ancestors, *bëhkëro* (T), a term in which we recognise the name *behkára*, the Desana designation for the Arawakan Kuripáko in recognition of the historical fact that it was mainly the Tapir People who first provided the Tukanoan invaders with women and so became their fathers-in-law and their ancestors. It is interesting to note that the Desana verb *vehkári* means "to join, to aggregate, to bring together"; in other words, the cluster of terms for tapir–Kuripáko–father-in-law implies the idea of alliance and partnership, not necessarily on very friendly terms but in recognition of a historical relationship.

This relationship is also indicated in some idiomatic expressions that are found in shamanic texts referring to Tapir as an ancestor. One expression is *yurá vehkë*; *yurá* means "thread, twist, interwoven object," and a literal translation would be 'twisted thread–tapir'. In discussing this term, several people rephrased it as *yurá seró vehkë*, which expands the translation to 'twisted thread–forked object–tapir'. Now, on the one hand, any bifurcate object (*sẽro*), be it a forked branch, a bifurcation in the river, a forked house post, or a fork-shaped drawing, symbolizes a crotch with sexual associations. On the other hand, the term *yurá* (thread) refers to a "line," a line of descent; and the translation is thus 'descent line–copulation–tapir', an expression that clearly indicates legitimate kinship with Tapir. Here we might add the following ethnographic detail: many women married to Desana men wear woven knee bands that are called by the very same name — *yurá seró vehkë*. The bands are adorned with a pattern of opposed triangles forming small hourglass designs that symbolize a male-female union. Another detail is that until quite recently Tukanoan girls were put into a first-menstruation enclosure constructed of six large tapir hides to symbolize their transformation into marriageable females, fit to join the Tapir People.

Another expression for Tapir is *nyamíri vehkë* (literally, 'nights-tapir'); in Desana, *nyamí* is 'night' and *nyamíri* the plural form. According to the Indians, the word *nyamí* is derived from *nyaári* (to become transformed) and *miríri* (to become satisfied, saturated). The meaning of this expression was explained as referring to Tapir as a female element, the female counterpart in the marriage alliance. In shamanic language, Tapir Women (Arawakan women) are creatures of night; they inhabit the west, the regions of the setting sun. They are *nyamíri nomé* (nights-women), who transform and satisfy men. The Desana are *ëmëkóri mahsá* (Day People) because they came from the east, with the rising sun; and indeed the sun is their father and ultimately the creator. In these two idiomatic expressions, then, Tapir comes to stand for the exogamous union between Day People and Night People, between east and west, and whatever else might be associated with these two opposing but complementary concepts.

Although the tapir is found in some forest areas and, at times, in the riverine environment, the Indians rarely hunt it. Among the Desana, Pira-Tapuya, and Tukano there exist no formal prohibitions to kill or eat tapirs, but people are reluctant to do so and will give numerous reasons why they are not being hunted. First, there is a strong belief that the spirits of game animals might try to harm the hunter and cause him or his family to fall ill. Apart from this, people will talk a great deal about the supposed dangers of eating tapir meat; it always has to be smoked and it is said to be difficult to digest, to be too tough, too strongly flavored, too rich, or too fat. People say that one would need special permission from a shaman, a special spell or some other ritual protection. Needless to say, all these arguments are unconvincing; the fact remains that the largest game animal of the forest is rarely hunted. From a practical point of view this is of minor importance because protein sources are abundant in the Vaupés territory; there is plenty of other game to be had, and fishing, of course, is a major food resource. So the problem of tapirs being restricted game does not affect the nutritional status of the community.

I shall transcribe here the words of a Tukano hunter, a young man who occasionally went out to kill a tapir and who gave me an account of his thoughts on tapirs and tapir hunting. I quote him at some length because this man, who is not a shaman, states in a very precise fashion what others have said in a less coherent way. This text is crucial to an understanding of tapir symbolism and avoidance.

The hunter first described how tapirs wander about and feed in the forest and then how they go to the river to visit their watering places. At this point he began to speak of tapirs as if he were talking of human beings. "When they go to drink water," he said, "they drink their beer and behave like people at home." He then went on: "Formerly, in the beginning, they too were progenitors; they too had descendants when each group of people [Tukanoan invaders] arrived; thus, some tapirs belong to the Barasana tribe, others to the Tuyuka, and others to the Bará.[7] Each group of tapirs had their properly named place of origin; they evolved like people." The text continues with a lengthy description in which the seasonal cycle of the tapir's feeding resources is compared to a common household routine. The narrator then said, "They [tapirs] are people like us; they have their houses, their tapir houses." The hunter said that by this he meant the supernatural abodes in hills and rock formations in the deep forest, where all game animals in spirit form are said to dwell under the care of the Master of Animals. I shall return to this image. The text continues: "But we kill them; we lie in ambush for them when they come to drink."

The narrator then established certain differences between categories of tapirs, some of which he described as zoological species, but compared others, which he called "true" tapirs (*vehkëa varoo*), to human beings. He said, "Those that go to feed in our fields are not important; they merely steal food. They will sleep anywhere; they belong to the forest. But those that have houses do not go about like this, they stay in their houses. . . . The tapirs that steal food from the fields are their servants. . . . This is why we lie in ambush for them when they eat manioc. . . . A tapir never knows in advance when he might go to a salt lick; he gets a warning from others; a tapir is like a person, I tell you. But if we think of this and ponder it, then tapir will see us in his thoughts. When we think of her [sic] she becomes aware of us [of our intentions] and knows. . . . If we want to kill one, we must think of other things."[8]

The hunter then explained in detail that, if one went for a tapir, one should always concentrate on its animal nature; otherwise the tapir would read one's thoughts. "If we think of a tapir as a person, the others will take revenge. This happens to shamans, but to an ignorant person like me, this won't happen. Tapirs take revenge only on those who think of them as people. His [the hunter's] children will fall ill. They [tapirs] take revenge and kill. So we kill her [sic] and eat her. If we were thinking like shamans, we would be eating human beings, but for us it is not dangerous to eat tapir."[9]

After another description of how tapirs go to their watering places, the hunter explained that these locations, the same as salt licks, were like imaginary longhouses where tapirs gathered to talk, take coca, imbibe narcotic potions, and drink their fermented beer. "They go to their watering places," he said, "just like women drawing water," and drink "as if it were beer." The hunter ended his talk by saying, "They have various greenish beverages; this is their *yajé* [a hallucinogen].[10] If we were to drink the potion of the true tapir, we would turn into tapirs . . . and, transformed into tapirs, we would go to where they are and enter where they live."[11]

The hunter's account throws new light on the problem of tapir avoidance. While this document provides a confirmatory context for the point I have made already, that a "tapir component" is present in many Tukanoan tribes, a number of new elements have been added to the original situation. In the first place, there now are two kinds of tapirs: the zoological species and one that consists of transformed human beings who live in supernatural longhouses. The narrator commented that it was difficult to tell the difference between the two at sight and that there always remained a dangerous uncertainty. In the second place, man-tapirs were said to take revenge upon the hunter's family; and third, if a hunter should think of a tapir as a person, the tapir would read his thoughts and punish him; but if he took the tapir for an animal, no harm would come from killing and eating it. As we can see from the narrator's switching from he- to she-tapirs, male and female personifications are involved here and, in order to become a prey, a tapir must be thought of as "someone else." Reportedly both male and female tapirs appear in dreams, nightmares, and drug-induced hallucinations, sometimes to accuse the dreamer of overhunting, at other times in a context of social relationships and an atmosphere of intense anxiety. Shamans are much interested in patients' tapir visions and say that the visions mirror the quality of a person's social problems.

To get a truer perspective of these images I shall briefly summarize some general attitudes toward game resources, their shamanistic implications, and their psychological projections. The Indians believe that certain isolated rock formations, deep in the forest, are ghostly abodes wherein game-animal spirits dwell under the care of the Master of Animals (Reichel-Dolmatoff 1971). These "hill houses," as shamans call them, have a womblike character; they are the places where game animals are said to multiply and from whence they emerge to roam in the forest; they are the spirit houses inside which a continuous process of gestation is going on. Shamans say that they visit these places during their narcotic trances because they must converse with the Master of Animals in order to ask him to release some of his charges so that the hunters may kill them for food. When shamans say these places are wombs and places of gestation, they mean that these are places of transformation, which can be recognised as such because, hovering over them, a spiral-shaped cloud formation or a large funnel-shaped dust devil can sometimes be seen. These spirals or funnels are compared to vaginae, entrances to the womb, which is the house inside the hill.

The cosmic fertilizing force that enters vertically into the house consists of what shamans call "color energies" (dári), which are said to be derived from the sun (Reichel-Dolmatoff 1978). In the opposite direction, rising from the subterranean abode to the surface, run what shamans call "wind threads" (miru dári), which transmit particular odors that emanate from the animals. As a matter of fact, the hunter who approaches such a hill can perceive the penetrating scent of certain aromatic herbs together with the musky estrous smell of game animals, such as tapir, deer, or peccary.

In a trance induced by hallucinogenic drugs, a shaman will enter a spirit house to negotiate with the Master of Animals, who is a jealous protector of his charges. The shaman will not ask for individual animals but rather for herds or troops of a certain species. He must always recompense the Master of Animals, and the payment consists of human souls. In fact, the shaman promises to kill a certain number of people, whose souls then enter the hill houses where they replenish and invigorate the energy of the game animals that have been released by their Master. Inside a hill house two categories of animals exist. One is formed by the spirit manifestations of the zoological species that multiply and breed inside the hill and are then released to fall prey to the hunters; the other category of animals consists of people who have been transformed, who are "like animals" because during their lifetime they did not obey social norms, especially those related to exogamy. When these people die, their souls, instead of leaving this earth and returning to the dimension of solar energy, remain in *deyóri turi*, the "visible world," and enter a mountain or hill, where they live in animal form. The purpose of their continued existence is two-fold: in part, their vital energy contributes to fomenting the community of game animals; and in part, they suffer punishment for their misconduct and are occasionally sent out into the forest, where a hunter might mistake them for fair game and kill them. As a precaution a hunter must always cut out the tongue of game animals, such as tapirs or deer, so they cannot tell their kin about their fate at his hands in case his victim was a transformed human who went unrecognized. Another Tukano text of interest that refers to this matter says in part: "They [the hunters] are fearful and immediately after killing [the game] they cut out the tongue and throw it away because they [the game] would tell their kin. They [people] say that their spirits would tell them. The tapir of the true house would take revenge, they say. And I always do the same; rapidly we cut out the tongue of any tapir we are going to eat."

From a number of statements made by shamans and other people, it is possible, then, to summarize the situation as follows: Most people believe that there are two categories of tapirs—the common game animal and transformed people. If the prey is a common

backward-pointing wings and a long and deeply forked tail. Its head, underparts, and wing linings are white like the sun at noon, and its beak, back, wings, and tail are black. It has red-brown eyes, light blue feet, yellowish talons, and a glossed green or purplish interscapular region.[6]

The Warao see in the swallow-tailed kite a model for the persistent archer on the hunt. The bird "represents the ultimate perfection of graceful and sustained flight. . . . Its only rival would be the Frigate bird" (Brown and Amadon 1968, 220). The kite hardly ever alights, feeding on the wing. Circling patiently high over the land, it quarters the ground for lizards, frogs, tree snakes, birds' nests, and hives of Hymenoptera before swooping down on its target with lightning speed. Devastating pirate that it is, the kite tears out entire birds' nests in flight, demolishes them, and feeds on eggs and brood.

The Primordial Archer

The Heraldic Raptor is depicted in the myth as the primordial archer and rattler whose paraphernalia are emblematic of the kite's high-altitude stalking and fulminating striking abilities.

As for the image of the Primordial Archer, he is believed to be capable of hurling unerring projectiles. For that reason his agent, in the person of the *bahana* shaman, is also referred to as a *hatabuarotu*, "archer."

The kite's reputation as an archer derives from its nesting behavior. During the mating season, with spectacular aerial acrobatics, the swallow-tailed kite builds its aerie in the top of green trees. While in flight he breaks off dead twigs for nesting material, and those that result in being too large or otherwise unsuitable are let drop from the sky to the ground.

Bahana shamans consider these sticks to be the arrows of the Primordial Archer and claim to engage the bird in shooting duels. Upon tossing a light arrow of *temiche* petiole into the air, the kite is said to intercept the missile in midair (sea gull fashion) and then return it to his challenger below. Whoever, bird or man, fails to catch the arrow forfeits his life and dies a sudden death.

The bow and arrow has a distinctly male connotation in Warao mentality. Women are reluctant to touch the weapon so as not to render the bowstring flaccid and the arrow aimless. Young girls refrain from manipulating a bow and arrow for fear that they may irritate their clitoris and make the organ grow large. But in the hands of the hunter and especially in those of the solar archer, the bow and arrow connotes generative prowess as expressed by the verb *hatakitani* which at the same time means "to shoot with bow and arrow" and "to copulate."

The swallow-tailed kite strikes its prey, such as bees, wasps, and flying termites, not with its beak but with a sudden thrust of one foot or the other. Similarly, the shaman dispatches his magic arrow through an opening in the palm of each hand. In his projectile-shooting capacity the *bahana* shaman is also known as *mohokarotu*, "he who discharges through the hand."

Other missiles associated with the Primordial Archer and his shaman are quartz pebbles. For instance, parents call their children inside when they see the kite circling overhead: the bird is said to carry a pebble in its beak which it shoots at children playing and especially those eating in the open. Similarly, top-ranking *bahana* shamans are capable of launching their quartz pellets accompanied by an effigy of their avian master. A shaman of this elevated status is referred to as *daunonarima*, "Father of the Wooden Mannequin."

The effigy is a twelve-centimeters-tall and two-centimeters-thick sculpture in the round, fashioned either in the stylized form of the kite's head and neck or in the naturalistic rendering of an adolescent boy. The anthropomorphic figure is provided with a neckband to which two parrot feathers (*Pionus* sp.) are attached as wings (Wilbert 1975d, 67–78; 1979a, 294–99). When activated by the tobacco-smoke-blowing shaman, the mannequin becomes as frenziedly aggressive as the swallow-tailed kite it represents and the estrous *Pionus* parrot. The shaman sends it forth to annihilate the entire child population of a band. It takes "to the wing," closely following behind three quartz pebbles that fly in a triangular formation emulating the kite. Hovering over the village with the sound of a strong wind, the preying foursome selects its victims, swoops down, and kills the children one by one. Even adults succumb to the siege that often lasts for days; and as the kite may devastate a nest of birds, so may its effigy lay waste a settlement in the fashion of epidemics that ravage Waraoland.

The Warao listener to the myth associates the kite's bow and arrow also with the "new song" of *bahana* shamanism. Recall that upon approaching the oval house in the sky, the journeying novice became fascinated by the music making inside the house where the creator bird played his musical bow. In a similar fashion the Warao hunter uses his bow and arrow as a lure to attract his prey. Holding the bow with the hand of his outstretched left arm horizontally and pointing away from him, he takes the free end of the bow between his teeth while his right hand taps the string with an arrow to produce a series of twanging sounds. With the animal in shooting range, the hunter quickly converts the musical bow into a deadly weapon and lets fly. As shall increasingly become clear, this dual function of the bow and arrow as a stalking and striking device makes it a highly appropriate metaphor of the nature of the swallow-tailed kite and of the Heraldic Raptor's order of *bahana*.

Finally, it merits pointing out that within the shamanic context of the myth the kite's bow and arrow becomes a symbol of magical flight and transcendence. Replacing the shamanic drum of other regions, it attracts a sorcerer's pathogens like game. But it also prepares, through music and dance, the trance experience of the shaman's arrowlike flight across the celestial bridge, prefigured in the bow, to the sky house of *bahana*.

The Primordial Rattler

Turning now to the image of the Primordial Rattler it is important to point out that his is a dancing rattle (*habi sanuka*) and not the large ritual rattle (*hebu mataro*) used by other Warao shamans in a different context (Wilbert 1974). Like the bow and arrow, the rattle is a composite symbol consisting of a phallic axis and a uterine calabash denoting conjunction. This finds linguistic expression in the word for calabash, *mataru* or *mataruka*, "hymen," a word that refers to a virgin womb that is deflowered by a *mataruka aiwatu*, "someone who pierces a calabash."

The natural model of the kite's rattle is the ovoid termitary or apiary built around the branch of a tree and whose rustling interior teems with termites' known reproductive power (figs. 2, 3). Warao dancers shake the small rattles of the Heraldic Kite during the "Dance of the Little Rattle" that features rites to secure fertility in man and animals. Animal pantomimes are performed by means of steps, postures, and the little rattles, until at one point enormous straw images are presented of a vulva (by men) and of a phallus (by

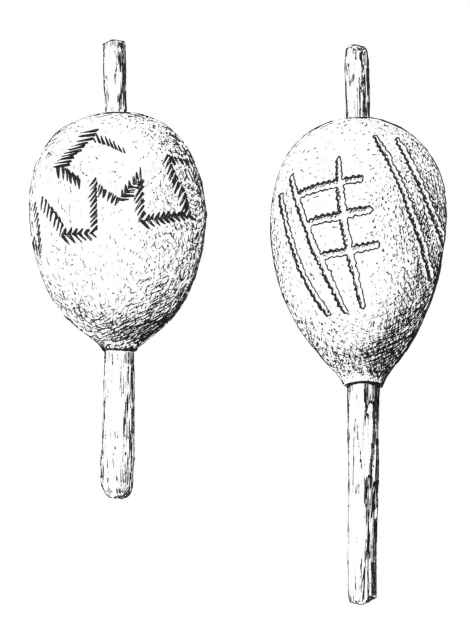

Figure 2. The Little Rattle of *bahana* ritual (*habi sanuka*) made of a tree calabash (*Cresentia cujete*). The rattle head is decorated with incised design patterns. (Drawing by Helga Adibi)

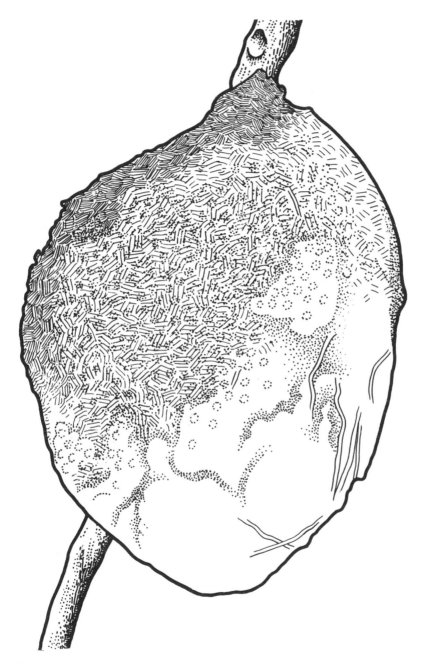

Figure 3.   The termitary mounted on the branch of a tree resembling a
Little Rattle. (Drawing by W. Patrick Finnerty)

women). In the ensuing melee the bearers of these effigies are clawed by members of the opposite sex who will not rest until the images are shredded and destroyed.

During the ritual of the kite's rattle the affinal kin ties between spouses become suspended and replaced by ritual bonds known as *mamuse*. Husbands agree to exchange wives, and upon payment of a substantial price, called *horo amoara*, "skin payment," the partners are free to engage in dancing and sex. *Mamuse* relationships are considered honorable and are believed to exercise a fortifying influence on the woman's offspring.

The Cosmic Egg

The next three episodes (2–4) of the myth present the image of the Cosmic Egg, created by the Heraldic Raptor through the power of thought (fig. 4). Endowed with a proper rhythm of continual self-generation, the Cosmic Egg represents a central metaphor of the *bahana* paradigm.

The peculiarity of the flowers alongside the celestial bridge between the zenith and the egg is that they consist only of the stems and the florescences of tobacco plants. The harvested leaves are understood to have contributed the construction material, in the form of tobacco smoke, for the Cosmic Egg and its inventory and to have served as the spiritual food of the occupants. Remember that although distinctly varied in form, all actors and accessories of the scenario are uniformly made of tobacco smoke with their telluric realism in narcotic suspension. Thus, while they do not do so in *bahana* context, potentially the flowers produce the nectarial food, that is, sex (see below), for the apian companions of the kite in exchange for pollination. This interrelationship is not lost on the Warao who, by employing the verb form *tokoyokitani* of the noun *tokoyo*, "flower," metaphorize it to connote "blossoming" in the sense of an estrous female exhibiting chromatic and odoriferous attractants (Barral 1979, 430). Thus the flowers along the celestial bridge are a vignette of the *bahana* paradigm, imitating the essential (food) and formal (sex) characteristics of flower symbolism.

Before commenting on the social model of the kite's community, let me first indicate that the architectural prototypes of the Cosmic Egg itself are the nest of the honey wasp (*Brachygastra lecheguana* Latreille) and the testis. The Warao refer to the wasp as *ono*,

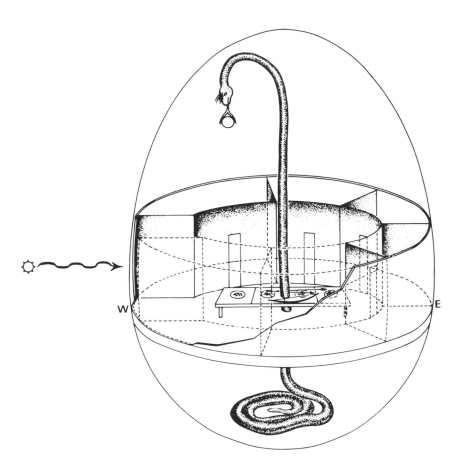

Figure 4. Cross section of the House of the Swallow-Tailed Kite showing two-story layout. From the lower story a plumed serpent with a luminous ball on her tongue penetrates the floor of the upper story and rises above the table of the *bahana* game. Notice the division of the *mesa* into four fields, each with its marker. The arrows are distinguishable by their different points. Surrounding an inner room is a ring of six quarters inhabited by the insect spirits. The room north of the entrance is inhabited by the primordial shaman and his (bee) wife. The room south of the entrance is occupied by the Creator Bird and his (frigate) companion. (Drawing by Noel Diaz)

"testis," in reference to the shape of its nest and to the extraordinary fertility of the insect. More than 15,000 individuals may inhabit a single nest; and, when the nest is destroyed, the wasps will regenerate their home repeatedly as long as some of its base remains intact (Schwarz 1929, 424). If it had a *bahana* game, say the Indians, the *ono* wasp would enjoy the same status as the swallow-tailed kite.

Built of grey paper, the 2-by-1½-foot ovoid nest of the honey wasp resembles the House of Tobacco Smoke in form and color. The testis is also oval in shape and of grey-white appearance. Inside and along the distal wall of the genital gland there are a number of chambers separated by septa which are like the combs that honey wasps fasten to the inside of the envelope of their nest and not, like other wasps, in parallel tiers. The nest does not have a central brood chamber with a single queen as do the nests of the other Hymenoptera and the termite of the *bahana* set of insects. Instead, within the honey wasp's hive there are several reproductive individuals at work on different combs, just as there are several insect actors in the rooms of the Cosmic Egg (fig. 5). It is precisely this absence of a central space of generation that excludes the model of the wasp's nest from *bahana* status, but it is in the presence of such a space where both the Cosmic Egg and the testis coincide. The architectural and anatomical layout of the house and the gland features a number of peripheral rooms and lobules that connect in a space of convergence where they interact. Even the bundle of convoluted ducts that leads away from the hilar side of the testis resembles the rope-bridge that connects the Cosmic Egg with the zenith and the central world axis.

The image of the coresident animal cohorts in the sky house causes a measure of consternation in the native listener. In the first place, there are the insects and the animosity that exists between them and man. The black bee, *hoi* (*Trigona hyalinata branneri* Cockerell), and the wasp *tomonoho simo* (*Stelopolybia fulvofasciata* DeGeer), in question are fiercely aggressive creatures in nature.[7] The former, although stingless, bites the scalp and twists the hair of those who dare disturb it. Worse still, black bees of this kind crawl into the facial orifices and torture their imprudent visitor with scores of painful bites. The wasp, in turn, is apt to attack a human passerby even at considerable distances away from its nest; and as few as three of its stings are purported to cause a fever in man. The termite, *ahi simo* (*Nasutitermes corniger* Motschulsky), displays the same

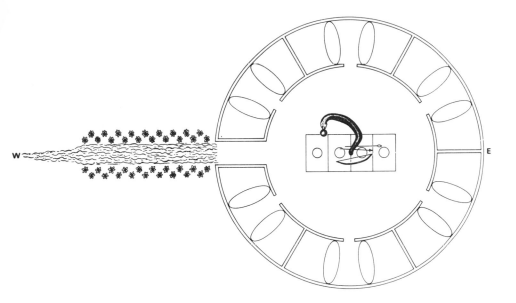

Figure 5. Floor plan of the House of the Swallow-Tailed Kite with an inner (ceremonial) game room, its table, and serpent, and an outer circle of living quarters. The bridge of ropes of tobacco smoke is indicated as well as the lines of tobacco flowers on both sides. (Drawing by Noel Diaz)

stamina as does the wasp in the face of overpowering odds; it returns to the site even after its nest has been completely razed. Termites are also powerful invaders of houses, and are reputed to be child snatchers.

A second reason for the Warao listener's uneasiness about the insects in the sky house is that he connects each of them with an insect family that mirrors the human family and its interpersonal relationships. This very complex model is best illustrated with reference to Blue Bee.

Blue Bee, *asebe* (*Trigona capitata* F. Smith), with the kite's white mark in the center of its face, is the master of the Cosmic Egg. He keeps two nonsororal wives, *aroida*, "long neck" (*Melipona scutellaris lateralis* [Erichson]), and *atekoro*, "cowife" or *kurakasi*, "engorged vagina" (*Melipona puncticollis ogilviei* Schwarz). *Asebe*'s father-in-law is *arahi sanuka* (*Trigona melanocera* Schwarz), as his name indicates, and his daughter, *daihene*, "yellow back" (*Trigona paupera* [Provancher]), is wooed by the bachelor *simowata*, "honey penis" (*Lestrimelitta limao* [F. Smith]), who also goes by the name of *dariamo*, "warrior."

The adult Warao listener knows about the frailty of such family relations and about the tensions that build up between a son-in-law and his parents-in-law, between a husband and his wives, and between a wife and her cowife; but he also knows about the fears of the wooing bachelor who, upon marriage, faces uxorilocal residence and bride service for the lifetime of his spouse. To the Warao the image of nest solidarity vaunted by the myth masks a cohering but severely stressed net of family relationships that, in the face of many odds, persevere only under the kite's protection. How bad the odds of survival are can be seen in the example of the bachelor wooer *simowata*. He is the robber bee, who is apt to rape the nest of his *Trigona* parents-in-law, *asebe*, by forcing them out of their home and by usurping their food and offspring. In addition, there are the fears that govern interfamily relationships within the band as exemplified by Black Bee, who counts among his kin, *kohora*, "the musty one," (*Trigona fuscipennis* Friese), an enemy of Termite, whose nest he invades to occupy it in forced symbiosis. Then finally, there is the snake of the lower compartment of the Cosmic Egg that contributes its share to the volatile atmosphere within the *bahana* house by being modeled after a species of blind snake (*Leptotyphlops* sp.) which bores its way into the bulbous arborial termitary to feast on the brood and to deposit its egg inside this temperature-controlled environment. In other words, given a chance, the various animals and their kin of the Cosmic Egg tear into one another, invade one another's houses, and cannibalize one another's offspring. The swallow-tailed kite destroys the nests of birds and bees and wasps, the black bee, *kohora*, enters the termite's nest, the robber bee usurps the hives of Blue Bee, and the blind snake breaks into the termitary.

In short, the image of peaceful coexistence in the Cosmic Egg of such unlikely companions as the swallow-tailed kite, the insects, and the snake is foreboding, not only because of the animosity between the insects and man but also because of the piratical nature of the kite's cohorts and especially because, rather than as friends, the inmates of the Cosmic Egg relate to one another as members in an ecological food chain. Starting at the bottom: the bees eat the nectar and the pollen of the flowers; the wasp feeds on the brood of the bees and the termites; the snake eats the brood of the termites and wasps; and the kite, at the top of the pyramid, eats the bees' and wasps' honey and eggs, as well as the flying insects and the snake. In fact, Warao imagination could scarcely have assembled a more varied set of natural models to create such a highly charged image of latent antagonism. To the Warao listener, any peaceful coexistence among the members of the Cosmic Egg community must depend on the magic power of the Heraldic Raptor.

The Celestial Gamblers and Tobacco

The image of the Celestial Gamblers makes it clear that by assembling the motley group of occupants in the sky house, the kite pursued a purpose other than mere coexistence. Aware of their piratical disposition and the conflict inherent in their mutual dependence, he called them to the gambling table to enact the "dance" of survival the way they know how to perform it best. Not surprisingly, therefore, the rules of play of the *bahana* game are truly second nature to its players.

The name of the game is *bahana akotubu*, which means "*bahana* game" or "dance" but also "to take excessive sexual liberties" with someone's wife. Accordingly, the objective of the game is invasion of the checker-house of their fellow "dancers" according to the chances dictated by the kite's arrow dice. The players deposit in the foreign houses their calabashes with seminal content like larvae in a comb. At the end of each game the plumed serpent erects itself like a central house post, and its power fills the winner with renewing life energy.

The secret of the Heraldic Kite's success in gaining the cooperation of the antagonistic gamblers is hidden in the plant that he created. The swallow-tailed kite is the Spirit of Tobacco, and tobacco the sine qua non of *bahana*.

The word *bahana* connotes "to smoke," "to suck." And the *bahanarotu* is the shaman who sucks smoke through hyperventilation from two-foot-long cigars.

From the point of view of its insect occupants, the House of Tobacco Smoke presents a constant image of death. Nicotine, the principal active ingredient in tobacco, is the most potent insecticide in nature; and the Warao are well aware of its deadly effect on bees, wasps, and termites and of its soothing influence on the mind of their shaman. Thus, the wisdom of the Creator Bird in choosing tobacco smoke for the construction of his sky house lies in the knowledge of its effect on insects, and the tobacco alkaloid is his secret magic power that overcomes the innate animosity of his house guests.

From the point of view of the *bahana* shaman, tobacco is also an image of transcendental life. The kind of tobacco used by the shamans is preferably the especially nicotine-rich *Nicotiana rustica* with powerful psychotropic properties (Wilbert 1975b). Saturated and engulfed in tobacco smoke, the Celestial Gamblers experience the illumination of a tobacco trance in whose flash the telluric conditions of their animal nature are transcended. The image of the ophidian master of ceremonies who marks the rhythm of the game is a sign of hope that the inexorable conditions of mundane life may become sublimated by the gambling odds of the kite's game of chance.

The "Quest of Bahana Power" and the "Origin of Bahana Shamanism" sections of the myth describe a shamanic celestial journey and the acquisition of *bahana* power as a result of the creative dream of a child during which he received the knowledge as a gift. The meaning of the episodal imagery is less culture-specific and its symbolism more generally accessible.

The World Axis

In the mystic center of the universe a four-year-old child, the product of two semiconscious protohumans, awakens to his riddle-solving destiny. The virgin fire in whose heat he ascends to the zenith must only be produced by men with the aid of a fire drill. The Warao see this operation as a simile of the sex act, and women feel inhibited to use it. Through the heat of the fire the youth achieves his ecstatic state and ascends the world axis. The base of this *axis mundi* rests on the bottom of the underworld, below the floating earth disk, and penetrates the earth at its center to rise to the apex of the sky. At the nadir the Warao picture the world axis entwined in the coils of an enormous four-headed serpent with deer horns on its heads. The heads of this all-seeing monster point in the four quarters of heaven, and the coils of its body support the buoyant earth. Thus the image of the three-tiered Warao cosmos produces the common cosmological schema of a solar bird at the top of the central world tree-pillar and a snake at its roots.

Connecting nadir and zenith, the world axis serves as a pathway of communication between man and the Supernaturals that frequent the sacred space above, below, and around it. Initiated men and women travel this *axis mundi* upward to the zenith and from there to destinations at the cardinal and intercardinal points, where their respective patron deities reside. Similarly, the gods descend along the world axis to visit earth. Also the world snake, at its base, can leave the netherworld and wind its way up to manifest itself by projecting its torso through the central earth hole or by emerging fully in the shape of a woman sitting astride a fallen tree.

The Warao do not think of the world axis as a solid column, but rather as a bundle of conduits, each one specific to its destination. For instance, one of these lines (before it was destroyed) was an artery that carried human blood from the earth to the land of the setting sun, to nourish there the cannibalistic god of the West and his retinue. Other channels are jets of heat or curls of ascending tobacco smoke. Thus the world axis of the Warao universe represents a dynamic bundle of pathways, one of which leads to the anchor point of the rope-bridge that conducts *bahana* shamans from the top of the sky to the House of Tobacco Smoke.

The Mother of Honey

Overcoming his earthboundness through the heat of a fire and his need for food by smoking tobacco, the as yet reproductively inactive youth is acceptable to the kite and his associates as one of their kind. He is capable of receiving the kite's gifts and of nurturing in his breast the gestating offspring of the four insects. Only upon reaching spermatogenesis at the age of sixteen does he have intercourse with his bee wife, introducing her gradually to the laws of "human" reproduction.

The young *bahana* shaman's wife was a daughter of Blue Bee (*aroida*). She is the Mother of Honey who releases man from the bonds of hunger and sex. Her sweetness is referred to as *diaba*, and experiencing it is *diabaia*, "orgasm." Etymologically, therefore, eating honey and nectar connotes copulation.

In actual life this is explainable by the high levulose content of
stingless-bee honey, which is of an intense and exquisite sweetness.
"A delight more piercing than any normally afforded by taste or
smell breaks down boundaries of sensibility, and blurs the registers,
so much so that the eater of the honey wonders whether he is savour-
ing a delicacy or burning with the fire of love" (Lévi-Strauss 1966,
52). The marriage of the first *bahana* shaman to a bee girl and other
Warao myths take note of this (Wilbert 1970, 175–77). And so does
a nubile girl in making an unequivocal overture to a man by passing
the tip of the tongue across her lower lip while sipping honey. According to several of my male informants, men are attracted to the
taste of honey with the same passion that they long for the
"sweetness" of a young girl.

One additional aspect of honey consumption among the Warao
Honey is considered a food, like tobacco, rather than a drink. In
fact, in preagricultural times, when the Warao lived extensively on
fish and honey, they were aware of the long-lasting satisfaction they
derived from a meal of these staples. According to one of my informants, "We would breakfast on fish, insect brood, and honey and
go all day without getting hungry again. Sometimes we even turned
in at night without feeling hungry enough to eat. Honey was the
blood of the Warao." There is no reason to doubt the veracity of this
statement, for a meal of fish, insect larvae, and honey would be rich
in proteins and high in carbohydrates.

One additional aspect of honey consumption among the Warao
bears mention in connection with *bahana* imagery. Honey is con-
sumed in its raw state only by the shamans and, through extension, by the gods. Commoners ingest it diluted in the form of honey
water or, during the ritual of the Little Rattles, fermented as mead.
The Warao are on record as having collected hundreds of liters of
honey at a time when the shaman sent out the families to prepare an
offering of propitiation for the Supernaturals. Macerated honey
would ferment on these occasions so that the gift of the Mother of
Honey contributed, besides natural food, the levulose and alcohol to
foster the congeniality conducive to procreation just as the gift of her
shaman husband contributed, besides spiritual food, the nicotine to
enhance friendship and spiritual well-being.

In a later episode (9), the honey wife of the first shaman, upon
entering the Cosmic Egg, changed into the form of a frigate bird and
cured the Heraldic Kite from a seizure he suffered in her presence.

The wife of a *bahana* shaman is invariably recognized as a *bahana* shaman in her own right who identifies with the Mother of Honey in her guise of the magnificent female frigate (*Fregata magnificens*). With its forked tail and especially because of its white breast, this otherwise black bird resembles the swallow-tailed kite in flight.

I have already referred to the similarity of the kite and the frigate in flight. Just like the kite, frigates are relentless pirates. Rather than foraging on their own, they prefer to rob other sea birds, such as boobies, grabbing and shaking them with their long beaks until their victims regurgitate their catch. Before the falling fish reach the surface of the ocean, the frigate swoops down and pilfers them.

Another characteristic frigates share with swallow-tailed kites is their aerial acrobatics and fighting. Constructing their nests from sticks, frigates either pick up sticks from the ground or purloin them from the kite's or from other birds' nests. In flight several of these birds can be observed fighting with one another over the possession of a stick, letting it drop on one occasion and catching it in midair on another. As in the case of the kite, *bahana* shamans see in these sticks magical arrows that the shamanic bird shoots at them. Also the stakes are the same in this game of chance, and frigates may even come down to catch the "arrow" a shaman hurls back at them.

Of additional analogical significance is the behavior of frigates in mating. The male bird sits on the nest and inflates its gular sac into an enormous scarlet balloon the size of a rattle. It spreads its wings and throws back its head, presenting a strutting body. Attracted by this display, the female descends and engages in much body contact, touching the male's wings, neck, and gular pouch. Eventually such behavior results in mating, which, in turn, releases the male bird from this seizurelike state. Hence the name "Mother of Seizure," which the Heraldic Kite bestowed on the bee wife/frigate bird when she cured him in the Cosmic Egg.

Frigates are great rattlers. Sitting on their nests, which they must defend constantly from encroaching neighbors, they fence with their beaks and produce a clattering noise that can be heard from afar. Again, the symbolic interrelationship of the rattle (in the form of a long beak and inflated gular balloon) and reproduction is alluded to in this most startling analogy. The Warao call a bird's dewlap or gular sac (or a man's larynx) *habi* as in *habi sanuka*, "Little Rattle" of *bahana*.

There is one other detail still to be mentioned. But, so far, a case has been made to suggest that Mawari, the swallow-tailed kite, had indeed found a most compatible counterpart in the female frigate, when he invited her to share his room that is south of the entrance to the House of Smoke and to become the first female *bahanarotu*.

THE SHAMANIC HEALERS

The last two episodes of the myth (10 and 11) explain the origin of *bahana* shamanism and why the modern shaman is less powerful than the first *bahana*; he carries only two insect tutelary spirits in his breast and only the two younger brothers (Termite and Blue Bee) of the two fraternal pairs in the Cosmic Egg.

The male shaman cures by extracting pathogenic "insects" that were sent to invade a patient's body by a malevolent colleague of his. The wounds such attacks cause are especially apparent in females, and although the shaman attends to both sexes he nevertheless treats in particular women with menstrual problems, general vaginal bleeding, and cases of protracted deliveries—in other words, gynecological problems which, although lingering, often take care of themselves. Consequently, healers of this kind of women's disorders have a high rate of success. The shaman, upon consultation with the two tutelary spirits that reside in his breast, finds out whether, in the game the Celestial Gamblers play over the patient (the "stake" of the round), one of his tutelary spirits (Termite or Blue Bee) won or whether one of the two more-powerful spirits that remained in the Cosmic Egg (Black Bee and Wasp) was victorious instead. In the latter case there is nothing a shaman can do. If one of the shaman's tutelary spirits wins the gamble, the shaman sends the winner from his breast, through the lumen in his arm and the hole in the palm of his hand, to effect the cure and, possibly, to claim the patient's body in a kind of peonage, called *ateho wabia*, "selling of the body."

Suffering from a protracted ailment frequently means that the patient is unable to pay the shaman's fee. Payments used to be made in tobacco that a woman obtained through trade in exchange for her products such as hammocks and baskets. Because tobacco does not grow in the Orinoco Delta, its acquisition is costly and women work hard to procure it. Furthermore, tobacco is indispensable for Warao shamanism (Wilbert 1972) since its smoke represents the staple food for the supernatural patrons of the practitioner. And if a patient is

incapable of providing the required remuneration for repeated se-
ances, she/he has no choice but to offer her/his body in payment for
the cure. This relationship between shaman and patient often lasts
for the recovered person's lifetime; and, although shamans have
several male *neburatu* clients of this kind, there are invariably also a
number of females among them. Significantly, however, these
"earned bodies" are considered "sons" and "daughters" of the
shaman, who, accordingly, may not have sexual relations with the
women. They address him as "father" and he calls them "daughter" and treats them as such.

To illustrate the control the "selling of the body" institution
gives a *bahana* shaman over the reproductively active female
"bodies" of the local group, let me briefly point out that the average
uxorilocal and endogamous Warao band consists of thirteen women,
twelve men, and twenty-five children. In the case of a *bahanarotu* of
my acquaintance, the practitioner has two wives and four married
daughters. A seventh woman, the wife of his son, lives virilocally
owing to adoption. In addition, the shaman has acquired four
women as ritual daughters through his practice as a healer. These
four women belong to other bands of the same subtribe. In this case
then, one *bahanarotu* has stewardship over eleven women: six in-laws,
one stepdaughter, and four ritual daughters. Altogether their number is almost the equivalent of a full contingent of adult females in a
band.

The *bahana* shaman has certain "paternal" obligations toward
his ritual daughters, but he also exercises fatherly rights over them.
For example, when visiting their respective villages, he may inquire
into the comportment of their husbands as providers. He has the
right to reprimand the men or to withdraw the women if complaints
of sustained neglect are not adequately redressed. He will also take
revenge on a neighboring *bahanarotu* should one of the women en-
trusted to him die suddenly—that is, suffer a typical *bahana* death.
Of course, all his affinal and ritual sons-in-law render bride service
for the lifetime of their spouses, so that *bahana* shamans, because of
prevailing residence rules and ritual kinship, may build self-suffi-
cient, maximally secure, and well-managed settlements with op-
timal conditions for individual and group survival.

Female *bahana* shamans also have a high success rate with patients suffering from seizures, although there are fewer of these than

there are patients with ailments cured by her husband. The source of her healing power lies in the pharmacological cause of the type of seizure in question—that is, nicotine poisoning. As mentioned in connection with the House of Tobacco Smoke and its metamorphosed occupants, nicotine is the most toxic insecticide in nature. In addition, however, nicotine is also one of the most toxic natural substances for man, producing tremors as symptoms of low-level poisoning and convulsions and death as a result of medium to high levels of poisoning.

Seizures among the Warao as a result of tobacco consumption occur in men because they, rather than women, ingest massive doses of nicotine for ritual purposes. Tobacco seizures have a sudden onset, which explains why *bahana* sicknesses, like the outbreak of exotic epidemic disease for instance, are characterized by the abruptness of "falling ill" without any previous symptoms. The Warao word for seizure, *sinaka*, is derived from *sinakakitani*, "to drop to the ground"; and the patient, *sinakabaka*, feels oppressed and shaken at the hands of Juru, the Earthquake spirit.

Furthermore, the pharmacological basis of the nicotine seizure also explains its origin in the tobacco-saturated environment of the Cosmic Egg and why the primordial female shaman's first patient was the Supreme Spirit of tobacco himself. Then as in modern times, she cures by leaning over the patient to prevent a more violent catathymic crisis; she may stroke the man's body and blow over it. Meanwhile the nicotine seizure runs its natural course and the spasms subside in replication of the cure effected in the Cosmic Egg and in accordance with the mating behavior the female frigate adopts in response to the strutting display of her partner. Since nicotine metabolism in humans is fast, women *bahana* shamans enjoy a high degree of success as curers, although the relatively brief therapy and recuperation period of the patient does not call for his "selling of the body" to her.

The Bahana Paradigm

In light of the preceding text and commentary it is perhaps justified to suggest that *bahana* imagery bespeaks the intense preoccupation of the Warao with the concerns of personal (sex) and societal (food) survival. *Bahana* symbolism begs the hypothesis that its pervasive imagery of fertility and fecundity signifies the cooperative-competitive tensions inherent in sexuality and attendant cultural behavior. No doubt, psychoanalytic theory of myth could profitably be engaged to analyze the emotional conflict and its resolution within the *bahana* complex. The application of structural theory to resolve the intellectual contradictions inherent in the myth should also be promising. However, my purpose here is to examine by means of the principles of similarity and contiguity the hypothesized pansexual dimensions of the myth so as to derive the meaning of its key symbolism (see Lounsbury 1959; Ortner 1973).

The paradigm of the *bahana* origin myth includes the phallic, conjunctive, and uterine imagery of eleven episodic *frames* and three —telluric, cultural, and cosmic (or metaphysical)—types of *form* (table 1). In general, the imagery of episodic frames may include that which is overtly presented in the myth and that which is covertly associated with it in Warao thought as revealed in the preceding commentary.

Table 1. Forms of Similarity and Frames of Contiguity

	P	C	U	P	C	U
Telluric Forms	Component	Image	Component	Component	Image	Component
Cultural Forms	Component	Image	Component	Component	Image	Component
Cosmic Forms	Component	Image	Component	Component	Image	Component
		1. Frame			2. Frame	

P = Phallic
C = Conjunctive
U = Uterine

Taking the first episode of the myth as an example (table 2), the conjunctive column contains two telluric images: (1) the *tepui* mountain and a cave (containing two eggs) as phallic and uterine attributes respectively, and (2) the vertical soaring flight patterns of the nesting swallow-tailed kite, with the nesting sticks and the nest itself serving as phallic and uterine attributes respectively.

Table 2. Substitution Class of First Episodic Frame
Axis Mundi and Heraldic Raptor

	Phallic	Conjunctive	Uterine
Telluric Form	*Tepui* mountain	*Tepui* mountain and cave containing eggs	Hollow mountain cave
	Swallow-tailed kite	Fulminating vertical and soaring flight	Nest
	Nesting sticks	Flight of mating season	Nest
Cultural Form	Rattle staff	Rattle; vertical and rotating movement	Calabash
	Taut bow string	Braced bow; musical bow	Arch of bow
	Arrow	Bow and arrow	Arch of bow
Cosmic Form	World Pillar	*Axis mundi* piercing cosmic planes with coiled serpent at base	Bell-shaped cosmic vault; circular cosmic planes
	Heraldic Archer	Heraldic Raptor with bow and arrow and rattle	Heraldic Rattler Cave of emergency

Also, the conjunctive column of the cultural form contains two images: (1) the rattle, with staff (and seeds) as phallic and the calabash as uterine attributes; and (2) the braced hunting or musical bow, with the arch of the bow as female and the taut bow string and the arrow as male attributes. (The similarity between the imagery of the vertical and rotating movements of the rattle in use and the image of the kite's flight patterns is perhaps particularly noteworthy.)

The conjunctive column of the cosmic form contains again two images: (1) the *axis mundi* with its simile, the World Pillar, as male and the bell-shaped cosmic vault and circular cosmic planes as female attributes; and (2) the Heraldic Raptor, brandishing his arrows as phallic and his rattle as uterine attributes. On the cosmic level the telluric cave turns into the image of the cave of emergence.

The telluric, cultural, and cosmic forms of the first episodal frame are not identical but are semantically similar in varying degrees of closeness. The fit depends, in part, on the sophistication of the listener with regard to his/her naturalistic and cultural knowledge and, in part, on whether comparisons of similarity are made in immediate relative context or in total context. Thus, as bundles of connotative meanings, the *tepui* mountain construes in a manner similar to that of the *axis mundi* and the axis of the rattle in immediate relative context, and so does the Heraldic Raptor with the flight pattern, the rattle, and the bows and arrows. The relationship between the *tepui* and the kite construes within the total form class of the myth because of their common androgynous nature. Although loose fits of this kind may appear too imprecise for scientific discourse, intrinsically, the notion of similarity relates to overlapping of less than complete resemblances rather than to idiosyncrasy. At the same time that the notion of similarity introduces statistical considerations of aggregates and particles, it permits general statements about what is more important and what is less important in form comparisons. And it is by recognition of the validity of tendencies rather than by entirely pervasive generalities that correlates and key symbols in mythic thought systems are derived.

The tendency of the conjunctive images and attributes contained in the episodic frames is toward signification of the necessity for coexistence for the sake of survival through harmonious sexual relations and the joint procurement of food. The redundancy of images demonstrates the potential, in myth, for multiple representations of the same theme or message. This characteristic permits the forms of a given context to substitute for one another and to construe with their frame in a similar manner to constitute a substitution class.

Phallic imagery associates with male humans (like elder and younger brothers, grooms, husbands, fathers, and shamans), with erect snakes, and with male birds and insects. It also relates to fire, heat, the sun (solar bird), flight (tobacco trance, plumed serpent), and the upper world. Masculinity is rigid (like nesting sticks, fire drill, arrow, rattle staff, flower stems, quartz pyramid, bow string, bridge rope, rectangular game table, cigar) and is expressed in such phallic images as the World Pillar with a hollow of eggs, the world axis with the Cosmic Egg, the erect serpent with a glowing ball of smoke, and the hollow shaman's arms each attached to a lung and inhabited by a pair of younger and elder brothers. *The summarizing symbol that compounds the imagery of fertility is the world axis with its scrotal appendage of the Cosmic Egg.* In its concrete form, the symbol recurs in the feathered arrow and particularly in the stick-rattle, consisting of a two-meter-long staff with a string of seed husks wound around its upper end. Officiating shamans carry the stick-rattle like a verger or crosier during ritual dances.

Uterine imagery associates with female humans (such as brides, wives, mothers and shamans), with coiled-up snakes, and with female birds and insects. It also relates to the family quarters and the underworld. Femininity is round-featured (bow, arch) and is expressed in vaginal images (flowers, perforated world disks, the bell-shaped cosmic vault), in pregnant images (bulbous and hollow hives, termitaries, calabashes, and the Cosmic Egg), and in specifically uterine images such as rooms, cups, and nests. *The summarizing symbol that synthesizes the imagery of fecundity is the calabash of the ritual rattle.*

Conjunctive imagery unites these male and female components into such major images as the World Tree Axis piercing cosmic planes, the Heraldic Raptor brandishing his paraphernalia, the Bridge to the Otherworld, the Cosmic Egg, the Divine Gamblers, and the Sky Journey of the ecstatic shaman. These images combine the summarizing symbols of the male stick-rattle and the female calabash into *the key symbol of bahana: the ceremonial rattle.*

With four exceptions, the episodic frames are completely filled with telluric, cultural, and cosmic forms so that, generally speaking, the frames have a tripartite distribution (table 3). There is considerable overlap in the contents of the frames from one row to another in form distributions, and the totality of frames constitutes the frame class or mode of *bahana* imagery. This does not imply, however, that the forms have the same distribution; they are unique in every contextual instance. But parts of the distribution of a particular form may occur also as the distribution of some other form. As one would expect in myth, rather than systematic absolute correspondence where every form fits in every frame, there are only approximations in kind that reveal the contextual tendencies of the myth. Take, for instance, the multiple occurrence of quartz pyramid, oval pebbles,

Table 3. Episodic Frames of the Bahana Myth and Distribution of Forms

	1. World Pillar and Heraldic Kite			2. Cosmic Egg		
	P	C	U	P	C	U
Te	Tepui mountain	Tepui mountain and cave containing eggs	Hollow mountain and cave	Flower stems, quartz pebbles, oval pebbles, hair, tobacco smoke	Stems and florescence Calabash cups with white content	Flower Calabash cups
	Swallow-tailed kite	Fulminating vertical and soaring flight	Nest	Ropes of bridge	Youth on bridge	Arch of bridge
	Nesting sticks	Flight of mating season	Nest			
Cu	Rattle staff	Rattle; vertical and rotating movements	Calabash	Checkerboard with white pieces	Calabash cups with white content on game table	Calabash cups as pieces
	Taut bow string	Braced bow; musical bow	Arch of bow			
	Arrow	Bow and arrow	Arch of bow			
Co	World Pillar	Axis mundi piercing cosmic planes with coiled serpent at base	Bell-shaped cosmic vault; circular cosmic planes	Upper level of Cosmic Egg	Floor level with central orifice; rectangular game table in circular room	Lower level; round floor with central orifice
	Heraldic Archer	Heraldic Raptor with bow and arrow and rattle	Heraldic Rattler Cave of emergence			

	3. Occupation of Cosmic Egg			4. Divine Gamblers		
	P	C	U	P	C	U
Te	Insect pollinators	Brood chambers	Hollow and bulbous hives	Quartz pyramid, oval pebbles, hair, tobacco smoke	Calabash cups with white content	Calabash cups

3. Occupation of Cosmic Egg (cont.)

	P	C	U
Cu	Chiefs and workers	Insect families	Family quarters in the round
Co	Plumed erect serpent with ball of wisdom	Female serpent coiled in lower compartment	Cup-shaped lower compartment

4. Divine Gamblers (cont.)

	P	C	U
Cu	Insect husbands at gambling table	Insect families	Insect wives in family quarters
Co	Plumed erect serpent with ball of wisdom	Penetration of floor and oval house by serpent	Cosmic Egg; round floor with central orifice

5. Shamanic Flight

	P	C	U
Te	Fire	Fire on hearth	Round hearth
Cu	Fire drill Father of youth	Fire drilling Son	Fire board Mother of youth
Co	World axis Rising youth	World axis penetrating cosmic tiers Novice on celestial bridge and in bell-shaped cosmic vault	Bell-shaped cosmic vault Bell-shaped top of the world

6. Mystic Enlightenment

	P	C	U
Te	Quartz pyramid, oval pebbles, hair, tobbaco smoke	Calabash cups with white content	Calabash cups
Co	Novice ascending Plumed erect serpent	Novice in Cosmic Egg Penetration of floor and oval house by serpent	Cosmic Egg Cosmic Egg; round floor with central orifice

7. Shamanic Transformation

	P	C	U
Te	Shaman's arms attached to lungs		
Cu	Husband-Shaman	Marriage	Wife-Shaman
Co	Radiant Shaman	Youth on celestial bridge	Bee wife

8. Shamanic Union

	P	C	U
Te	Man	Copulation	Woman
Cu	Husband	Intercourse	Wife
Co	World axis	World axis in zenith	Bell-shaped cosmic vault

9. Mother of Seizures and Honey

	P	C	U
Te	Swallow-tailed kite	Mating flight	Frigate
Cu			
Co	Male seizure patient	Female shaman joins male patient	Female shaman
	Solar creator	Cohabitation of Heraldic Raptor and Mother of Honey	Mother of Seizures and Honey

10. Initiation

	P	C	U
Te	Shamanic cigar with quartz pyramid, oval pebbles, hair, tobacco smoke		
Cu	Shaman	Initiation	Novice
Co	Projectile-shooting shaman in sky	Projectiles penetrating breast of novice	Body cavity of novice

11. Origin of Bahana Shamanism

	P	C	U
Te	Shamanic cigar with quartz pyramid, oval pebbles, hair, tobacco smoke		
Cu	Shaman	Initiation	Novice
Co	Projectile-shooting shaman in sky	Projectiles penetrating breast of novice	Body cavity of novice
	Ropes of celestial bridge	Youth on bridge bordered by flowers	Arch of bridge
	Spirit sons	Spirit sons in breast of shaman	Body cavity of shaman; Cosmic Egg

Te = Telluric, Cu = Cultural, Co = Cosmic, P = Phallic, C = Conjunctive, U = Uterine hair, and tobacco smoke in telluric frames 2, 4, and 6 as phallic attributes of the conjunctive form of the gambling table with uterine calabash cups as counter pieces. In association with these three frames the seminal character of the four kinds of contents remains somewhat concealed, suggested only by their form and color. However, in frames 10 and 11, where they occur in modified contexts, they are lifted, so to speak, out of their uterine cups, placed into a shaman's phallic cigar, and shot into a novice's lungs.

The major tendency of form distribution within the *bahana* myth is a series of androgenous images appearing in a diachronic continuum from macrocosmic to microcosmic models. More specifically, the episodic frames provide three different environments for the images, displaying them in the transcendental context of the cosmos, the social context of the house, and the personal context of the human body (table 4).

Table 4. Episodic Frames and Context Models

Episodic Frames	Context Models
1. World Pillar and Heraldic Raptor	Cosmos
2. Cosmic Egg	Cosmos
3. Occupation of Cosmic Egg	House
4. Divine Gamblers	House
5. Shamanic Flight	House-Cosmos
6. Mystic Enlightenment	House
7. Shamanic Transformation	House
8. Shamanic Union	Body
9. Mother of Seizures and Honey	House
10. Initiation	Body
11. Origin of *Bahana* Shamanism	Body

Thus the frame class of the *bahana* myth is characterized by a three-tiered general model: (1) There is the cosmos with its sea serpent of the underworld, its earth disk with a village of insect tribes around the shaman's house, and the top of the world with the Cosmic Egg and a bell-shaped cosmic vault. (2) The house model has two images: (a) *the Cosmic Egg* houses a blind snake in its lower compartment, and has a round floor with family quarters around a gambling table and a bell-shaped upper compartment with a glowing ball in the serpent's mouth; (b) *the traditional Warao-style stilt dwelling,* built over the water, is inhabited by the anaconda, and has a floor with family quarters and a bell-shaped (traditional) or pyramidal (modern) vault of rafters for a roof. (3) The anatomical model of the human body features the abdominal region with intestines and reproductive organs, separated by the diaphragm from the thoracic region with lungs and heart and a bell-shaped rib cage, and the head.

The three regions of the human body are considered to be the seats of four different kinds of self (Osborn n.d.). The lower abdominal region is occupied by *obonobu,* the "potential-self." It endows a person with special capabilities and talents and the ability to ponder and to reflect. The designation of the self is related to *obonobuai,* "to love, to desire," and is associated with the reproductive potential of the lower body.

The thoracic region is occupied by *kobe,* the "emotional-self." It produces a person's feelings of guilt, fear, and anxiety as well as those of remorse and shame. The primary meaning of *kobe* is "heart," and it is through the action of this four-cameral organ that the individual acquires the properties of "strong blood" or "weak blood." The emotional-self determines whether a person's potential will be realized, since mismatched sexual partners cannot procreate. Only couples with strong bloods can.

The head is the seat of *obohona,* the "personality-self." It is a person's source of inspiration, knowledge, consciousness, and will power. The personality-self is immortal and pertains to the supernatural world, where it survives after a person's death.

The fourth self of a human being is *mehokohi,* the "likeness-self." It is located in the thorax but reflects the entire body; it is the shadow image of the person.

Projecting the properties of the abdominal, thoracic, and cerebral personal selves into the three-tiered house, the Cosmic Egg, and the universe, it becomes apparent that *bahana* and its underlying homology of "human body/house-cosmos" as one of mankind's most archaic thoughts relates to the problem of self-realization within the physical, cultural, and metaphysical conditions of life. Its key symbol, the rattle, is also three-tiered, featuring a "leg" (handle), a "body" (calabash), and a "head" (upper part of the calabash and distal end of the axis). In other words, the rattle is the collocative expression of the *bahana* myth's substitution-distribution matrix, which amalgamates the meanings of a plurality of forms and frames into the singularity of a key symbol.

NOTES

1. The bulk of information on *bahana* shamanism has been collected intermittently since 1954 on numerous field trips. I concentrated my research on the Winikina-Warao of the Central Delta where my principal informant, Antonio Lorenzano, happens to be a *bahanarotu*. I have also studied with Manuel, the *bahanarotu* of an Arawabisi subtribe, who is known as a famous *daunonarima* (highest ranking *bahanarotu*). Additional information pertaining to the animals of the *bahana* complex was collected over the past ten years by my Warao field assistant, Cesáreo Soto. He employed eleven informants originating from almost as many different settlements dispersed throughout the Intermediate Delta. At the time of recording, the informants were estimated to be between thirty-five and eighty years old. The data collected by C. Soto were recorded in the Warao language. My own data were recorded in Waraoan and Spanish.

I am very grateful to my colleagues Philip L. Newman and Gerardo Reichel-Dolmatoff for their helpful suggestions and constructive criticism, and to Alan Dundes for his manifold advice concerning form and content of the paper. Floyd Lounsbury of Yale University discussed with me at length the application of the principles of similarity-contiguity to the analysis of myth, and Peter Rivière from Oxford University had several very helpful conversations with me regarding the methodological implications of the model. Danny Chalfen was my research assistant for the project. A grant from the Ahmanson Foundation covered the research expenses.

2. I published a shaman's personal account of the *bahana* complex on an earlier occasion (Wilbert 1972). It is necessary here to give a brief summary of the same and to add some further detail that facilitates clarity and comprehension. Although closely following the original account, the wording of the present narrative is my own.

3. In Venezuela known as *gavilán tijereta*: scissor-tailed kite (Waraoan: *hukonomana* or *hukono kahamana*).

4. Hearing Mawari's name pronounced for the first time by a Warao shaman came as a surprise to me, inasmuch as the name is associated with Carib-speaking Indians. For the Waiwai, for instance, Mawari is the

Creator (Fock 1963, 35–36). This is not the place to enter into a discussion of the related ethnohistorical question (Wilbert 1981). Suffice it to say that the Warao have been a very mobile and seafaring nation for thousands of years and probably have assimilated cultural traits not only from the South American mainland but from Mesoamerica and the Caribbean as well.

5. In Venezuela the first group of birds are known as *alcatraz* (W.: *yoroa*), brown pelican, (*Pelecanus occidentalis*); *gaviota guanaguanare* (W.: *nabakabara*), laughing gull, (*Larus atricilla*); and *piapoco* (W.: *hari* or *hebu hari*); toucan (*Ramphastos tucanos*). The vernacular, Waraoan, and scientific terms of the second group are: *cucarachero* or *picua* (W.: *bikaroana*), wren (*Troglodytidae*); *cristofué* or *garrapatero* (W.: *keribitabu*), greater ani (*Crotophaga major*); and *pico de plata* or *picoplata* (W.: *sonson*), silver-beaked tanager (*Ramphocelus carbo*). I am grateful to Dr. Thomas R. Howell (UCLA) for his assistance with the identification of the birds. I am deeply indebted to Dr. Charles Hogue (Natural History Museum, Los Angeles County) and Dr. Edward O. Wilson (Harvard) for their instruction and guidance.

6. The kite's colors (black, white, red, yellow, green, and blue), albeit in different sets, are repeated in the flowers, the rooms, the gambling table, and the plumes of the serpents as the creator bird's signature.

7. Hymenoptera identification by Dr. Roy R. Snelling (Natural History Museum, Los Angeles County) based on author's collection. Dr. Snelling's assistance is gratefully acknowledged. Termite identification by Dr. Kumar Krishna (American Museum of Natural History, New York). Color of mythological insects does not always correspond to color of natural prototype.

REFERENCES

Barral, Basilio de
    1979   *Diccionario Warao-Castellano, Castellano-Warao.* Caracas: El Políglota.
Brown, Leslie and Dean Amadon
    1968   *Eagles, hawks and falcons of the world.* Vol. 1, 228–30. New York: McGraw-Hill.
Cohen, Percy S.
    1969   Theories of myth. *Man* (n.s.) 4(1):337–53.
Coomaraswamy, Ananda K.
    1935   *Elements of Buddhist iconography.* Cambridge: Harvard University Press.
Fock, Niels
    1963   *Waiwai: Religion and society of an Amazonian tribe.* Nationalmuseets Skrifter, vol. 8. Copenhagen: The National Museum.
Lévi-Strauss, Claude
    1966   *From honey to ashes.* New York: Harper and Row.

Lounsbury, Floyd G.
1959   Similarity and contiguity relations in language and culture. In *Report of the Tenth Annual Round Table Meeting on Linguistics and Language Studies*, ed. Richard Harrell, 123–38. Georgetown University Institute of Languages and Linguistics, Monograph no. 12. Washington, D.C.

Matthäi, Hildegard
1977   *Die Rolle der Greifvögel, insbesondere der Harpye und des Königsgeiers, bei ausserandinen Indianern Südamerikas.* Münchener Beiträge zur Amerikanistik, vol. 1. Munich: Klaus Renner Verlag.

Morey, Robert V.
1979   A joyful harvest of souls: Disease and destruction of the Llanos Indians. *Antropológica* (Caracas) 52:77–108.

Ortner, Sherry B.
1973   On key symbols. *American Anthropologist* 75:1338–46.

Osborn, Henry.
n.d.   The Warao self. MS.

Schwarz, Herbert S.
1929   Honey wasps. *Natural History* 29(4):421–26.

Wilbert, Johannes
1970   *Folk literature of the Warao Indians.* Latin American Studies, vol. 15. Los Angeles: Latin American Center, University of California.
1972   Tobacco and shamanistic ecstasy among the Warao Indians of Venezuela. In *Flesh of the gods: The ritual use of hallucinogens*, ed. P. T. Furst, 55–83. New York: Praeger.
1974   The calabash of the ruffled feathers. *Artscanada* 4:90–93.
1975a   Eschatology in a participatory universe: Destinies of the soul among the Warao Indians of Venezuela. In *Death and the afterlife in pre-Columbian America*, ed. Elizabeth P. Benson, 163–89. Washington, D.C.: Dumbarton Oaks Research Library and Collections.
1975b   Magico-religious use of tobacco among South American Indians. In *Cannabis and culture*, ed. V. Rubin, 439–61. The Hague: Mouton.
1975c   El violín en la cultura Warao: Un préstamo cultural complementario. Trans. R. Acuña. *Montalbán* 4:189–215.
1975d   *Warao basketry: Form and function.* Los Angeles: Museum of Cultural History, University of California.
1979a   Gaukler-schamanen der Warao. In *Amerikanistische Studien*, ed. Roswith Hartmann and Udo Oberem, vol. 2, 294–99. Anthropos Institut, Collectanea Instituti Anthropos, vol. 21. Sankt Augustin.
1979b   Geography and telluric lore of the Orinoco Delta. *Journal of Latin American Lore* 5(1):129–50.
1981   Warao cosmology and Yecuana roundhouse symbolism. *Journal of Latin American Lore* 7(1):37–72.
1983   Warao ethnopathology. *Journal of Ethnopharmacology* 8:357–61.

THE LION IN THE CITY:
ROYAL SYMBOLS OF TRANSITION IN CUZCO

R. TOM ZUIDEMA

During the last six days of the initiation rituals in Cuzco, celebrated in the month of Capac raymi (royal feast) and ending with the December solstice, the noble youths were reintroduced to Inca society by men dressed with a puma head and skin over their heads and backs, playing the four "drums of the Sun" (Zuidema 1974–1976, 1982c; Zuidema and Urton 1976). The chroniclers Molina and Cobo give detailed descriptions of the ceremony, probably based on observations of the informants (Molina 1943, 48–60; Cobo 1956, 207–12). They give Quechua words for the puma skins, the dresses of the players, and the dances that were executed, and they venture an explanation of the purpose of the ceremony. These data, however, do not tell us why puma skins and drums were used or why the feast had to coincide with the December solstice. For an answer to these questions we must turn to other rituals and to Inca mythology, where the puma is associated with times and places of transition and transformation. The puma shares this trait with other animals like the *amaru* (serpent, dragon) and the *uturuncu* (jaguar).

One symbolic use of the puma, the American lion, or his head, is to allow the sun or the rainbow to emerge from openings in the earth as if from springs of water. Similar ideas are expressed in other indigenous cultures of South America (e.g., Reichel-Dolmatoff 1975, 169–73). Moreover, examples from the ancient Middle East abound demonstrating that Western culture was also familiar with this concept of the lion (e.g., Wit 1951; McCall 1973–1974). Such knowl-

Reprinted by permission from *Journal of Latin American Lore* 9:1 (1983), 39–100.

edge may have oriented the interest of the Spanish chroniclers in the Inca symbol, but it also influenced their rendering of the myths that refer to the ritual. These they interpreted against the background of their own colonial society.

My principal aim in this article is to understand certain puma myths and rituals in their proper context: the symbolic use of felines by the Incas themselves. The study of the Inca calendar allows us to further explore the Andean use of puma skins and drums as part of "rituals that mark transitions between temporal periods, spatial zones or social states" (Turner 1977:53; c.f. Van Gennep 1960). I will concentrate on three variants of an Inca myth from Cuzco which discuss the transitional functions of lion skins and drums in the context of an Inca prince who defends Cuzco against an enemy and is subsequently crowned king by his father, who had fled the city. One variant relates the myth explicitly to the December rituals, which supports the conclusion that we are dealing with a royal charter myth for initiation rituals in which the crown prince, when available, would also participate.

In the descriptions of the ritual the specific Incaic word "puma" is used for the animal that the myths describe more neutrally as "lion." Connecting the myths and the ritual brings into focus two issues of critical importance for the study of Inca culture and society in Cuzco at the time of the conquest. While one of our two earliest variants of the myth, given by Cieza de Leon, refers to the prince as wearing a lion skin, the other variant, by Betanzos, uses the lion symbol when he refers to the body politic of the valley and city of Cuzco: the future king has to be its head and the people are its body. A similar religious and legal concept of "body politic" was well known in Europe at the time Betanzos wrote (1551). Although in Europe the metaphor of the body used the human form, the connection of kingship to the symbol of the lion also had a long trajectory in Middle Eastern and European history. Spanish influence is obvious in colonial paintings from Cuzco depicting Inca kings, and on painted wooden beakers (*queros*) belonging to the indigenous culture of the same period. They connect Inca royalty to European heraldic lions or lion heads. The analysis of the version given by Betanzos must concentrate on the extent to which his European perspective has reinterpreted and changed the Inca myth.[1]

The understanding of the Incas' metaphorical use of the puma is

especially hampered by the development of the comparison of Cuzco to a puma, which took place after Betanzos's original presentation. Twenty years later, Sarmiento reinterprets Betanzos's original data by comparing the fortress of Sacsayhuaman above Cuzco to the lion's head, and the city to its body. A metaphor that was originally intended to explain problems of social structure, of royal succession, and of borders, lost these characteristics and, in turn, became a problem of political history and of physical architectonical shape. In recent years, Rowe (1967) has suggested that the layout of the central part of Cuzco has the precise shape of a puma. His reconstruction is not based on reasoned argument and is only partially supported by a chronicler, Sarmiento, whose own argument is spurious. Nonetheless, Rowe's presentation is uncritically accepted by archaeologists and in the popular literature. I will return to the original issue as presented by Betanzos, and then review Rowe's suggestion.

One reason that led Sarmiento and Rowe to their ways of comparing Cuzco to a puma is the well-attested Inca toponym of Pumapchupan (tail of the puma), or Pumachupa, for the confluence of the two rivers that encompass the ceremonial center of the city. They use a metonymic argument by extending the concept of "tail" for the confluence to that of "body" for the whole city, an argument that Betanzos himself, remarkably enough, does not use. Moreover, they ignore the reasons why the confluence itself was called "Tail of the Puma." One reason is alluded to by the calendrical rituals. While the men dressed with puma heads and skins had a function of presenting the noble initiates to Cuzco society, the ritual of *chupay huallu*, "waggling the tail," stresses political connections to society outside Cuzco. This ritual was carried out in Pumachupa, just after the first full moon that followed the December solstice. A general study of the Inca ritual and agricultural calendar supports the conclusion that there is a close connection between the two rituals that involve, respectively, the puma-men and the use of the place Pumachupa. Both references to puma can be trusted as truly Incaic. But while the first mentions actual puma skins, including their tails, the second only makes a metaphorical comparison to the puma's tail. There are no Inca data to confirm the metonymic extension that Sarmiento and Rowe allow themselves to make.

Betanzos describes the ritual use of Pumachupa in conjunction with his association of the puma with the body politic. In fact, they are discussed in the same myth. From these data we can derive some idea of the territory that was involved in each. The concept of body politic does not use the central part of the city of Cuzco but its valley, as circumscribed by the initiation rituals leading to the presentation of the youths to their elders in Cuzco by the puma-men. The ritual of Pumachupa extends to a much wider area.

The data that are pertinent to the theme all refer to calendrical and initiation rituals, and rituals of royal consecration and of borders that the initiated youths, including the future king, have to defend. The "body politic" metaphor, as used by Betanzos, derives its importance from these rites of transition, which allow us to evaluate its pre-Columbian roots.[2]

In this paper I will argue that Betanzos's use of the lion for describing the body politic metaphor and his placing it in the context of the future king who will defend the valley of Cuzco against an enemy has to be studied in the context of the ritual whereby older men reintroduce the initiates into Cuzco society. As the puma head and skin are the distinctive marks of these elders, I will treat this theme first in more general Andean terms.

CAPAC RAYMI AND THE PUMA-MEN

The Ritual Use of Puma and Fox Skins

The use of the puma skin was not limited to Capac raymi. One description of a harvest ritual near Lake Titicaca mentions their use by young women, representing at that time the Earthmother who had given their people a good harvest (Cieza 1945, ch. 117). The distinctiveness of Capac raymi, then, was that the puma skins were worn by men who had families and owned llamas and cultivated fields (Molina 1943; 60; Avila 1952, ch. 2, 10). Certain other animals were also related to agricultural rituals because of their behavior (Huertas 1981, 79; Agustinos 1952, 84; Urton 1981a, 1981b). The skins of foxes and pumas had a form of homeopathic value, being used to counteract the destructive influences associated with these animals.

In Paracas and Nazca art we see men depicted with fox heads and skins on their heads and backs. Guaman Poma illustrates repeatedly the guardians of the cultivated fields defending these by shouting and using rattles against thieves and wild animals, like foxes (figs. 1, 2, 3).[3] The word *ararihua*, which refers to the guardians, derives from the Aymara term *huararihuasita*, "to shout very much when people catch the fox or wolf who steals" (Bertonio 1956). Guaman Poma depicts a young man dressed as *arariva* (*ararihua*) for the month of October. Elsewhere (1980, 285 [287]) he explains his specific reasons for doing so. In October, or Umaraymi (Aymara: *uma*, water), people would ritually plead for the water of the coming rains and boys—probably those to be initiated in December—had to "ask God for water and to paint their faces" (Guaman Poma 1980, 285 [287]). But the harmful effects of receiving rain also had to be averted. Processions were held against hail, frost, and lightning, calling them, like the fox, "thief" and shouting *Astaya, zuua, runa nacchac chachac cuncayqui cuchuscaayque. Ama ricuscayquecho* ("Ay, ay! Thief, robber of people, I will cut your throat! That I will never see you again!"). In his drawing (fig. 4) of a man who sees a fox with a serpent in his beak he comments: *atoc zupayta ayzan camaquita ayzan* ("the fox drags along the demon, drags along his creator") and in the text next to it he says (282 [284]):

Hearing the howling of a fox or any animal, the indians who tell omens say that the heads of the living people go out, or the arms or legs or entrails of men and women. They said that these indians or their wives or husbands or the children of their mothers and fathers will die. Or that they will die, drowning in the river or falling from a rock or burning in a fire or that they will commit suicide like today the Chancas do when they are very drunk and thus the demons and Satan will take them to their house in Hell.

The *ararihua* derives his distinctive dress from that animal which is specifically associated with the forces he is to combat.

Similar data exist about the use of the puma skin. Today in northern Chile a herder will hold a puma skin responsible for his llamas, beating it when a live puma has killed an animal.[4] In a dance called *huantaycocha* (from the sixteenth-century province of Huarochirí), owners of llamas were allowed to wear a puma skin during the time of the reappearance of the Pleiades in celebration of the ripe harvest in early June (Avila 1952, ch. 10; Zuidema 1982b). At that

11059

TRAVAXA
CHACRAMÃTAPISCO
carcoy pacha tienpo deoxean dela sementera enpieRayno
utubre · oma raymi quilla ·

pasian · ararnico · pachaca
o jeador

o tubre — o mo raymi   otubre

Figure 1. The *ararihua* in October. (Guaman Poma 1980, 1159 [1169])

Figure 2. *Ararihua* with sling and rattle. (Guaman Poma 1980, 859 [873])

Figure 3. The *ararihua* in March. (Guaman Poma 1980, 1138 [1148])

Figure 4. The fox used in prognostication. (Guaman Poma 1980, 281[283])

time boys, whom we can compare to the initiates in Cuzco, danced
for the first of three times in the year.

Two myths, also from Huarochirí, further describe the puma
dances of the llama owners. In the first myth, the god Coniraya
Viracocha pursues the woman Cavillaca who has fled from him along
a river down to the coast (Avila 1952, ch. 2). On the way, he
classifies six animals: three good ones—the condor, the puma, and
the falcon—who say that she is nearby, and three bad ones—the
skunk, the fox and the parrots—who say that she is already far
ahead. Coniraya promises the puma that he will be honored and that
he will eat the llamas of guilty people, saying, "He who kills you will
put you on his head and will dance with you in a great feast. He will
repeat this every year, sacrificing a llama to you and he will dance
with you." However, he also condemns the fox, saying, "Even if you
pass by at a distance, people will hate you and will treat you as a fox
of bad luck. When they kill you they will throw you and your skin
away as being worthless" (Avila 1952, ch. 2). In the other myth two
brothers-in-law compete, challenging each other (Avila 1952, ch. 5;
Zuidema 1982d). One challenge is won by dancing in a red puma
skin that was found near a spring of water. During the dance a rainbow appears. In this myth, then, the relation of a red puma with
water is stressed, whereas in the first myth this same animal is
associated with llamas (although the dance is called *huantaycocha*,
cocha meaning "lake"). This double purpose is also expressed in
other Andean myths and rituals which stress the relation between
llamas and water. Avila himself translated the first part of his
Quechua manuscript which includes the two myths, and gives a description of the puma skin as used in both cases. There he says (Avila
in Loayza 1952, 19):

> When they kill you, they will strip off your skin without cutting off the
> head and they will fill this up in a way that it has the form of a head,
> and they will put your eyes in the holes that will look alive; your feet
> and hands will be hanging from the skin and also the tail with at the end
> a thread to adorn it, and they will tan and soften the skin and after that
> they will lift you, in that way prepared, up over their heads, putting
> yours above theirs; and the skin, feet and hands will cover the back of
> he who puts you on, which they will do in the most important feasts in
> order that you will be honored in such a way, and I add to this: that he
> who wishes to adorn himself with you, first must kill a llama and thus
> have to walk and sing with you at the back.

This description implies that the puma is always honored, although ethnographic facts are more ambiguous. For instance, in Ayacucho I was told that when a puma is killing cattle or llamas around the villages men will hunt it accompanied by one woman, whose presence is thought to weaken the puma. Once the puma is killed, its blood is immediately drunk raw; then they insult the puma and carry it back to the village. The first myth recognizes a similar attitude toward the puma but instead concludes that if it eats a llama, then the owner of that llama surely had been sinful (*hucha*). Apparently, puma masks are still used today in the town of Acomayo, southeast of Cuzco, which specializes in hunting pumas. Men and woman take part, using only sticks. After they capture the puma, they eat it, as the meat imparts strength. The same people make the puma masks and dance in them, though they would not show them to other people, who "would get too scared by them."[5]

There are more data on pumas and foxes which demonstrate continuing patterns in Andean concepts about these animals. In Pacariqtambo, also south of Cuzco, pumas are referred to, among other terms, as "son of the earth." This is related to the belief that they are able to communicate with the earth, will "hear" about things through the earth. The fox is also called "son of the earth." Both animals are often observed eating together during the day what the puma has hunted during the night. They are related, each in his own way, to the rainy season. While the pumas are said to enter the village only during this time of year, foxes predict in October and November the outcome of the next year's crop. If they howl loudly during these months, it will be a good year with plenty of rain and a large harvest; if they howl weakly it will be a bad year. One of the principal functions of the *ararihuas*, which still survives in Pacariqtambo, is to guard against foxes and pumas.[6]

As Guaman Poma shows the use of fox skins in October and in March, we can understand his and other ethnohistorical data in the light of modern practices. In October foxes howl, predicting the outcome of the harvest, and in this way they also have a propitious influence; in March, when the crops ripen, their interest in eating them has to be forestalled.[7] The habit pumas and foxes have of eating together demonstrates a certain dependency of the latter upon the former and supports an apparent ranking of fox skins, which are worn by young men in the year of their initiation,[8] under puma skins, worn by their elders, who supervise them.[9]

These ethnohistorical and ethnographic data may suffice to give us an idea about the richness of Andean concepts concerning the puma, on the use of its skin, and on puma masks.[10] My intention, however, is to analyze what use Cuzco society made of the puma symbol for the purposes of its own political organization. These purposes are best expressed in the rituals of Capac raymi, the royal feast.

The Puma-Men in Capac Raymi

During the month of Capac raymi, when all the foreigners had left, twelve- to fifteen-year-old boys belonging to the Inca nobility learned about the mythic origins of their ancestors and participated in various rituals commemorating those origins. First they went to Huanacauri mountain, from where their first ancestor and Inca king had observed the valley and taken possession of it. Then the boys competed in a race from Anahuarque mountain, also on the southern side of the valley, in memory of the fact that only this mountain had risen with the waters of the Flood and remained dry. Near the end of the month they went to Yahuira, a hill near the town that had been the sacred mountain of the people who owned the valley before the Incas. There, the boys received their last badges of manhood and nobility: the *huara*, or loincloth, and the golden earspools. Then they went back to the plaza where they would sit facing the rising sun, for the first time according to their *ayllu*s, social divisions belonging to Hanan or "upper" Cuzco and Hurin or "lower" Cuzco. At this time their ears had not yet been pierced. For this they had to wait six days, during which time the men with puma skins played the drums. Their wait over, the noble boys went out to the *chacras* (cultivated fields) near sources of water and had their ears pierced. Apparently this was a private ritual, yet other boys had it done at home (Albornoz, see Duviols 1967, 27).

> When this was finished, on the same day, the priests of the Creator, the Sun, the Thunder and the Moon and the herders of the Inca occupied themselves in counting the cattle [i.e., llamas] of the Creator, the Sun, the Thunder and the Moon, so that the animals would increase. This was done in the whole kingdom on the same day. (Molina 1943, 60)

Returning to the rituals with the drummers and their puma skins, Molina describes the skins—as does Avila for Huarochirí—

adding that the puma heads had golden earspools and teeth, and that the men were also adorned with golden headbands and golden *chipana*s, or bracelets. The pumas were called Hillacunya, Chuquicunya. Whereas according to Molina it was other men, Cobo states that it was these puma-men who performed the dance Cayo dressed in long red shirts, *pucacaycho uncu*. This was followed by another dance, called Huallina. Many sacrifices were made of llamas and of other things so that those who were "knighted" would be lucky in war and in all other endeavors. At the end of these days, when the boys were to bathe and put on new dresses, each boy's "most important" uncle would give him a shield, a sling, and a club for going to war. Other relatives would present him with other special objects to make him rich in all things. When a crown prince was knighted the important people of the empire gave him large presents, as well as herders for the llamas that he received. People would offer burnt sacrifices of certain birds so that those who were knighted would be lucky in war. Then the ears were pierced.

The ritual period (from the moment when the boys were given their earspools to when their ears were pierced) with the puma-men playing the drums, demarcated various transitions. During the December solstice the sun reversed its movement from south to north and heavy rains commenced. The age of the boys suggests that ear piercing was a symbolic opening for sexual life. During this month they were helped by girls of the same age who had already passed the celebration of their first menstruation (Zuidema and Urton 1976, 85). Fertility was important to men as well as to llamas and the Earth. The latter concern is expressed in the name *pucacaychu uncu*, "the red dress that drags over the earth" (González Holguín 1952: *kaychuni*, to sweep; *kaychuykachan pachacta*, or *ppacchanhuan*, to drag along one's dress), referring to the Earthmother whose name, besides Pachamama, was Suyrumama, "Mother of the long dress that drags over the ground (*suyru*)" (Molina 1943, 74). In harvest rituals young women with long dresses and puma skins would impersonate Pachamama Suyrumama (Cieza 1945, ch. 117), whereas during the December solstice rituals the impersonators were men. The names Hillacunya Chuquicunya for the puma skins mean "lightning (*illa*) thunderclap (*cumya*)" and "golden (*choque*) thunderclap," an interpretation which is appropriate in the light of the myths to be dealt with next.

The female, private, family interest in agriculture and fertility that started with planting in August (Zuidema 1982a, 1982c) was transformed into a male, public, political interest, stressing *ayllu* and moiety organization, the state organization of llama herds, warfare, and the political relations of the Incas to other states. This public interest comes out most clearly in the dance Cayo (Molina 1943, 58; Polo 1916, 21; Santacruz Pachacuti 1950, 227, 234), a dance that Cobo, probably correctly, calls Aucayo. At this time the foreigners were invited back into the city and all people came together on the plaza for "rejoicing" and dancing (Cobo 1956, 211).[11] The priests called Tarpuntay (*tarpuy*, to plant) gave all those present a small loaf (*bollo*) prepared of maize and the blood of sacrificed llamas to eat, and said: "This which has been given to you is food of the Sun, and it has to be in your body as a witness to manifest that you will be punished when at any time you will talk badly about Him or about the Inca [king]" (Cobo 1956).

The Drums

While the maize bread as host stressed spiritual unity, the drums played during the dance (Au)cayo can be understood in terms of political borders. Santacruz Pachacuti repeatedly refers to them (1950, 238, 251). When, according to Inca epic tradition, the Chancas attacked Cuzco, the prince Inca Yupanqui rallied the people to the defense of Cuzco by having the big drums played in ten different locations, probably on the outskirts of town. Later, his son Tupa Yupanqui went out to conquer the Collas around Lake Titicaca, but these, "in order to terrify the people of the Inca, began to sing, hanging eight drums in four wooden racks, all dressed up with gold, feathers and silver." This provenance of the drums is confirmed by Guaman Poma (1980, 324, 325, [326, 327]). He uses the drums to characterize, in general, dances and songs from Collasuyu (one of the parts of the empire) and gives the drawing of a woman playing the drum, while men play the flutes (fig. 5). In the accompanying text he repeats that women play the big drum. Herrera (1945, Década 5, book 4, ch. 6), in a very interesting description of a dance which is probably from around Lake Titicaca, involving *curaca*s (chiefs), their sons as successors, and their wives, confirms that it was the latter who played the drum. However, puma-men played these drums during the December solstice and they wore the female dress *pucacaychu uncu.* At this time a male interest reigned in a female domain, the Earth, while in the Colla case, female cooperation was needed in a male affair: the defense of the border against enemies.

In two descriptions of rites of passage Santacruz Pachacuti also discusses the drums (1950, 228, 233–34). In one case, the birth of a crown prince, a male interest (that of the king) is expressed in the female activity of passing a son from the private female womb to a public male position. In the other case, Santacruz Pachacuti mentions death as a rite of passage when, at the time of Capac raymi, a new image of the Sun is placed in his temple (he adds the famous drawing of the latter). King Mayta Capac renews the image of the Sun that his great-grandfather, Manco Capac, the founder of the Inca dynasty, had placed there. By bringing in the large drums for Capac raymi, he wished, "to know only the creator as powerful Lord, despising all the highest things, elements and creatures like men, the sun and the moon that here I will paint as they were placed till the holy Gospel came into this kingdom." He then elaborates on this theme, which touches a central issue to be discussed in the myths:

> They say that Maytacapacynga was very learned, who knew all medicines, and the past and the future; at the end of the feast of Capac raymi Viracochan pachayachachi that he had celebrated for a whole month, he had said to his people in those days of feast, when it became dark "Oh, how soon ended the feast and now remains for us only death, because death has to come, like now it becomes dark, like a dream, an image of death!" And he said many times "because the feasts are also the image of the real feast rational creatures are blessed that in the future they will obtain and know the eternal feast and the name of the Creator." And they say that many times he said that men did not die like animals. Remembering this he went to fast in Ttococachi, weeping, and eating one row of maize kernels in one day. And thus he passed a whole month with its nights fasting in midyear.

Fasting and eating one row of maize kernels was a ritual practiced by the Inca king (or brother of his who was assigned this task [Bertonio: *Sasiri ccapaca*]), when he had killed an enemy. It is therefore important to know that Santacruz Pachacuti relates the custom to Capac raymi.

Figure 5.   Woman playing big drum and men playing flutes. (Guaman
            Poma 1980, 324 [326])

In these last two descriptions, Santacruz Pachacuti, like Molina, mentions the hymns and songs of *ccayo* and *uallina*, together with a third song, *ayma*. This Aymara word—Santacruz Pachacuti was a *curaca* in an Aymara-speaking province—can help us to understand the word *huallina*, which is not mentioned by the Quechua dictionaries or by other chroniclers. Ayma derives from *aymatha*, "to dance in the old way, especially when people go to work in the fields of their chiefs" (Bertonio 1956). The ceremony of Ayma is also referred to in this context by Polo (1916, 25). We might, therefore, look for a derivation of *huallina* from *huallatha*, "to dance as they did in the time of the Inca when they received him, the men giving each other a hand and the women behind them playing" (Bertonio 1956). The translation refers to the dance described by Herrera where the women played the big drums, as did the puma-men in Capac raymi during the Huallina.

We now come to a final appreciation of the drums, and the women or puma-men playing them. The drums were used in two circumstances: at political borders and at political centers. The first circumstance also implies war. Beating the drum with sticks, which Bertonio refers to in Aymara as *nuatha*, *lekatha*, or *sakatha*, was done in imitation of beating their enemies with weapons.[12] However, as playing the drum in Andean culture generally was and is a female prerogative (fig. 6), we have to understand why men played them in Capac raymi.

Andean rituals made a direct comparison between agriculture and warfare. For instance, planting and harvest were celebrated with victory songs called *aucaylli*, a word derived from *auca* (enemy) and *aylli* (victory song). The December solstice, when the sun is strongest and it changes its course, also makes the most important changes in the agricultural cycle. Planting stops, as by December young plants have to be strong enough to withstand the onslaught of the coming heavy rains. Water that has been used in irrigation canals is returned to the rivers as the rains take over the function of providing water for agriculture (Molina 1943, 63–66). Maize flowers transform into seeds (Agustinos 1952, 60). But while people now depend on rain for their crops to grow, they also have to fight against hail, snow, and thunder. This task is given to the *ararihua* who, moreover, must keep pumas and foxes out of the fields (Condori 1977:38). Victory is not so much over the earth, but has to be obtained over the weather, as one

Figure 6. Woman with drum defending crop, in February and at night, against fox, deer, skunk, and birds. (Guaman Poma 1980, 1135 [1145])

of the following myths explains. This myth also supports the interpretation of the names of the puma skins as *illacunya chuquicunya*: the
sound of the drums imitating thunderclaps. The initiation rituals of
the noble boys were related to this central moment of change in the
agricultural cycle. Instead of women it was men, wearing the puma
skin and the long dress and playing the drums, who introduced boys
from their parents' houses into society, and who reintroduced them
into secular life after a month of contact with the ancestors.[13]

THE BODY OF THE LION

Three myths further explain the use of puma skins at the end of
Capac raymi. The first two myths refer to the epic story of the attack
of the Chancas on Cuzco, their defeat, and the resulting reorganization of the city and its subsequent conquest of an empire. The Sinchi,
or warleader, who led the Incas to victory is here glorified as a
Puma. The third myth—with details about space very similar to
those found in the second—mentions the same hero, but in his capacity as defender of Cuzco against the destructive aspects of weather.
This myth also mentions the month of December and its rituals.

For a full understanding of the first two myths, an analysis of the
whole epic of the Chanca war would be necessary, something beyond
the scope of this article. Another problem that will not be considered
is that of possible historical elements about this war. No archaeological evidence has yet been discovered in support of it ever having
taken place (Rowe and Menzel 1966; Zuidema 1978, 1055–
56; Duviols 1979a, 83) and many elements of the extant accounts
would, on first sight, appear to be purely mythical. Place names refer
to actual sites of archaeological importance. Nevertheless, these
names are the strongest evidence that the war did not play the
historical role it was supposed to have had. Whereas later chroniclers
confuse the mythical Chancas with the historical ones from present-
day Andahuaylas, in the second myth they are said to derive from
Paucara, in Huancavelica, a place of much earlier archaeological
importance (+600 A.D.) and outside the historical Chanca territory.
Also, the myth describes how the Chancas are defeated a second
time in a place called Jaquijahuana, a hill separating the valleys of
Anta and Ichubamba, and how their bodies were left there for the
foxes, but archaeology demonstrates it to be an important pre-Inca
town, with bones still strewn over the ground from that much earlier

occupation. Central to the argument of the myth is another town Jaquijahuana, distinguished from the first by being called Caquia Jaquijahuana. This is one of the best-preserved Inca cities, next to
which are pre-Inca ruins. The myth explains why the Inca city was
built here (see map).

Thus, the myth attempts to draw into the Inca context places
that originally had a different meaning in local history. Moreover,
these places were used by the Incas for constructing a war of ex-
emplary significance in the initiation rituals. In this context the war
can be treated as myth. However, the problem of the Chanca war as
political myth does not end with this, since the Spanish colonial
historians used it as a framework for expressing their own opinion
about Inca conquests and the Spanish right to conquer Peru.

The Myths of the Chanca War

The detail of the "Body of the Lion" is given by the two chroniclers, Pedro Cieza de León and Juan de Betanzos, who in 1551 were
the first people to write a well-argued account of the epic history of
the Incas.[14] The dynastic sequence, of which they themselves apparently were not entirely convinced, presents all the data on Inca
culture and religion, myth and ritual, as though screened through a
historicized framework. Betanzos points out in his introduction,
"how differently the conquerors talk about [the deeds and customs of
these Indians of Peru], far from what the Indians were used to
doing" and that "the common Indians talk out of whim and as in
dreams." In accordance with these observations he interweaves
history and the ritual calendar, giving one as a comment upon the
other. In the version told to him, Inca history did not have a
chronological but a cyclical and moral importance for his informants. He and Cieza are the first and the last to be aware of this
problem of myth and history, and to reflect upon it. After them, the
Inca epic is just assumed to be "history" (Zuidema 1982d).

The general framework of the myth about the Chanca war is as
follows: The king Viracocha Inca has conquered the town of Calca,
some seven leagues (35 km) north of Cuzco and on the other side of
the Villcanota river. One of his feats was to set the town afire, throwing a heated stone with his golden sling from the site where he would
later build the town of Caqui (Caqui Jaquijahuana). (The aerial distance from Caqui, south of the river, to Calca is approximately 5

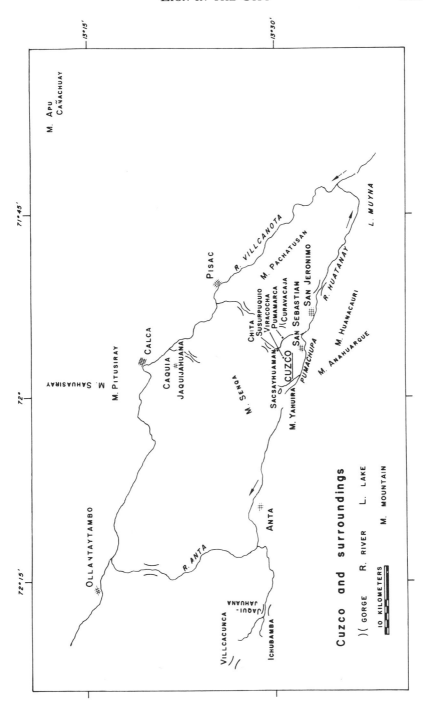

Cuzco and surroundings

)(GORGE   R. RIVER   L. LAKE
                M. MOUNTAIN

10 KILOMETERS

km). Together with the crown prince Inca Urco he later returned to this spot when fleeing from the Chanca attack on Cuzco. A younger son, Inca Yupanqui, organized the defense of Cuzco. In the night before the battle he prayed outside the town to the Sun god, who appeared to him. During the battle he was helped by stones turning into soldiers. These soldiers, known as Pururaucas, were sent to him either by the god Viracocha—identified as the Creator by the Spaniards—or by his father, Viracocha Inca, who took this name after having a vision of the god (Duviols 1977a). Inca Yupanqui withstood the Chanca attack on the outskirts of town. Later he defeated them a second time in the Jaquijahuana to the west of Cuzco. He reorganized not only the city of Cuzco, its political organization, calendar, and religion, but also its history, by dressing up certain mummies and identifying them as his ancestors (Sarmiento 1947, ch. 30–32). Upon being crowned, he adopted the name of Pachacuti Inca and began the conquest which would lead to the formation of the empire.

Cieza's Version

Both Cieza and Betanzos use the lion symbol while discussing the problem of royal succession. Inca Yupanqui claimed the throne, not by right of birth, as was the case with the crown prince Inca Urco, but by defending the town that was abandoned by his father and brother. In the version given by Cieza, Inca Urco was crowned when his father fled town. Inca Urco himself then left "in order to enjoy himself in the pleasures of the houses built for that purpose," keeping Inca Yupanqui in Cuzco as his lieutenant (Cieza 1967, ch. 44). In the meantime the Chancas were approaching and the Cuzco nobles asked Inca Yupanqui to defend the city. He denounced them for not having crowned him earlier, but was appeased with their promise to do so after the war. And, says Cieza, "After this had occurred, the captain Inca Yupanqui came out on the plaza where was the stone of war, having placed the skin of a lion on his head, giving to understand that he would be strong like that animal" (Cieza 1967, ch. 45). Inca Yupanqui thus identifies himself with the puma during the interim period in which he led the Incas to victory but was not yet crowned. During this time Inca Yupanqui held the position of lieutenant.[15]

Betanzos's Version

Bentanzos refers to the puma symbol in a similar interim position, but his story is quite different and he gives the symbol another meaning. When Inca Yupanqui had defeated the Chancas the first time, he sent prisoners and the spoils of war with an emissary and two thousand soldiers to Viracocha Inca in Caquia Jaquijahuana, asking him to step on the spoils in his dignity of king. The king refused, insisting that Inca Urco, as crown prince, should carry out this ritual act, keeping alive the latter's right to succession. Vicaquirao, the emissary of Inca Yupanqui, did not allow this to happen and returned with the prisoners and the spoils. Viracocha Inca planned to ambush Inca Urco on the road in a gorge coming out from their residence—a gorge in which Inca defenses are still very much in evidence—but this was averted. Inca Yupanqui sent an emissary a second time, this time with three thousand soldiers, in order to convince his father to come to Cuzco, and there step on the spoils. But the latter again refused, claiming to be ashamed of having fled and wishing to die in Caquia Jaquijahuana. After these events, Inca Yupanqui defeated the Chancas in Jaquijahuana, the one west of Cuzco, and let the people and their curacas who had helped him return to their lands. They, however,

> implored him to receive them under his protection and to favour them as his vassals. They wished that he would take the tassel of State [that is, the Inca crown] and be Inca [king]; for all of which Inca Yupanqui thanked them and answered that at the moment his father and Lord was still alive and that it was not just, while his father lived, that he should take the tassel of State. If he was there [in Cuzco] at the moment, it was because he was captain of his father. He asked them to do two things for him, the first being to go to his father and respect him and do everything that he [his father] ordered, being that he was their Lord; and they said that they would do so. And the other was that they would consider him [Inca Yupanqui] as their friend and brother, and that everybody, whenever he sent to them a request, would comply. They said that they had no other Lord than he, and that he could do with them as he wished and deemed best as [they were] his vassals; and he thanked them. (Betanzos 1968, ch. 10)

From then on, Viracocha Inca did not want to use the tassel anymore, neither did he go back to Cuzco. He made use of the people sent to him to build the town of Caquia Jaquijahuana. Inca Yupanqui, however, reconstructed and organized Cuzco, beginning

with a temple of the Sun to commemorate the vision that he had had
before the battle against the Chancas. Here, Betanzos describes the
organization of Cuzco, the irrigation system, and the feasts, especially that of Capac raymi.

He then comes to the theme of the puma, couching it with
elaborate detail. When Inca Yupanqui had sent his people away to
work their fields he traced, or planned, the town and made figures of
clay (Betanzos 1968, ch. 16). Thus, when they returned they found
him, "painting and drawing bridges and how they should be made
and constructed; and in the same way he drew certain roads that left
town and that went to those bridges and rivers." In this way he gave
names to all the places and groundlots and, "he called the whole city
together 'Body of the Lion,' meaning that the inhabitants and people
who lived there were the members of the Lion, and that his person
was the Head of it." The people were greatly impressed, but they
considered that they had to place on his head the tassel of State as an
insignia of king(ship) and that they had to give him a new name. Inca Yupanqui protested that he would not do so, "because he thought
that his father had to give the tassel to Inca Urco when he died and
that he [Inca Yupanqui] would take it from his head and that he
would take the head with it." And thus he repeated his curse, "he
took a beaker of *chicha* [corn beer] in his hands and emptied it on the
ground, saying that his blood [of Inca Urco] would be well spilled
like he [Inca Yupanqui] had emptied the beaker with *chicha* on the
ground." The lords then went on their own account to Viracocha
Inca and brought him to Cuzco. Taking the tassel from his own
head, he said to Inca Yupanqui, "you are really the son of the Sun; I
name you King and Lord. And it was a custom among these Lords,
that when this was done, together with placing the tassel on the head
of the other, he had to give him a new name." Viracocha Inca said:

I name you from now on, and your people and the other nations that
you will subject will call you, Pachacutec Yupanqui Capac Indichuri,
which means "Turn of Time, King Yupanqui, Son of the Sun." Inca
Yupanqui then had brought a used vessel as people would find it in a
house without washing . . . and he ordered it to be filled with *chicha* as
dirty as it was . . . and he made his father Viracocha drink it without
leaving anything in it. Viracocha Inca did as ordered and lowered himself and asked forgiveness. The new Lord answered that he did not have
to pardon him, but that he was satisfied if he [V.I.] said it was for the
people that he had sent out to kill him [P.I.] and that he had done this

only in the name of the city of Cuzco and of the Lords of it who were present; because of the things that he [V.I.] had done as a woman, and because he was [a woman], he had to drink from such vessels as the one he had drunk from. During all this Viracocha Inca had his head lowered on the ground and said *chocayun* which means "My cruel father!" and "I know my sin!"[16]

Pachacuti then lifted up his father. As was customary during the feast that followed the crowning, the king was married. Sacrifices were given to all the idols and *huacas* (sacred places) around the city; many male, female, and young llamas and deer were sacrificed for the feast, as well as all the other animals which could be found:

[There were] many birds like eagles, falcons, partridges, ostriches and all the other brave wild birds, and also ducks and other tame birds; and many other animals [such as] tigers, lions, wild cats, except foxes, because they hate those and when they see them in similar feasts and make the sacrifices they consider them as bad luck. And in the same way they sacrificed many children . . . whom they buried alive, always a boy and girl, with many golden objects, and these were children of caciques and principales. Viracocha Inca returned to Caquia Jaquijahuana and when he died his mummy was brought back to Cuzco. (Betanzos 1968, ch. 17)

Betanzos deftly weaves a description of Inca culture into his account of Inca Yupanqui's ascendancy to the throne. This ascendancy begins with the moment that the Chanca menace forces him to come forward as a war leader; goes through the time that he, as a law giver, defines the structure of Inca society; and ends when he is crowned and married and his father becomes a mummy. The puma symbol is used to explain the legal problems of succession. During this time two capitals are built: Caquia Jaquijahuana, with the crowned king, and Cuzco with the *segunda persona* (second person), in what effectively is the center of the kingdom. The motive of stepping on the spoils of war is not to reconfirm the king, because Viracocha Inca will not step on them, but to decide between his two sons who will be the successor.

Viracocha Inca uses the legal argument for succession, but Inca Yupanqui wants to force upon him the argument of right of conquest, or, more accurately, the "right of defense." First, he sends Vicaquirao as his emissary and wants Viracocha Inca himself to step on the spoils in the presence of Vicaquirao, thus recognizing Inca

Yupanqui as the conqueror. Second, he wants Inca Urco to be
crowned, which will give him a chance to defeat the latter without
having to rebel against his father as the lawful king. In this way, he
will contest the right of his father to crown a son who had not been a
conqueror. Third, he obliges Viracocha Inca to come to Cuzco and
crown Inca Yupanqui. Fourth, in the aftermath, Inca Urco will start
a war out of Caquia Jaquijahuana. But now he is the rebel and not,
as in the second step of the argument, Inca Yupanqui. When Inca
Urco is defeated and killed, the soldiers of his army will be brought
into Cuzco as prisoners of war, in long dresses with tassels, like
women (Sarmiento 1947, ch. 33, 37). They are treated like Viracocha Inca, who, as a woman, had to drink *chicha* from a dirty vessel.

    Although Cuzco and Caquia Jaquijahuana form the two spatial
poles of the argument, an important role is given to the other place
called Jaquijahuana. The account of the war indicates some reasons
for this correspondence in names.[17] The latter two places clearly
functioned as borders. At the western border, Inca Yupanqui defended Inca territory a second time and defeated the Chancas. Betanzos uses this occurrence to describe the treatment of prisoners of
war and how they were killed. Later, he also associates Caquia Jaquijahuana with the treatment of prisoners of war (Betanzos 1968,
ch. 10). These motifs of border and death in the tale have something
to do with the name of both places. *Kahuana*, as derived from the verb
kahuay "to see," means "lookout, a high place to look out from like a
watchtower"; that is, a place used by a *kahuak* "guard, sentry, spy,"
for *kahuariy kahuariy* "guards warning each other of danger"
(González Holguín 1952). *Caquia* is an onomatopoeic word for
thunder.[18]

    The story of how Viracocha Inca conquered a town from Caquia
Jaquijahuana, using a golden sling and a hot stone, refers to the connection of his attack with the Thunder, since he used the sling as
special weapon of the Thunder god. We might consider it as an in-
congruent element that the king who was associated with the god
Viracocha used a weapon that we would expect to find in the hands
of Inca Yupanqui, as the Inca more closely associated with the
Thunder god (Sarmiento 1947, ch. 31, 47). We must take into account, however, the dilemma expressed in the epic. On the one
hand, Viracocha Inca had to be an Inca, a conqueror, and the father
of Inca Yupanqui within the royal dynasty; on the other hand, he

had to represent the non-Inca outside who was conquered by Inca Yupanqui as the real founder of Cuzco. The device of the epic here was to describe the father when he was a young conqueror using attributes belonging to the son.[19]

Turning to the word *jaqui*, González Holguín (1952) gives *"haqquini*, to leave something behind; to leave an inheritance after death,"* and indicates some idiomatic uses that imply the sense of "to repudiate [a woman], to abandon." From another part of Peru, Huarochirí, Avila describes the custom of carrying the mummies of the ancestors to a mountain from where they could see the snowcapped mountain and god of Pariacaca, who also was their god of Thunder (Avila 1952, ch. 9). We may speculate that Caquia Jaquijahuana had a similar function. When Viracocha Inca used his golden sling to conquer Calca on the other side of the river, he was facing the snowcapped mountain of Sahuasiray Pitusiray (fig. 7). Of all the *nevados* near Cuzco, this mountain plays the most prominent role in terms of Incaic mythological origins. At the same time, Caquia Jaquijahuana was their most important fortress to the North (López de Velasco 1971, 245). Many stories about the other side of the Villcanota refer to the "non-Incaness" of the people living there and to their association with felines, serpents, and the jungle (fig. 7). Thus, the name Jaquijahuana could mean "lookout on the abandoned place," and Caquia Jaquijahuana may have been a place from which the dead looked out toward Sahuasiray Pitusiray. In fact, just after their conquest of Cuzco, the Spaniards found the mummy reputed to be that of Viracocha Inca in Caquia Jaquijahuana, where he was worshiped and implored for rain (*Relación* 1934).

The Theme of the "Body Politic"

We now come to the central theme of the myth, the metaphorical use of the puma. For Betanzos (1968, ch. 17), its use summarizes his entire description of the organization of Cuzco, including both its material and its social aspects. We recognize two distinct uses of the metaphor: Cuzco in a spatial sense and Cuzco as the body politic of which Inca Yupanqui was the head and its inhabitants and neighbors the limbs. Betanzos is very explicit about what he is referring to in both cases (Betanzos 1968, ch. 7, 8).

Figure 7. Anti Indians worshiping Sahuasiray Pitusiray mountain and the jaguar. (Guaman Poma 1980, 268 [270])

In terms of the spatial metaphor, we have the following data. With the approach of the Chancas, Inca Yupanqui asks his three generals to seek the help of all people within a radius of 3 leagues (15 km) around Cuzco. While praying for help to the god Viracocha, "twenty squadrons of people emerged that never had been seen by Inca Yupanqui or his people, who came from the directions of Collasuyu [S.E.], and from the road to Acha [Antisuyo, N.E.], and from the road to Condesuyo [S.W.]." Other chroniclers identify these people with the Pururauca, stones that became warriors and helped to defend Cuzco. When Inca Yupanqui had the war drums played in ten different locations, the Pururaucas were sent by his father, Viracocha Inca, who had already fled (Santacruz Pachacuti 1950). Certain stones in the valley were later recognized as the mythical Pururaucas, and one such stone was known with the name of Viracocha.[20] Betanzos does not mention the element of warriors turning into stone, but it is not difficult to recognize them in his twenty squadrons and in "the 10 lords and 20 nobles" who were later assigned, along with their villages and provinces, to help Inca Yupanqui in the reconstruction of Cuzco (Betanzos 1968, ch. 16). They received lands within a perimeter of 5 leagues (25 km) of Cuzco.

In this context, we have to understand how Inca Yupanqui "designed the city and made figures of clay" while "giving names to all the places and ground-lots" (Betanzos 1968, ch. 16). He called the whole city "Body of the Lion" when "he was painting and drawing bridges as they had to be build," and when "he drew certain roads that from one village went to another and that went to those bridges and rivers." We can also compare this description to that which Betanzos gives of the marriage of Inca Yupanqui, who is now called Pachacuti, "the turn of time." Then the king gave sacrifices to all the idols and *huacas* that were around the city, and where the llamas and wild animals, especially felines, were sacrificed.

In all these cases, Betanzos clearly alludes to the organization of the *ceques*, the forty-one "lines" or directions that together described the topography of the valley of Cuzco by way of the 328 *huacas*, which are mentioned as place-names within a perimeter of 15 to 25 km (Cobo 1956, 169–86; Rowe 1979; Zuidema 1964, 1982c). By 1567 Polo de Ondegardo already knew about this system and Betanzo's informant apparently implied this knowledge in 1551. Comparing the data given by Betanzos with those on the *ceque* system, it is of particular interest to read in the latter about the two last *huacas* on the sixth *ceque* of Antisuyu (III 2c):[21]

> The sixth was a house called Pomamarca (house of the puma). . . .
> Here they kept the body [mummy] of the wife of Inca Yupanqui, and
> they offered her children with all the other things. . . . The seventh
> was called Curavacaja, it is a high place, on the road to Chita, where
> one loses sight of Cuzco, and it was assigned with a stone marker as the
> end of all the huacas of this ceque. They kept there a dead lion and told
> its origin, but that is [a] long [story].

We can reconstruct the story referred to here to some extent, because Pomamarca is mentioned in Santacruz Pachacuti's version of the myth as the place to which Viracocha Inga fled and from whence he sent the Pururaucas.[22] This description of the mountain pass with the puma skin is crucial for an understanding of the spatial concept implied by the metaphor of "Cuzco as a puma," for "Cuzco" was the entire area described by the *ceque* system.

The *ceque* system was also the administrative instrument used by the Incas to describe the political organization of Cuzco. The care of *huacas*, *ceques*, groups of *ceques*, and *suyus* was assigned to increasingly larger political groups. The spatial expanse of the *ceque* system, therefore, referred to the body politic of which Pachacuti Inca became the head. While the myth of the Pururaucas discussed the physical transformation of men into stones and vice versa, we can now see how the Pururaucas and *huacas* symbolically and spatially represented social units, subject to the Inca king and belonging to Cuzco as a city.

The idea of "body politic" had a great influence on the intellectual climate of Europe at the time Betanzos wrote (1551). In 1544, Bishop Zumarraga introduced into Mexico the Paulinian simile of the mystic body of Christ of which He was the head and the faithful its limbs. Betanzos mentions in the introduction to his chronicle how he had just "finished translating and abridging a book called 'Doctrina christiana,' which includes the Christian doctrine and two vocabularies, one of words and the other of notes and complete phrases and a confessional." The latter was probably in Spanish and Quechua. Therefore, the manuscript may well have been one of the

Christian doctrines published by Zumarraga between 1543 and 1546 (Bataillon 1966, 823–26).

The Christian influence in Betanzos's concept can also be detected in another way. Fischer (1973), in his analysis of Paul's Letter to the Ephesians, observes the religious and historical importance of the concept of "the body growing out from the head" (Eph. 4:16). A similar idea is still alive in the modern Andean myth of Inkarri, the Inca king who was (in the popular concept) beheaded by the Spaniards. His head is said to be kept as a prisoner in the palace of the Peruvian president. When his body is fully grown onto his head again, Inkarri will lead the Indians to freedom (Wachtel 1971, 74–75; Ossio 1973). The myth seems to have been influenced by the same Paulinian idea that led to the concept of the "mystic body."

In another way, Betanzos's use of the puma's body seems to connect with medieval legal ideas about the "mystic body" as "body politic." Kantorowicz (1957), in his book *The King's Two Bodies: A Study in Medieval Political Theology*, analyzes the history of the concepts that lead to distinguishing a king's natural body from his metaphoric body, the State. One concept, for example, is how the king was, in legal terms, "the father and the son of law," meaning that as head of state he was above the law, but as a person he was under it.[23] In a study of Inca kinship (Zuidema 1977a) I made use of certain statements expressing similar ideas. One example is Guaman Poma's discussion of royal succession. He mentions that, at the death of a king, his sons would go in to a "conclave" to choose the new king. Although this might be a younger son, after his election all the brothers would call him "father," "grandfather," or "uncle" according to their new rank. (Guaman Poma 1980, 288 [290]; Zuidema 1977a, 276–77). In the light of these examples we may consider the context of Betanzos's data: how Pachacuti Inca, at the time of becoming the head of state, obliged his father to call him "father."

Spanish ideas of Medieval legal theology (Kantorowicz's subtitle) may also have influenced Santacruz Pachacuti when he distinguishes between the feast of Capac raymi and the "real, eternal feast" or between Inti, the sun as we see it, and the "real Sun," which is Viracocha (Santacruz Pachacuti 1950, 228).

At the moment, my interest in these data is to indicate how Betanzos's intellectual background may have made him especially sensitive to certain Incaic concepts. In the case of his use of the expression "Body of the Lion," he does not give us an original Quechua word, or a description of an observed ritual. We are dealing—necessarily so—with his Spanish interpretation of Incaic data. Our task is to connect his reflections upon these data to the data themselves.

Before concluding this section, I would like to indicate the possible importance of two details in Betanzos's account as controls, in order to discover to what extent he transmits accurate ritual data of Inca culture. Both details have to do with drinking *chicha*. In the first passage, Inca Yupanqui threatens to kill his brother Inca Urco, cutting off his head, in the same way he is now spilling *chicha* on the ground from a beaker. This was his way of obtaining the "tassel of State," the *mascapaycha*. This Quechua name, although applied to the whole headgear or crown of the Inca, specifically referred to the lower part, the tassel, where each red woolen thread represented a conquered enemy and the blood of his severed head (Murua 1962, I, ch. 9). In this instance, Betanzos was correct in relating the acts of cutting off a head and spilling blood to the ritual of "taking the tassel of State."

In the other passage, Pachacuti Inca obliges his father to drink dirty *chicha*, out of an old vessel, like a woman. Betanzos (probably following his Inca informant) gives it as an example of insult to Viracocha Inca and this may well have been the case. The dregs of *chicha*, called *concho* ("unclear *chicha*"), were drunk by the priests Tarpuntay (from *tarpuy*, "to plant") in August, the month of planting. As male priests, they ritually supported the life-giving force of Pachamama, the "Earth-mother." Drinking the *concho* was meant to induce the coming of the heavy rains in January, a month of rituals symbolizing the turbulent, sediment-laden waters of the rivers.

The myth to be discussed next makes clear the position of Viracocha as god of the turbulent waters. We may therefore conclude that in Betanzos's passage Pachacuti Inca carried out a ritual act; on the one hand, he wrestled the role of king from Viracocha Inca, but, on the other hand, he conferred on him the status of ancestor to the high priest and to all priests concerned with agriculture. The themes of turbulent water, dirty rain, and fertility also constitute the central part of the myths of Inca Urco, the son who fled with Viracocha

Inca, which I will discuss elsewhere. These two passages about *chicha* seem to be interrelated in their meaning and to have a clear Incaic function in Betanzos's account.

The Myth of Capac Raymi

The myths of Cieza and Betanzos place the role of the puma, or his skin, in the context of royal succession, suggesting its importance for understanding the meaning of the feast of Capac raymi. In an indirect way they also refer to the theme of Thunder. The following myth, given by Murua, will make the two latter themes explicit. The place of action, chosen for a reason similar to that of Betanzos's myth, is close to Caquia Jaquijahuana. If, therefore, the myth of Murua mentions "Inga Yupanqui, called by another name Pachacuti Inga Yupangui," as captain and son of Manco Capac, the founder of the Inca dynasty, and not as the ninth king of the dynasty, then the spatial element allows us to consider this myth as a variant together with the first two. Murua's myth stresses the fight of Pachacuti against the forces of nature represented by a giant, coming from the north. Elsewhere, I have compared this myth to others from Cuzco and Huarochirí which involve either a son of Pachacuti Inca called Inca Amaru, "Inca Serpent," or, as antagonist, a serpent god. While these myths require further detailed analysis, they reinforce the discussion here (Zuidema 1982d).

The following is the version of the myth given by Murua:[24]

> The strong and valiant Inga Yupanqui, by another name called Pachacuti Inga Yupangui, was a Prince and son of the great Mangocapac, the first king in this kingdom; and thus this great Pachacuti was the first prince and captain and conqueror that existed in this kingdom; who conquered all around this great city of Cuzco; he made himself feared and called Lord. People say that he was more cruel than brave, because he was very harsh and the first who ordered that they worship *gauca*s, and how sacrifices to them should be made; and he apportioned them and ordered that they be worshipped in his whole kingdom. Some people say, although as a fable, that he was the cause that, in the time of this brave captain and prince Pachacuti, appeared above this city where it is called Chetacaca, and with another name Sapi, a very large person dressed in red, as he is in this drawing [a drawing which Murua does not include] with a trumpet in one hand and a staff in the other. Before he appeared it had rained very much during a whole month, continuously, day and night [and the inhabitants of Cuzco were

terrified and anxious], saying that the earth turned [and was destroyed], which they call Pachacuti. They say that this person had come on [by way of] the water to Pisac, four leagues [20 km] from Cuzco, and that Pachacuti went to meet him and where they agreed [and became friends]. He [Pachacuti] asked him not to play the trumpet because they feared that if he played the earth would be upset, and that they had to be brothers; and so he did not play it and after some days he [the giant?] turned into stone and because of this reason he [Inca Yupanqui] was called Pachacuti, which means to turn [upset] the earth, and also who is disinherited and from whom his property has been taken away. This prince and captain waged great wars with his enemies and he also won a victory as a brave and vigorous captain. Later he ordered that many feasts and sacrifices be held, and made the year begin in December, which is when the sun reaches the end of its road, because before this prince governed the year began in January. And the [musical] instruments that this strong captain Pachacuti Inga Yupangui and his captains and guards used in war were flutes of deer bones and big flutes of wood and small flutes of reed, big painted drums of wood and large calabashes. He was very cruel in war like all his people and soldiers. They also used trumpets of conkshells and rattles of shells and oysters. They ate their enemies and if these were thin they would make them fat and eat them: they killed with many [poisonous] herbs; their arrows were of strong wood, put in the fire and of strong reed; they had arrowpoints of stone and fishbones, they were brave warriors and went almost naked. They were so swift that they could catch deer by running. And so they were feared by their enemies.

The myth gives many confusing details, but by comparing it to the first two myths and accepting the calendrical context as mentioned, these may be sorted out. The two places of action in space are not Cuzco and Caqui Jaquijahuana, but Cuzco and Pisac, the latter being a fortress 30 km northeast of Cuzco with a position similar to that of Caquia Jaquijahuana—above the Villcanota river, although on the other side. The "gorge of Chita" (Chitacaca) performs a defensive role which corresponds to the gorge which defends Caquia Jaquijahuana. The giant takes the place of Viracocha Inca in the myth of Betanzos. We can compare him to this king, as well as to the god Viracocha, for three additional reasons: (1) he has a (probably long) red dress; (2) he holds a staff (bordón), as does the god (Santacruz Pachacuti 1950, 211); and (3) he comes down on the waters of the Villcanota river as does the god in the origin myth. More than any other similar Andean myth, this one makes clear that the giant represents the swollen waters of the river which arise during and after

the month of December, and that these waters are associated with
the sound of the trumpet. The waters will destroy Cuzco if the giant
sounds his trumpet. Even though the myth does not explicitly say so,
we can nonetheless understand that Pachacuti defends Cuzco, ward-
ing off the rains and the waters, with the same sound as that made
by the giant. For this reason, the myth presents the musical instruments, including the big, painted, wooden drums, as weapons to
be used against the forces of nature.[25]

The ambiguous details concern the relationship between the
giant and Pachacuti. It is not clear who turns into stone. If, as seems
most probable, it is the former, then we could consider the stone as
representing the Pururaucas, one of whom was, in fact, called "Viracocha." Pachacuti and the giant conclude a pact and call each other
brother; what were antagonistic traits in the first two myths are thus
used here as ambiguous similarities, uniting the two. The giant,
while not defeated, nevertheless agrees not to advance and not to
play his trumpet. Pachacuti is not only brave and victorious, but is
also called "disinherited" and "more cruel than brave." In fact,
both Andean understandings of the concept "Pachacuti" exist. Bertonio translates the word by "time of war" and by "boaster who says
that he will do [something] and who will say wonders, and then does
not do anything." Guaman Poma, who talks about the same "Ynga
Yupangui Pachacutichic ynga" as "son and captain of Manco
Capac," like Murua, says of him, on the one hand, that "he did not
conquer, and did nothing else than sleep, eat, drink, and go to
whores, around town" (Guaman Poma 1980, 146 [146]). On the
other hand, Ynga Yupangui Pachacutichic Ynga "was highly praised
[like a] hawk, lion, tiger, fox, vulture and they say that in one jump
he leapt from a high rock, that he flew better than a hawk and that
thus he was called *acapana*" ([red light on horizon of] dawn). A composite description is applied to one person which is otherwise divided
between two personages, Pachacuti, the ninth king, and his brother,
Inca Urco. But even though Guaman Poma, in his drawing of the
lazy captain Pachacuti, shows him lying in bed, he also draws the
rising sun seen through the window, thus comparing the dawn
(*acapana*) to the brave captain. Pachacuti is a warrior, like the dawn
that defeats the night. If, however, we associate the characteristic of
"being disinherited" (one from whom his property had been taken
away) to Inca Urco, then it confirms the interpretation of the term *ja-*

qui in the name Caquia Jaquijahuana as the place where Viracocha Inca and Inca Urco were left without their kingdom.

Murua and Guaman Poma both mention Pachacuti's feats of physical prowess, including comparisons to wild animals which in other descriptions of the Incaic initiation rituals are ascribed to the initiates. During competitive races in December and January (Molina 1943, 54–55, 66; Santacruz Pachacuti 1950, 221) the first boys to arrive were given names of swift and brave animals, such as "eagle" and "puma," whereas the last to arrive were assigned names like "fox," "serpent," and "toad." The first animals refer to Pachacuti's position, whereas the latter are related to those of Viracocha Inca, of the giant, or of Inca Urco.

The existence of ambiguities in Murua's myth is important for interpreting the presence of men wearing puma skins and playing drums. They are not only to be compared to brave warriors—to the Pachacuti who defeats the Chancas—but also to the giant representing the natural forces of fertility that are warded off, and whose defeat leads to the incorporation of those forces into the political unit that is thus defended. Murua's myth also mentions the political concept. His Pachacuti organized the cult of the *huaca*s, and the myth refers to Chitacaca. The gorge overlooking the valley of Cuzco was one of the borders of Cuzco as defined by the *ceque* system. The month of December Murua mentions is the Incaic month of Capac raymi, which ends with the December solstice (Zuidema 1982b, 1982c). His myth allows us to understand the myth of the epic war against the Chancas in terms of Capac raymi, the "royal feast."[26]

THE TAIL OF THE PUMA

Betanzos's Description of Pumachupa

Looking back at the myths given by Betanzos and Murua we recognize the importance of water in both of them. The giant in Murua's myth comes down on the Villcanota river to Pisac and crosses the mountains to Cuzco, bringing with him the heavy rains. Betanzos explains what constitutes Cuzco as the body of the puma: the valley including the roads as they go to bridges and to rivers. By mapping the *ceque*s in Cuzco, I came to the same conclusion about the importance of rivers and irrigation canals (Zuidema 1978).

These data oblige us not only to read carefully what Betanzos says about "the body of the lion," but also to take into account the full context in which he places the toponym Pumachupa, "the tail of the puma." His description of the latter helps us to further define the concept of "border" in Cuzco's body politic.

Betanzos specifically deals with the rituals in the months of July and September. According to the Inca calendar, the irrigation canals were repaired in July and a first irrigation was done in order to make the fields ready for plowing and planting in August and September (Molina 1943; Cobo 1956; Guaman Poma 1980). Cobo (1956, 216) also mentions the sacrifice made at that time to the beginning and end of the irrigation system in the Cuzco valley. Betanzos's description for September poses a problem if we compare his data to those of Molina and Cobo. They are consistent with what Molina and Cobo describe for January. The analysis shows, however, that similar rituals were carried out in both months. Therefore, I will use Betanzos's description of September, comparing it later to those of Molina and Cobo for January.

Betanzos refers to canals and rivers twice. In the first reference he mentions the distribution of lands to the people who helped Inca Yupanqui in the defense of Cuzco:

> And then another day he [Inca Yupanqui] ordered that all the people of Cuzco who had obtained land should come out to repair and to make their tubes [or sewers] and irrigation canals, all of which was repaired and made with building stones, because the construction was made in such a way that it would persist forever, ordering them to make their borders and high border markers, made in such a way that they never would loose them, and putting under each of the markers a load of charcoal, saying that if the marker should fall down, they would recognize the borders of those lands by way of the charcoal found there. (Betanzos 1968, ch. 12)

Inca Yupanqui lets the people go to their own lands and orders them to return within exactly one year. His next concern is the two streams running through town that destroy the land each year when flooded with the coming rains. He wants to repair and strengthen the banks of those two streams:

> He showed them the places where the streams originated and where, in his view, they had to start to make the repairs and reinforcements down to where the streams join at the end of the city, called Pumachupa

which means "tail of the lion," and from there he ordered that the reinforcement and repair would reach "Machina" [Jiménez de la Estrada
reads this word as "Muyna"] which is four leagues [20 km] from the
city. And thus the lords caciques measured with their ropes the space
from the beginning where Inca Yupanqui told them to where the
streams joined. Measured in such a way they divided among
themselves the part of the work that was assigned to each. . . . And he
ordered that the work and reinforcement would reach to "Machina."
(Betanzos 1968, ch. 13)

In both accounts Betanzos discusses borders of land in terms of
water and canal repair. Distribution of work as described here is still
common, especially in the Department of Ayacucho, where it gives
occasion to the elaborate rituals of Yarqa aspiy (e.g., B. J. Isbell
1978, 138–45; Pinto 1970, 72–84). The meeting place of two rivers or
canals (González Holguín: "Tincuk yacu"; Guaman Poma: "Tin-
coc yacu") played (Guaman Poma 1980, 297 [299], 274 [276], 785
[799]), and still plays (Earls and Silverblatt 1978, 311–14) a crucial
role in the cults of the water and of the dead. Pumachupa in Cuzco
had a similar ritual role; Coricancha, the temple of the Sun and of
the ancestors, was founded nearby.

The second reference to canals and rivers is in Betanzos's two
descriptions concerning the month of September. In the first of these,
he discusses the feast of "Porapuipia" (Betanzos 1968, ch. 15); a
badly transcribed word, it is given by Gutiérrez de Santa Clara and
Cabello Valboa as Pura opiayquis, meaning "the month of full moon
of drinking."[27] Betanzos says of Purap Upyay:

And he ordered to celebrate the other feast called Porapuipia [*purap
upyay*], also in this month [of September, Cituayquis] to be done for the
waters with sacrifices. In these sacrifices he ordered that many cloths
and sheep [i.e., llamas] and coca be offered, together with flowers of all
the herbs and plants in the fields. All this should be offered to the waters
in the following way: they should take large quantities of cloth and
throw them in the part where the rivers join. They also should bring
many sheep and young sheep and offer them to the water and cut their
throats in the place where the cloth was thrown, making a large fire to
burn these sheep and young sheep, and throwing the ashes in the water
in that same place. Then they should throw the flowers as you have
heard, and after this he ordered that they should throw much ground
coca into the water.

The other description is a further comment on the one just given
and is also the most interesting (Betanzos 1968, ch. 18). Pachacuti

Inca, now king, requests 100,000 soldiers within three months. Betanzos explains the social mechanism necessary to obtain the cooperation of these people: "And Pachacuti Inca Yupanqui was glad [with their cooperation] and ordered them to take care to have in their lands chiefs and functionaries. Each of the nobles of Cuzco should throw *chicha* in the river [out of] certain beakers, and at the same time they should give them [the other chiefs] beakers of *chicha*, pretending that they were drinking with the waters of the rivers." And after describing the general custom of two people visiting each other, drinking to each other out of courtesy from two beakers (*queros*), he continues:

> And in the same way Inca Yupanqui ordered that, when this sacrifice was done, two lords from Cuzco would go, one on one side of the river and the other on the other [side], each taking with him ten Indians or the number that he wanted. These Indians should have long poles, taking care that the sacrifices would not get stuck at the borders of the river . . . and that the sacrifices would go some 30 leagues [150 km] down the river. And as they observed that the land gave fruits by way of the waters, he ordered that in that month the same sacrifice was done everywhere, and that for that day they brought from all their lands food. . . . This was brought to the plaza of Cuzco and from there distributed over the whole town. . . . This feast was celebrated in this month [of September] . . . from half moon to full moon and the sacrifice and feast took four days.

The use of flowers, the communal meals, and the period from half moon to full moon support his identification of the feast as Situa. According to Molina, four hundred warriors would run in four directions to certain points on the two major rivers, the Villcanota and Apurimac, defining in that way the territory occupied by the peoples living around Cuzco, who were recognized as "Incas-by-privilege" (Zuidema 1964, 1978, 1983). Warriors drove out evil and sickness. At the same time, people would clean their houses and invite each other to eat and drink.

On the one hand Betanzos's description is an elaboration on the feast of Situa. On the other, however, it refers to the rituals of the month of January. While in September warriors would drive out evil and sickness with the fire of burning faggots (Betanzos 1968, ch. 15; Guaman Poma 1980, 252, 253, [254, 255]; Molina 1943, 32), in January men would perform the sacrifices in the river as Betanzos describes. The following ceremony, given by Molina for January, which also takes place during full moon, elaborates on the symbolic significance of the place Pumachupa in this context.

The Ritual of Mayucati, "Following the River"

After the time when the puma-men had played the drums, and Cuzco was open once again to foreigners, the January rituals stressed the political bonds to the people living around Cuzco (Molina 1943, 64–66). On the nineteenth day of this lunar month (that is, some four days after full moon), they began the ritual of Mayucati, "following the river." The dams, which had been placed in the river above Cuzco for obtaining irrigation water, were broken and the waters allowed to retake their natural course, carrying everything that was in their way. The ashes of sacrifices, which had been collected throughout the year, were thrown into the river in Poma-pichupan ("the tail of the puma"), and people followed them to Ollantaytambo, some thirty leagues downriver. From there it was expected that the river was strong enough to carry the ashes unaided down to the Mother Ocean where they would reach the Creator. People thanked the Creator for the good last year and prayed for the year to come in the hopes that it would be equally good. The men who had followed the ashes then ran back through the mountains to Cuzco, carrying objects made of salt in their hands. Those who ran best carried lances or falcons of salt while the slowest ones bore toads of salt. Molina does not mention pumas of salt; although Bertonio specifically refers to them, calling them *hayupuma*.

The complete context of the ritual is too complex to be dealt with in its entirety here, and I will refer only to the elements most relevant to the present argument. First, we observe that the ashes were followed along the river Huatanay from Cuzco to the Villcanota river and then, passing by Pisac and Caquia Jaquijahuana, down to Ollantaytambo. This was done during the heavy rains. In this month, or in the one before, the giant of Murua's myth came down riding on the swollen waters of the Villcanota. The idea of swollen waters was further enhanced in Cuzco by the breaking of dams. Betanzos described how the river was channeled from the dams to 20 km below the town in order to circumvent the destructive forces of the water. But it also appears that the further the ashes could be carried on the waters, the further the political influence of Cuzco would reach. Ollantaytambo was a limit. In a myth that continues the story, Inca Urco, the son who fled with Viracocha Inca, first battles against Pachacuti from Caquia Jaquijahuana. When he has to retreat, he falls into the river, is carried by the water to Ollantaytambo and killed there. Ollantaytambo was the last town along the river occupied by "Incas-by-privilege." Just below this town is the ecological boundary at which the cultivation of tropical products begins.

During the days of the ritual of Mayucati, the people in Cuzco, as well as those reaching Ollantaytambo, carried out the *taqui*, or dance, of Chupay guallo. This dance helps explain the meaning and the purpose of the name of Pumap chupan. Chupa means "tail." *Huaylluy*, in both Quechua and Aymara, means "to love" and "to swing." A detailed analysis of *huayllu* would demonstrate the connection between the two meanings and, moreover, the extreme importance that ideas connected to *huayllu* had in Andean culture and art. Here I give only those meanings directly related to this argument.

González Holguín: *huayllun cuscuni*, to swing (on a swing); *huayllun cuscuy*, swing.

Bertonio: *huayllutha*, to let somebody down with a rope; *huayllu-casitha*, to let oneself down with a rope, to go down from a slope of a mountain; *huayllusitha*, to swing, of boys, from a rope. (Under "to swing," Bertonio gives, as a synonym, *kapahalatha*, "to twist much the two ropes so that the poor boy turns around like a top.")

The meaning of "swinging" as a metaphor used in relation to *mayucati*, "following the river," becomes clearer if we look at the following words in Quechua.

González Holguín: *mayo*, river; *mayuini*, to stir a liquid; *mayuiccun chupanta*, to swing the tail.

We can interpret the expression of *chupay huayllu* then as "swinging the tail," comparing a river and its turbulent waters to a swinging tail. The river as a tail began in Pumachupa. It was not this place of *tincuc*, however, which represented the tail, but the river that from there went down to Ollantaytambo. In the modern use of the name it is still applied not only to the confluence of the rivers, but also to the first section of the river below. When Betanzos mentions Pumachupa he discusses the channeling of the river Huatanay, probably down to where it enters the Villcanota river. The *chupay-huayllu* dance was performed in Cuzco, where men began to follow the ashes in the river, and in Ollantaytambo, where they ended this ritual. Each description of political extension is combined with another concept of a geographic and ecological border. Thus, we can distinguish three expanding areas: the city of Cuzco, its valley, and the surrounding area where those people lived who were given the "privilege" of calling themselves "Inca" (Rowe 1946; Zuidema 1983). These "Incas-by-privilege" helped Pachacuti Inca rebuild the city and to channel rivers and irrigation canals making the valley habitable. They were the people with whom the Inca drank from two *queros* and whose cooperation and political relationships were symbolically and spatially represented by the river as it extended through space.

The term *huaylluy*, meaning "to love" and "to swing," probably had a specific reference related to pumas as well. Like other felines, pumas move their tails when sexually aroused. While the winds brought the fertilizing rains to Cuzco, the swollen, rushing waters of the river returned that gift to its place of origin. Swinging the puma's tail symbolized the marriage relations that the youths, after their initiation, could establish with the peoples living around Cuzco, thereby confirming their political alliances (Zuidema MS).

If the puma represented the body politic with the Inca as the head and the people as the limbs, it was the tail which defined its border. We understand why the puma skin, as described by Avila and Molina, not only had a stuffed head adorned with golden earspools and teeth, but also a tail adorned with colored woolen threads. The connection between the head and the tail, being, respectively, the center and border of the body politic, was an active, fluid one, represented by the river of Cuzco. Its water went from the center (Cuzco) to the border of that section of the empire in which the Incas of Cuzco still had an active ritual interest.

Cuzco as a Puma

We can now address the crucial question of Betanzos's metaphor of "Cuzco as a lion": does it stem from a genuine Inca way of thinking about Cuzco? The data on the tail can be accepted as Inca, supported as they are by the names Pumachupa and Chupayhuayllu. But do we have similar data on the pre-Columbian origin of, or Quechua words referring to, the body politic itself as a puma? I think we have sufficient data to discuss this problem. Here are three examples to support such an argument.

The first comes closest to Cieza's idea of Inca Yupanqui, dressed with a puma skin like the puma-men playing the drums. When Molina describes how Inca Yupanqui prepared himself to defend Cuzco against the Chancas, and how he went to visit his father Viracocha Inca in Caquia Jaquijahuana, he gives us the account of the meeting of the prince with the Sun god, rising out of a spring of water in a place called Sursurpuquio (Molina 1943, 20; Zuidema 1977b, 1982b, 1982c). "Out of his head came three shining rays [of light]; at the shoulders there were intertwined serpents; he had the headband, earspools and dress of an [Inca] king. In between his legs was a lion's head and above his shoulders another lion, whose arms seemed to embrace him from shoulder to shoulder, and there was a serpent that seemed to go from his shoulders down." Inca Yupanqui met the Sun, "his father," at this place located in a direction from Cuzco (+ 24° NE) that was significant in the astronomy of the Incas. As seen from the temple of the Sun, this direction indicated sunrise on May 25, the date which, according to Molina (1943, 25), marked the beginning of the year. Close to that direction were also Pumamarca and the place Curavacaja, where the puma skin was kept. We can speculate that Betanzos came to formulate his concept of "body politic" through information like this. The Inca idea was that Inca Yupanqui met the "mystic body" of the body politic that he was going to form; that he met his "father" the Sun at sunrise during a time of transition when he himself claimed the right of being king.

Another argument can be made by looking at the concept of "tail" in mythology and pre-Columbian art. I will analyze the comparison which the myth of Susurpuquio makes between a puma's tail and a serpent in more detail elsewhere. Inca art derived this powerful symbol of the tail from earlier Andean art styles, and represented it in ritual beakers with the hollow body of an animal on their rims. This animal "drinks" the liquid from the beaker. The water then passes through its hollow body and tail, and back into the bottom of the beaker. Although the puma is generally represented in Andean art with a well-developed tail, it is not the only such animal. One myth, given by Avila (1952, ch. 3), explicitly refers to the importance of the tail in relation to water. When a mountain with all species of animals on it rose with the waters during the Flood, the fox was at the edge of the mountain, his tail waggling in the ocean. From then on the fox's tail has been rotten and black. This explanation of the tail of the fox (a despised animal) points to the general importance of the tail as a link between the body politic and water, from which the body politic derives the fertility necessary to continue and renew its existence. The beaker with a tailed animal on its rim —the puma being one animal used for that purpose—is a perfect metaphor for this hydrological concept: recycling water through river, ocean, and rain.

The last argument shows perhaps the most promise for further development. At the beginning of the valley of Curahuasi, some 100 km west of Cuzco, the famous sculpted granite stone of Sayhuite is found. Carvings in its upper part represent terraces, irrigation canals, pumas, and other animals, such as lizards. The underside is plain. The two parts are separated by a heavy carved line with a large puma head sticking out at one end. The irrigation system of the valley begins below this stone. Visitors have interpreted the upper part of the stone, which is the back of the puma, as a model of the valley with its cultivated lands, terraces, and irrigation canals. Although there is no documentary evidence to support such an interpretation, a comparison with Betanzos's myth would enable us to argue for it. We could compare the stone to the model Inca Yupanqui made for reorganizing the valley of Cuzco. The city itself is also situated at the upper end of its valley. The stone of Sayhuite, however, in no way seems to present an actual map of its valley. Rather, it is a symbolic representation of it. Therefore, if the puma stone represents the valley as a political unit, we can consider the irrigation system to be its tail. Inca kings each had a lithic representation, called their *huauque* or brother, which symbolized their permanent place in society. Cultivated plots of land, *chacras*, similarly had their *huanca*, or owner, in the form of a stone erected in it (Duviols 1979b). The stone of Sayhuite was such a *huanca* for its valley. The model of the valley of Cuzco of which Betanzos speaks may have been such a *huanca*, inspiring him to compare Cuzco to a puma stone like the one in Sayhuite.

The three examples suggest an approach to the investigation of the pre-Columbian roots of Betanzos's metaphor. The later Middle Ages in Europe developed the religious concept of the mystic body of Christ and his Church into a secular one that came to mean "body politic." This development also led to the distinction between two "bodies" in the king: one considered to be the state eternal, and another which was that of the mortal king who would die and be succeeded by a new king. A rite of passage not only transforms a social person into a new form of life, but it also renews and preserves continuity. In the case of Cuzco, the State was the "Body of the Puma" and the Inca the Head of it; the rituals of the puma-men helped to preserve them; stones like the *huauque* of an Inca or the *huanca* of a territory expressed the idea of their permanence. Betanzos probably fused European concepts of the "mystic body" and "body politic" with Incaic concepts concerning the Puma.

PUMA AND JAGUAR (UTURUNCU)

The principal aim of this study is to understand Betanzos's reference to Cuzco as the "body of the Puma." His concern was not to define specific political borders in Cuzco. Nevertheless we could extract from his data references to the city with its public buildings; to the valley with its roads, rivers, and canals that served Cuzco; and to the "Incas-by-privilege" who cooperated directly in the civil and economic functions of Cuzco. Water, in the form of channeled rivers and irrigation systems, as well as ritual drinking, symbolized social cohesion. Nonetheless, water represented not only the forces of nature but also the disruptive forces which originated outside the body politic. Of equal interest to that which symbolizes the body politic is that which symbolizes what lies outside it. I will briefly mention in this respect the role of Uturuncu, the jaguar. Through the opposition of puma-jaguar, not only will we be able to analyze the borders which define inside-outside oppositions, but also to study the internalization of this primary opposition in the hierarchical divisions and spatial subdivisions of the state.

Guaman Poma mentions that Inca Roca, the sixth Inca king, was a conqueror of the lowland Indians living northeast of Cuzco. Inca Roca was

> a tall and large man, who talked a lot and who talked with the Thunder, a great player of games and whoremonger, always willing to take away the property of the poor. . . . He conquered the whole of Andesuyo [toward the northeast and the tropical jungle] and people say that he turned into an *otorongo* [jaguar], he and his son, and thus he conquered all the Chunchos [jungle Indians]. . . . People say that he has sons and descendants in the Chunchos because most of the year he was there, but others say that he did not conquer them but that they became friends. (Guaman Poma 1980, 103 [103])

He also gives the same kind of data about Inca Roca's son Otorongo
Achachi, or Tiger Grandfather (see fig. 8):

> Otorongo Achachi . . . was a son of Ynga Roca. This captain con-
> quered Andesuyo, Chuncho, the whole *montaña* [the Eastern slopes of
> the Andes and the jungle]. People say that in order to conquer he
> turned into an Otorongo; he and his father turned into tigers and he
> died in the Andes [in the original meaning, the jungle northeast of the
> mountains] and he has a son in the Andes from a Chuncho woman and
> for that reason the [these?] Yngas were called Otorongo Achachi
> Amaro Ynga [Tiger Grandfather Serpent Inca] and he has them
> painted on his coat of arms and these Incas brought coca and they ate it
> and taught the other Indians about it because in the mountains it is not
> grown. (Guaman Poma 1980, 154, 155, [155, 156])

Inca Roca turned into a jaguar because he conquered outside the
highland habitat, fighting the savage Anti or Chuncho Indians,
headhunters who themselves worshiped the jaguar as an animal
which eats people (Guaman Poma 1980, 268, 269 [270, 271]). Guaman Poma also implies that Inca Roca turned into a jaguar because
he ate coca and tobacco. Coca in Aymara means any green tree,
besides the specific coca tree of which the green leaves are chewed;
and *coca haque* means savage (man). Guaman Poma describes Inca
Roca with a green mantle. Green was associated with the rainy
season; with the spirits of the dead (in the form of green flies); with
love amulets and, in general, with forces from the outside. We can
see in these data, then, a contrast between puma and jaguar.

PUMA	JAGUAR
highlands	lowlands (jungle)
established society	savagery (wild men; wild women)
red	green
king	priest
government	sorcery, drugs, love

This opposition also refers to a specific border between highlands
and lowlands. Toward the northeast, Apu Cañachuay mountain
was, and still is, worshiped because of its isolated position at the
border with the lowlands (Zuidema 1977b). From here an Inca road
went down to the lands of coca. Many Incaic and modern myths
refer to Apu Cañachuay, identifying it as a serpent or puma who
governs the rains and who is the lord of llamas. Guaman Poma calls

Figure 8.   The son of Inca Roca, as jungle Indian, fighting a jaguar.
(Guaman Poma 1980, 155 [155])

him, moreover, Apu Tinya, Lord Drum, confirming the association
of the puma with the drum. Together with Sahuasiray Pitusiray, it is
also one of the most sacred mountains of Antisuyu, one of the four
political divisions of Cuzco and the Inca empire (see fig. 8). These
data also oblige us to consider the opposition of puma and jaguar in
terms of the internal organization of Cuzco.

Inca Roca, the jaguar, with his son Vicaquirao, are twice involved in the opposition of Inca Yupanqui (Pachacuti Inca) to his
father Viracocha Inca and to his brother Inca Urco. Inca Yupanqui
sends Vicaquirao as an emissary to his father in Caquia Jaquijahuana. Later, when Inca Urco rebels, the general of Pachacuti Inca who defeats him is Inca Roca. Vicaquirao, the son of Inca Roca
in the dynastic image of the Inca mythology, gave his name (*vica*,
child's loincloth; *quirao*, cradle) to the *panaca*, or descendants, of Inca
Roca. Inca Roca and his son were chosen to represent a position between two opposing forces. I will analyze these forces in terms of the
spatial-hierarchical organization of Cuzco itself and not in terms of a
pseudohistorical dynasty (Zuidema MS).

CHINCHAYSUYU (Inside)	ANTISUYU (Outside)
high nobility	Viracocha Inca
low nobility: Pachacuti Inca	
commoners: Inca Roca, Vicaquirao	

Pachacuti Inca, Inca Roca, and Viracocha Inca all belonged to
the Hanan Cuzco moiety (Upper Cuzco, North). Within the three-
fold hierarchical division of each *suyu* (quarter) in this moiety,
Pachacuti Inca was considered to be the ancestor of the second group
in Chinchaysuyu, that is, of the lower nobility in the first of the two
quarters. Likewise, Inca Roca was considered the ancestor of the
third group in Chinchaysuyu, the non-noble people; and Viracocha
Inca was taken as the ancestor of the high nobility in Antisuyu, the
second *suyu*. Within Hanan Cuzco, Chinchaysuyu represented the
inside, Antisuyu the outside. Inca Roca and his son, then, being the
commoners in Chinchaysuyu, were conquerors of Antisuyu. Although the myths of Betanzos and Murua that I have used here do
not associate the latter two Incas with any specific animals, Viracocha Inca did have as his *huauque* (brother), a stone image of the
amaru (serpent, dragon). Guaman Poma depicts the jaguar and the
amaru as the heraldic animals of Antisuyu, drawn in a shield with a

walking jaguar in the upper position and an *amaru* in the lower. Given that he also uses an eagle and a rampant lion as similar heraldic emblems of Chinchaysuyu, we can reconstruct an opposition between Chinchaysuyu and Antisuyu (figs. 9 and 10).

CHINCHAYSUYU		ANTISUYU
vertical eagle (right half)	vertical lion (left half)	horizontal jaguar (upper half)
		horizontal serpent (lower half)

Although this opposition is not precisely equivalent to that discussed above, similar hierarchical principles of inside/outside and higher/lower are involved.

These data help us discuss the context of the group of animals within which the puma as animal was chosen to represent the body politic of Cuzco. Guaman Poma (1980, 694, 695 [708, 709], 899, 900 [913, 914]) includes the *amaru* (called a serpent, but drawn as a felinelike dragon), the jaguar, and the puma in the following hierarchy of major animals whose characteristics intrude on human society. He compares them to the Spanish and to the indigenous colonial government which tyrannizes the Indians (fig. 11). The order is:

The Spanish corregidor as the *dragon* (*amaru*).
The Spaniard of the *tambo* (guesthouse on the road) as the *tiger*.
The Spanish *encomendero* as the *lion*.
The Spanish priest as the *fox*.
The Indian cacique principal as the *rat*.
The Indian scribe as the *cat*.

The classification is from high rank to low rank, large to small, and outside to inside. Amaru and tiger are considered more "outside" than the lion. In terms of Andean ecology the puma, which belongs to the mountains, is "inside"; it lives near man and his cultivated fields and domesticated animals. Man, as conqueror of the puma, could make the animal the symbol of his polity. Moreover, the red, unspotted skin of the puma could be compared to the red waters of the rainy season, and his tail to the rivers.[28] Man tried to "domesticate" waters by building irrigation canals for use in the dry season and by canalling the river during the wet season.

Figure 9.   Eagle and rampant lion in the coat of arms of Chinchaysuyu.
(Guaman Poma 1980, 165 [167])

Figure 10. Jaguar and *amaru* (serpent) in the coat of arms of Antisuyu. (Guaman Poma 1980, 167 [169])

Guaman Poma's data bring indigenous ideas about the puma and the jaguar that are probably of pre-Columbian origin into contrast with each other. We should not lose sight, however, of the more elaborate classification of six "felines" which define the "estates" of human society, a classification derived from a European model (see, for example, J. Caro Baroja 1978, ch. 13). Somewhat later than Guaman Poma, the Augustinian monk Antonio de la Calancha applied a similar classification to define important Incaic cities (Calancha 1639, book 2, ch. 11, p. 373). "The Indians of the Andes, who live in the lands behind snow-capped mountains, where it always rains and where it is very hot (like in Panama and Cartegena), and the Indians who live in the mountains, worship Tigers, Lions, Bears and Serpents, because there is an abundance of these species in their countries. Those [people] of Guanuco [worship] a rampant Lion, those of Tiaguanaco a curled Serpent, those of Tomebamba [the present-day city of Cuenca in Ecuador] a Bear and those of Chachapoyas Tigers."

LATER DEVELOPMENTS OF THE "CUZCO AS A PUMA" METAPHOR

In this essay I have studied the concept of "Cuzco as Puma," as given by Betanzos in our oldest chronicle, in terms of Andean myths and rituals and by developing a critical method of analyzing their possible pre-Columbian origin. Betanzos's information was later repeated by Sarmiento in 1572 and paraphrased by Garcilaso de la Vega in 1609. While Betanzos wrote down his information in direct confrontation with Inca culture and couched it in an elaborate analysis of royal succession and law, Sarmiento reinterpreted that information, giving it a new bias that served the political aims of Viceroy Toledo, who had assigned him to write this chronicle. This is not the only case in which Sarmiento—an otherwise admirable chronicler —uses original data from Betanzos, reformulating their meaning and intent. Sarmiento writes how king Topa Inga Yupanqui, the son of Pachacuti Inca, "remembered how his father Pachacuti has called the city of Cuzco the Lion city, and that the tail was where the two rivers join that pass through the city, and that the body was the plaza and the settlements around it and that the head was missing, but that one of his sons would put it there" (Sarmiento 1947, ch. 53). Topa Inga Yupanqui then built the fortress of Sacsayhuaman as the head.

Sarmiento's interest in the story is to justify Tupa Yupanqui as

694

Figure 11. The colonial government that tyrannizes the Indians.
(Guaman Poma 1980, 694 [708])

the builder of the fortress. He no longer uses the metaphor to represent a body politic. He describes a real city, although he includes in its architecture the settlements around the political center. The fanciful nature of Sarmiento's reinterpretation is clear. He wants us to think that Pachacuti Inca had a city without a head, and that Pachacuti Inca himself was not the "head" at all. Worse, Sarmiento adds a head, the fortress of Sacsayhuaman, the name of which means Royal Eagle (González Holguín). Thus, we have a puma's body with an eagle's head.

The last reference we have in the chronicles to the use of the body metaphor is from Garcilaso. He separates it completely from this other metaphor, which compares Cuzco to the heroic qualities of a lion. I will discuss his two metaphors separately, beginning with the latter. His motivation is found in his enumeration of the twelve settlements around Cuzco and in his interpretation of the names of two of them: Huacapuncu and Pumapchupan (Garcilaso 1945, book 7, ch. 8). Of the first, which belonged to the northwest part of the city, he says:

> Then comes the neighbourhood called Huacapuncu: it means "door of the sanctuary," because *huaca*, as we will explain, means among other things "temple" or "sanctuary"; *puncu* is "door." They called it thus because near this neighbourhood the river enters that goes through the middle of the principal plaza of Cuzco, and along the river goes a broad and long street and both traverse the whole city, and a league and a half below it they come together with the royal road of Collasuyu. They called that entrance "door of the temple or sanctuary" because, besides the neighbourhoods dedicated to the temple of the Sun and to the house of the chosen virgins, which were their principal sanctuaries, they considered the whole city as sacred and it was one of their major idols.

And of Pumapchupan he says:

> Passing the neighbourhood of Rimacpampa, is another one, south [i.e., southeast] of the city, called Pumapchupan; which means "tail of the puma," because that neighbourhood ends in a point, by way of two small rivers that at the end join, making a point of the block of houses. They also gave it its name because that neighbourhood was the last of the city; they wanted to honor it by calling it "tail" and "end of the lion." Besides this, they kept there lions and other fierce animals.

On the names of both neighbourhoods Garcilaso then comments:

> And for these reasons they called the entrance of the small river [the first and central one, called Sapi or Huatanay] and of the street "door

of the sanctuary," and at the exit of the same river and street they said "puma's tail," as a way of saying that their city was sacred in its laws and vain religion and a lion in its arms and militia.

Garcilaso's text offers a curious mixture of some good and some rather naïve suggestions. But most are of a metaphoric nature. Of Pumapchupan he suggests that it was called thus (1) because of its shape; (2) because it was the last neighbourhood of the city; (3) because pumas were kept there.

The third argument is quite improbable. No other chronicler refers to such a fact. The interpretation of the name Huacapuncu is completely Garcilaso's own. González Holguín mentions in his dictionary the following regular Quechua words:

huaccapunco: a toothless person, said as an insult, or *cassaquiru*

kassaquiro, *huacapunco*: toothless, or *kassapallca*

Toothless: *cassaquiru*

These words give us a far better understanding of why the neighborhood was called Huacapuncu. It straddles the gorge out of which the river Sapi enters Cuzco, and seen from Cuzco it conforms to González Holguín's definition of "Notch, empty space or break in a continuous line (Cassa, or *allca*)."

Having become aware of his procedures, we can now take a close look at Garcilaso's symbolic interpretations of the words *huacapuncu* and *pumapchupan*. He calls the whole of Cuzco sacred because its gate was sacred, and militant because its lower end was the tail of a puma (and not the tail of a donkey or some other nonheroic animal). Although he makes associations with real pumas—which were kept in Pumapchupan—the name does not lead him to compare either the city of Cuzco or its shape to this animal. His comparison is metaphoric: the people of Cuzco are said to be heroic like the puma.

Even if Garcilaso does not use the body metaphor for Cuzco here, he does so in two other places, although he refers to the human body and not that of a puma. Discussing the name Tahuantinsuyu for the Inca empire, he says:

> The Inca kings divided their Empire into four parts, that they called Tauantinsuyu, which means "the four parts of the world," according to the four principal parts of heaven: East, West, North and South. They placed the city of Cuzco in the center, which [name] in the private language of the Incas means "navel of the earth": they called it "navel" for a good reason because the whole of Peru is long and narrow like a

human body, and the city is almost in the middle. (Garcilaso 1945, book 2, ch. 11)

And previously he states:

> In this way they started to inhabit our imperial city, divided into two halves that they called Hanan-Cozco, that, as you knew, means "Upper-Cozco" and Hurin-Cozco, that is "Lower-Cozco." Those that were attracted by the King came to live in Hanan-Cozco and therefore they called it the higher part, and those that were invited by the Queen were going to live in Hurin-Cozco, and therefore they called it the lower part. And he ordered that there would be only one difference and recognition of superiority: that those of Upper Cozco were respected and held as firstborn, elder brothers and those of the lower part as secondary brothers; and, in conclusion, that they were like the right arm and the left in any pre-eminence of place or office, as those of the upper part were attracted by the man and those of the lower part by the woman. (Garcilaso 1945, book 1, ch. 16)

These two passages contain the following distinctions:

HANAN	HURIN
king	queen
male	female
right (arm)	left (arm)
firstborn, elder brother	secondary, younger brother
high	low

By comparing the data of Betanzos, Sarmiento, and Garcilaso we can come to the following conclusions:

1. There is no evidence that the shape of Cuzco was seen as an animal (in this case, a puma), lying on its side.

2. Betanzos's and Garcilaso's understanding of Cuzco as a puma or a human was completely metaphoric; only Sarmiento's erroneous conclusion that Sacsayhuaman represents the puma's head suggests that Cuzco has the shape of a puma.

3. The name Pumachupa could evoke the image of Cuzco as a puma, but only Sarmiento makes use of this fact.

4. Garcilaso's use of Hanan and Hurin as right and left, respectively, demonstrates that he correctly interprets the body metaphor as a symmetrical representation. Betanzos and Sarmiento also implicitly recognize the importance of symmetry in their use of the metaphor. They picture Cuzco extending into all directions from the ceremonial center, as does Garcilaso.

Today, the metaphor of the body, whether that of a human, a bull, or a puma, is used by different Andean communities to describe the structure of their political organization. This usage, as attested by the chroniclers, implies possible European influences. In each case the metaphor was used symmetrically, as was done by Garcilaso (Bastien 1978; Bonilla and Fonseca 1963; Vellard 1943, 1963; Laurencich-Minelli 1981; Quispe 1969).

We can now evaluate the following statement by J. H. Rowe (1967) about "Cuzco as a Puma" against these ethnohistorical and ethnographic data.

> The area between the rivers was laid out in the shape of a puma (see plate XXXIV), the fortress representing the puma's head and the point where the rivers come together representing the tail. This point is still called "The Puma's Tail" in Inca. The space between the puma's front and back legs constituted a great public square used for ceremonies; it was paved with pebbles. The streets were straight but somewhat irregularly arranged to fit the topography of the site of the puma figure; in consequence, none of the blocks was square, and the blocks varied greatly in size.

As Rowe does not understand the metaphoric quality of the comparison, he completely misinterprets the element of symmetry in the metaphor which refers to the totality of Cuzco society. With his reference to plate XXXIV Rowe implies that the chroniclers—Sarmiento and Betanzos—say that Cuzco would have been shaped like a puma, lying on its side with the front legs joined, represented as one, and the back legs in a similar fashion, and that one reason for the irregular layout of the city was the desire of the Incas to represent a puma. He does not analyze the texts that he quotes; these do not say anything about the shape of the animal. Nonetheless, his unfounded opinion has been generally accepted by archaeologists and historians of architecture.[29] Seeing in Cuzco the shape of a puma dispenses with any consideration of Betanzos's intention in choosing to discuss the symbol: the shaping of a polity, royal succession, and the organization of agriculture and irrigation.

Conclusions

Betanzos's discussion helped us to analyze three themes of interest in Inca political organization. First, we were able to relate his concept of the metaphor of the puma's head and body to that of the *ceque* system, mentioned by Polo de Ondegardo and Molina twenty years later (although Matienzo [1967] had already referred to it in 1567). This system of directions describes the same area as the metaphor: the valley of Cuzco and its hydrological system. The concepts of "puma's tail" and "waggling the tail" implied the territory around Cuzco in which the "Incas-by-privilege" lived, and in whom the Incas were interested due to their immediate ritual contributions, involving economic, political, religious, and calendrical obligations (Zuidema 1977a, 1981, 1982a, b, c,).

The Valley also fulfilled a mediating role, situated as it was between the city and the area of the "Incas-by-privilege." This helps us to understand the contradictory statements about its people. On the one hand, those who lived there before Pachacuti's reorganization of Cuzco were said to have been expelled into the territory of the "Incas-by-privilege"; on the other hand, we know that these were represented by *ayllu*s in the valley who, according to myth, originated from their territory. We can understand the value of the apparently conflicting data by placing them in the mythological context of the contributions that Inca Yupanqui received for the defense of Cuzco (either the twenty chiefs and their people sent to him by Viracocha Inca, or the *pururauca*, or stones that turned into soldiers, also sent by his father). The economic and kinship ties between Cuzco and the "Incas-by-privilege" involved the latter having both temporary and permanent representation in the valley and at court (Zuidema MS).

The dynamic aspects of the relations between the Incas and "Incas-by-privilege," expressed by the calendar and by stories of political change, oblige us to study the importance of change as expressed in ritual and myth. Our ritual and mythological data combine and interrelate references to rites of passage of the noble youths, to seasonal change, and to political change. The last, in the form of royal succession, was described in a charter myth for the initiation rituals. In this respect the studies of Terence Turner on the problem of transformation in myth, ritual (rites of passage), and moiety organizations are especially useful for understanding why the Inca data on political organization mentioned here find their most cogent expression in the rites of passage of the noble youths in Cuzco (Turner 1977, 1979, 1980). I will outline briefly this aspect of transformation.

Any society must assure the renewal of its leaders in order to maintain its political structure. In Cuzco, the primary purpose of the December initiation rituals was to select the noble youths for their future roles in the Inca army, bureaucracy, and priesthood. These rituals, at the moment when foreigners had to leave town, separated the initiates from the latter, and especially from the children of the foreigners, who were initiated elsewhere and at another time. The distinction between elders and uninitiated youths was related, first, to the concentric opposition of Incas to "Incas-by-privilege." It also received calendric-ritual expression within the opposition of the northern half of the valley, Hanan-Cuzco, to the southern one, Hurin-Cuzco. Before their ears were pierced during the December solstice, the initiates visited sacred mountains to the south of Cuzco which had belonged to the pre-Inca population. After that, until June, they were involved in state rituals in which the northern sacred mountains were important. Within the context of these oppositions we must also consider the special services that the youths had to perform in the year of their initiation. (In this case the data from outside of Cuzco are more explicit.) The youths were the *ararihua*, wearing a fox skin, while their elders wore the puma skin during Capac raymi. The puma symbolized royalty, nobility, and the power of the Incas over the non-Incas.

In terms of the calendar, the month ending with the December solstice was the most propitious for carrying out the initiation rituals for practical and symbolic reasons: practical because it started the rainy season, when there was less travel (Guaman Poma 1980, 1134 [1144]); symbolic because it could be related to two important seasonal changes. First, Cuzco ended its dependency on outside irrigation water. From then on it released its rainwater through a channeled river. Second, plants, especially maize, passed from being young plants to setting seed and ripening during maturity.

The association of the puma symbol, in rituals and myth, to the dynamic, transformational aspects of Cuzco society was made possible through the importance of water, in the form of irrigation, rain, and rivers, for Andean people. We should once again distinguish the symbolic from the practical interest. The Huatanay river receives the water in the valley of Cuzco and from there it flows into the Villcanota river. It follows one course, although the Cuzco valley collects rain from different directions. The Incas used this hydrological cycle to symbolize their ritual relationships to the "Incas-by-privilege" who lived around them in all directions. The ritual of drinking to the nobility of the "Incas-by-privilege" was probably done on the occasion of the initiation rituals that ended with *mayucati*, or following the river. But the drinking was done into all directions, as was the expelling of illness and evil at the beginning of the agricultural season.

I mentioned the Andean mythological themes of the rainbow coming out of the earth through a puma's head, and that of the mountain Apu Cañachuay, on the border of mountains and jungle, which, as a god of rains, is associated with a puma and is called "lord drum." I also mentioned the actual border function of a puma skin, kept at the place where a road leaves the Cuzco valley; and of the mythical encounter (at a place nearby and in the same direction from Cuzco as the other place) of the future Pachacuti Inca with his "father" the Sun who came out of a spring of water dressed in a puma skin. In all these cases, the border function of the puma symbol had ambiguous characteristics. It referred to the fertilizing contributions of rain, brought by winds from beyond the horizon, as well as to the destructive forces of thunder, hail, and snow. The social group affected by these forces expressed its cohesion by way of the men, wearing puma skins and playing drums, who were the owners of "property": land, access to irrigation water, llamas, and a family. Defending their property against the destructive forces in nature and in society led the men to adopt the puma symbol, which is identified with those forces. In this sense the puma became "socialized" in Andean culture. In contrast, the jaguar, living outside the mountains, kept for Andean man its savage characteristics. These were the ideas about the puma which Betanzos used for his metaphor of the body politic.

NOTES

1. Because a central problem to be dealt with in this essay is Betanzos's understanding of the metaphor of the body politic and his use of the symbol of the lion, his term "lion" appears in the article title. Another purpose of the study, however, is to contribute to an understanding of the importance of the puma, the American lion, in Andean culture.

2. I wish to thank Gary Urton, Stephen Fabian, and Deborah Poole for their helpful criticisms and Deborah Poole for editorial assistance.

3. In using Murra and Adorno's edition of Guaman Poma, I have added their revised pagination in brackets.

4. Van Kessel, personal communication.

5. D. A. Poole, personal communication.

6. G. Urton, personal communication.

7. We can reach the same conclusions about the calendrical importance by observing the behavior of foxes from the following description by T. Platt (1978:1085 and 1980:146–47): ". . . if one sees the fox [atuj] in September [the time of sowing] moving towards the mountains, the year will bring a good harvest in the puna; but if one sees him coming down, the year will be good in the valley. In the same way, if the excrement of the fox has potato peels, the puna will be prosperous; but if it has corn husks, the valley will have an abundant harvest. Moreover, two nebulous spots in the southern sky are associated with the puna and the valley respectively; if one is clearer than the other, the year will be good in the corresponding area." Although we need a specific identification of both "nebulous spots in the southern sky," one might coincide with the "dark cloud constellation" of the fox which Urton identifies in between the Tail of Scorpio and Sagittarius (Urton 1981a, 70,71, 116, 188–90, and 1981, 123–24). The theme of the fox, traveling either to the puna or the valley, is, moreover, the opening theme of the second myth given by Avila, where the puma skin is also discussed in relation to a spring of water and the rainbow.

8. This is also stated in a description given in a document from Hacas, north of Lima, in 1656 (Hacas 1656).

9. Of course, the connection between lion and fox was also a traditional element in medieval European culture. See, for example, Lewis 1966 and Jacoby 1970.

10. I must leave for later analysis some extremely interesting data, found in Bertonio's Aymara dictionary (1612), on the use of puma heads in dances and on the context within which we could develop this analysis.

11. Although the name aucayo may have been derived from auca or "enemy," the fact that the dance was carried out on the plaza called Huacaypata, "the place of rejoicing," leads me to understand the word as haucayoc, "the dance of rejoicing."

12. In the context of the Chanca war, Betanzos also mentions the Inca drums made of the skin of defeated enemies. As an ultimate insult the drums were played using the arms of these flayed enemies.

13. The description of the rituals occurring at the birth of twins (Avila 1967) also stresses that, in response to this omen of death, illness, and bad weather, men have to play the drums that are normally played by women. The connection between agriculture and warfare is analyzed in detail by Duviols (1973, 1979b) in terms of the Andean myths of the first people who occupied a territory and cultivated the earth.

14. Cieza and Betanzos themselves were not completely convinced of the historical value of the dynasty (Cieza 1967, ch. 32; Betanzos 1968, ch. 5; Zuidema 1964, 137–38, 145–46; Duviols 1979,77).

15. The Spanish chroniclers also described the position of "lieutenant" as that of "second person" to the Inca in pre-Columbian society or to the "principal cacique" in colonial society.

16. The Quechua word used here is certainly copied incorrectly. As Betanzos translates it as "I know my sin," we can conclude that the root of the Quechua word was *hucha*, or sin.

17. Caquia Jaquijahuana was well known as a village which was inhabited until the end of the seventeenth century, after which it was abandoned. Only at the beginning of this century did local Cuzco historians rename the Inca ruins here Huchuy Cuzco, "the small Cuzco." They may have had a case for comparing them to Cuzco, because Cieza (1967) already implied to their similarity.

18. Lira writes this word as *kkhakkya* "thunderclap." Bertonio used a similar word Ccaca, metaphorically for "phantom that walks at night, and they take this name from the noise it makes like stuttering."

19. A similar argument is developed more elaborately by Duviols (1973, 160–63) to explain why in central Peru the god of the original inhabitants called Huari or Viracocha, with characteristics relating him to the earth, but also to the sun, was still considered to be a conqueror, even though they were later conquered by another group with its own Eagle-Thunder god. The opposition in Cuzco of Inca Yupanqui (Pachacuti Inca) with Viracocha Inca reflects that of the Thunder god with the god Viracocha. In Huarochirí the first conquest corresponds to Coniraya Viracocha (Avila 1967, ch. 2) and the second to the Thunder god Pariacaca (Avila 1967, ch. 5, 8; Zuidema 1982d).

20. This conclusion is based on two pieces of information. While in the *ceque* system the fourth *huaca* of the fourth *ceque* of Antisuyu is called Viracocha, a document from 1720 (included as the last two, loose pages to the document catalogued as Ciencias 27, cuaderno 4, "Aguas de Uca ucu," dated 1797, in the Historical Archive of Cuzco) calls the same place Pururauca. I have been told that today this place is called Angel caca, "the rock of the angel(s)."

21. See Zuidema (1964), 1982c) for the notation indicating the hierarchical organization of the *ceque*s.

22. The *ceque*s next to the one mentioned here are, moreover, associated with the Pururauca stone called "Viracocha" as well as with the vision of Inca Yupanqui when the Sun god appeared to him with the puma skin over his head and back, a myth I will refer to later.

23. This concept applied also to the distinction between the lands that a king held as a private individual and those that belonged to him as the head of state. The first were subject to taxes; the others not. The Spaniards

observed a similar distinction in terms of Inca royal lands (Murra [1955] 1978, 73; Wachtel 1980–1981, 309).

24. The Murua chronicle is preserved in the form of two manuscripts which occasionally differ greatly. I will use the Loyola manuscript (Murua 1946), as it is only in this version that we find the paragraph on the month of December. Minor details added in brackets point out where the Wellington manuscript (Ballesteros 1962) differs.

25. For the connection of water and music, see Barthel (1959) and Zuidema (1978, 1042–43).

26. Arriaga (1968, ch. 5) mentions the three principal feasts in the Andes as that of the first appearance of the Pleiades in early June, "to keep the maize from drying up"; that celebrated "at the beginning of the rainy season, at Christmas or a little afterward . . . addressed to the thunder and lightning, to beg for rain"; and that for the harvest of maize in April. In Cuzco, Capac raymi is, in fact, divided over two months, the first being Capac raymi proper as described now, falling before the December solstice, and the second, Capac raymi camay quilla, which takes place later. The description of this last month best conforms to that of Arriaga's second feast (see the next section). Murua's myth, then, seems to refer to both months: that of the initiation of the youths and that of their subsequent defense against the elements.

27. Jiménez de la Espada, the first editor of Betanzos, gave the erroneous interpretation of the month name as "purappucquio."

28. Today the river that a person has to cross after death in going to his ultimate abode is called Puka mayu, "red river" (Flores Ochoa 1974–1976, 257).

29. W. M. Isbell (1978), the only person to check the sources, accepts Rowe's idea, although we must conclude that his own interest in the puma is metaphoric because of the kind of comparison he makes to data from the Desana. Gasparini and Margolies stretch the legs of the puma to conform it to their concept of the architecture of Cuzco.

Agurto reprints Rowe's drawing of Cuzco as a puma, although, at a conference given at the Congreso del Hombre Andino in Cuzco in 1979, he expressed his criticism. He pointed out, for example, that the Inca city of Pisac may derive its name from Pisaca, or "partridge," without having the form of this animal. The last reference to this piece of popular modern folklore can be found in the map of South America published in the March 1982 issue of the *National Geographic* magazine.

REFERENCES

Agurto Calco, Santiago
    1980   *Cusco: La traza urbana de la ciudad incaica.* Cuzco: Proyecto PER 39, Unesco, Peru.

Agustinos
    1952   *Religión en Huamachuco.* Lima: David Miranda.
Albornoz, Cristóbal
    1967   See Duviols, Pierre.
Arriaga, Father Pablo Joseph de
    1968   *The extirpation of idolatry in Peru.* Trans. and ed. L. Clark Keating. Lex-
            ington: University of Kentucky Press.
Avila, Francisco de
    1952   *Religion en Huarochirí* (1608), ed. F. Loayza. Lima: David Miranda.
Barthel, T. S.
    1959   Ein Frühlingsfest der Atacameños. *Zeitschrift für Ethnologie* 84(1).
Bastien, Joseph W.
    1978   *Mountain of the condor: Metaphor and ritual in an Andean ayllu.* American
            Ethnological Society, Monograph no. 64. St. Paul, Minn.: West
            Publishing Company.
Bataillon, Marcel
    1966   *Erasmo y España: Estudios sobre la histórica espiritual del siglo XVI.* Mex-
            ico, D.F.: Fondo de Cultura Económica.
Bertonio, Ludovico
    1956   *Vocabulario de la lengua aymara* (1612). La Paz: Don Bosco.
Betanzos, Juan de
    1968   Suma y narración de los Incas (1551). In *Crónicas peruanas de interés in-
            dígena,* 1–55. Madrid: Biblioteca de Autores Españoles.
Bonilla Mayta, Heraclio, and César Fonseca Martell
    1963   *Jesús de Machaca.* Lima: Universidad Nacional Mayor de San Marcos.
Calancha, A. de la
    1639   *Coronica moralizada del Orden de San Augustín en el Perú.* Barcelona: n.p.
Caro Baroja, Julio
    1978   *Las formas complejas de la vida religiosa: Religión, sociedad y carácter en
            España de los sigloas XVI y XVII.* Madrid: Akal.
Cieza de León, Pedro de
    1945   *La crónica del Perú* (1553). Buenos Aires: Espasa-Calpe Argentina, S.
            A.
    1967   *El señorio de los Incas* (1551). Lima: Instituto de Estudios Peruanos.
Cobo, Bernabé
    1956   *Historia del Nuevo Mundo* (1653). Vol. 2. Madrid: B.A.E.
Condori Mamani, Gregorio
    1977   *Gregorio Condori Mamani: Autobiografía.* Ed. R. Valderrama Fernández
            and C. Escalante Gutiérrez. Biblioteca de la Tradición Oral Andina.
            Vol. 2. Cuzco: Centro de Estudios Rurales Andinos ''Bartolomé de
            las Casas.''
Duviols, Pierre
    1967   Un inédit de Cristóbal de Albornoz: ''La instrucción para descubrir
            todas las guacas del Piru y sus camayos y haziendas'' (*ca.* 1582). *Jour-
            nal de la Société des Américanistes* 56(1):7–40.
    1973   Huari y Llacuaz, pastores y agricultores: Un dualismo de oposición y
            complementariad. *Revista del Museo Nacional, Lima* 39:153–91.
    1977a   Los nombres quechua de Viracocha, supuesto ''Dios Creador'' de los
            evangelizadores. *Allpanchis Phuturinga* 10:53–63.

REFERENCES

247

1977b   Un symbolisme andin du double: La lithomorphose de l'ancêtre. *Actes du XLII* ᵉ *Congrès International des Américanistes* 4:359–64.

1979a   La dinastía de los Incas: ?Monarquía o diarquía? Argumentos heurísticos a favor de una tesis estructuralista. *Journal de la Société des Américanistes* 66:67–83.

1979b   Un symbolisme de l'occupation, de l'aménagement et de l'occupation de l'espace: Le monolithe "Huanca" et sa fonction dans les Andes préhispaniques. *L'Homme* 19(2):7–31.

Earls, J., and Irene Silverblatt

1978   La realidad física y social en la cosmología andina. *Actes du XLIIIᵉ Congrès International des Américanistes* 4:299–325.

Fischer, K. M.

1973   *Tendenz und absicht des Ephesers Brief*. Gottingen, FRLANT, III.

Flores Ochoa, Jorge A.

1974–   Enqa, Enqaychu, Illa y Khuya Rumi: Aspectos mágico-religiosos en-
1976   tre pastores (Perú). *Journal de la Société des Américanistes* 63:245–62.

Garcilaso de la Vega (El Inca)

1945   *Comentarios reales de los Incas* (1609). Buenos Aires: Emecé.

Gasparini, Graziano, and Luise Margolies

1977   *Arquitectura inca.* Caracas: Centro de Investigaciones Históricas y Estéticas, Facultad de Arquitectura y Urbanismo, Universidad Central de Venezuela.

González Holguín, Diego

1952   *Vocabulario de la lengua general de todo el Perú llamada lengua Qquichua o del Inca* (1608). Lima: Imprenta Santa Maria.

Guaman Poma de Ayala (Waman Puma), Felipe

1980   *El primer nueva coronica y buen gobierno* (1583–1615). Ed. J. V. Murra and R. Adorno. Mexico, D.F.: Siglo XXI.

Hacas

1656   Archivo Arzobispal de Lima. File 4, item 18.

Herrera, Antonio de

1945   *História general de los hechos de los castellanos* (1601–1615). Asunción del Paraguay: Editorial Guaranía.

Huertas Vallejos, Lorenzo

1981   *La religión en una sociedad rural andina (siglo XVII)*. Ayacucho: Universidad Nacional de San Cristóbal de Huamanga.

Isbell, Billie Jean

1978   To defend ourselves: Ecology and ritual in an Andean village. Latin American Monographs, no. 47. Austin: University of Texas Press.

Jacoby, R.

1970   *Van den vos Reinaerde: Legal elements in a Netherlands epic of the thirteenth century*. Munich: W. Fink Verlag.

Kantorowicz, Ernst H.

1957   *The king's two bodies: A study in Medieval political theory*. Princeton: Princeton University Press.

Laurencich-Minelli, Laura

1981   Gli Aymara della Bolivia visti atraverso alcune note di Mons. Federico Lunardi. *Terra Ameriga* 42:69–77.

Lewis, W.
1966   *The lion and the fox: The role of the hero in the plays of Shakespeare.* New York: Barnes and Noble.
Lira, Jorge A.
1944   *Diccionario Kkechuwa-Español.* Tucumán: Instituto de Historia, Lingüística y Folklore.
López de Velasco, Juan
1971   *Geografía y descripción universal de las Indias.* Vol. 248. Madrid: Biblioteca de Autores Españoles.
Matienzo, Juan de
1967   *Gobierno del Perú* (1567). Institut Français d'Études Andines. Paris-Lima.
McCall, Daniel F.
1973–   The prevalence of lions: Kings, deities and feline symbolism in Africa
1974   and elsewhere. *Paideuma* 19/20.
Molina, C. de
1943   *Fábulas y ritos de los Incas* (1573). Lima: David Miranda.
Murra, John V.
1978   *La organización económica del estado inca.* Mexico, D.F.: Siglo XXI.
Murua, Fray Martín de
1946   *Histórica del origen y genealogía real de los reyes incas del Perú* (1590). Ed. C. Bayle, S. J. Madrid: Biblioteca "Missionala Hispánica," Instituto Santo Toribio de Mogrovejo.
1962   *Historia general del Perú: Origen y descendencia de los Incas* (1611–1618). Madrid: Colección Joyas Bibliográficas, Biblioteca Americana Vetus 1.
Ossio A., Juan M., ed.
1973   *Ideología mesiánica del mundo andino.* Lima: Prado Pastor.
Pinto Ramos, E. G.
1970   Estructura y función en la comunidad de Tomanga. Ph.D. diss., Universidad de Huamanga, Ayacucho, Peru.
Platt, Tristan
1978   Symétries en miroir: Le concept de Yanantin chez les Macha de
(1980)   Bolivie. *Annales Economies, Société, Civilizations* 33(5/6): 1081–107. Also published as: El concepto de Yanantin entre los Macha de Bolivia. In *Parentesco y matrimonio en los Andes*, ed. Enrique Mayer and Ralph Bolton, 139–82. Lima: Fondo Editorial, Pontificia Universidad Católica del Perú.
Polo de Ondegardo
1916   *Los errores y supersticiones de los Indios sacados del tratado y averiguación que hizo el Licenciado Polo* (1584). Ed. Urteaga y Romero. Lima.
Quispe Mejía, Ulpiano
1969   *La herranza en Choque Huarcaya y Huancasancos, Ayacucho.* Lima: Instituto Indigenista Peruano.
Reichel-Dolmatoff, Gerardo
1975   *The shaman and the jaguar: A study of narcotic drugs among the Indians of Colombia.* Philadelphia: Temple University Press.

Relación del sitio de Cuzco
    1934   Second series, vol. 10. Ed. Urteaga y Romero. Colección de libros y documentos referentes a la historia del Perú. Lima.

Rowe, John H.
    1946   Inca culture at the time of the Spanish Conquest. *Handbook of South American Indians*. Vol. 2, 183–330.
    1967   What kind of settlement was Inca Cuzco? *Ñawpa Pacha* 5:59–76.
    1979   An account of the shrines of ancient Cuzco. *Ñawpa Pacha* 17:1–80.

Rowe, John H., and Dorothy Menzel
    1966   The role of chincha in late pre-Spanish Peru. *Ñawpa Pacha* 4.

Santacruz Pachacuti Yamqui Salcamaygua, Juan de
    1950   Relación de antigüedades de este reyno del Perú. In *Tres relaciones de antigüedades peruanas*, ed. M. Jiménez de la Espada, 207–81. Asunción de Paraguay: Guaranía.

Sarmiento de Gamboa, Pedro
    1947   *Historia de los Incas* (1572). Buenos Aires: Emecé.

Trimborn, Hermann, and Antje Kelm
    1967   Francisco de Avila (before 1608). In *Quellenwerke zur alten Geschichte Amerikas*. Vol. 8. Berlin: Gebr. Mann Verlag.

Turner, Terence S.
    1977   Transformation, hierarchy and transcendence: A reformulation of van Gennep's model of the structure of Rites de Passage. In *Secular Ritual*, ed. S. Falk Moore and B. Meyerhoff. The Hague: van Gorcum.
    1979   The Gê and Bororo societies as dialectical systems: A general model. In *Dialectical Societies: The Gê and Bororo of central Brazil*, ed. David Maybury-Lewis. Cambridge: Harvard University Press.
    1980   Le dénicheur d'oiseaux en contexte. *Anthropologie et Sociétés* 4(3):85–115.

Urton, Gary
    1981a   *At the crossroads of the earth and the sky: An Andean cosmology*. Latin American Monographs, no. 55. Austin: University of Texas Press.
    1981b   Animals and astronomy in the Quechua universe. *American Philosophical Society, Proceedings* 125(2):109–27.

Valderrama Fernández, Ricardo, and Carmen Escalante Gutiérrez, eds.
    1977   *Gregorio Condori Mamani: Autobiografía*. Biblioteca de la Tradición Oral Andina. Vol. 2. Cuzco: Centro de Estudios Rurales Andinos "Bartolomé de las Casas."

Van Gennep, A.
    1960   *The rites of passage*. Chicago: University of Chicago Press.

Vellard, J.
    1943   Un village de structure précolombienne. *Annales de Géographie* 52:206–18.
    1963   *Civilisations des Andes: Évolution des populations du haut-plateau bolivien*. Paris: Gallimard.

Wachtel, Nathan
    1971   *La visión des Vaincus: Les indiens du Perou devant la conqête espagnole*. Paris: Gallimard.

1980– Les Mitimas de la Vallée de Cochabamba: La politique de colonisa-
1981 tion de Huayna Capac. *Journal de las Société des Américanistes*
67:297–324.

Wit, Constant de
1951 *Le rôle et le sens du lion dans l'Egypte ancienne*. Leiden: E. J. Brill.

Zuidema, R. T.
1964 *The ceque system of Cuzco: The social organization of the capital of the Inca.*
Leiden: E. J. Brill.
1974– La imagen del sol y la Huaca de Susurpuquio en el sistema
1976 astronómico de los Incas en el Cuzco. *Journal de la Société des
Américanistes* 63:199–230.
1977a The Inca kinship system: A new theoretical view. In *Andean kinship
and marriage*, ed. Ralph Bolton and Enrique Mayer. Washington,
D.C.: American Anthropological Association.
1977b Mito, rito, calendario y geografía en el antiguo Perú. *Actes du XLIIᵉ
Congrès International des Américanistes* 4:347–57.
1978 Dynastie Inca et l'irrigation. *Annales Economies, Société, Civilizations*
5/6:1037–56.
1982a The Inca observations of the solar and lunar passages through zenith
and anti-zenith at Cuzco. In *Archaeoastronomy in the Americas*, ed. R. A.
Williamson. Los Altos, Calif.: Ballena Press.
1982b Catachillay: The role of the Pleiades and of the Southern Cross and
Centauri α and β in the calendar of the Incas. In *Ethnoastronomy and
archaeoastronomy in the American tropics*, ed. A. F. Aveni and Gary Urton.
Annals of the New York Academy of Sciences 385:203–30.
1982c The sidereal-lunar calendar of the Incas. In *New World archaeoastronomy*, ed. A. F. Aveni, 59–107. Cambridge: Cambridge University
Press.
1982d Myth and history in ancient Peru. In *The logic of culture: Advances in
structural theory and methods*, ed. I. Rossi, 150–75. South Hadley,
Mass.: Bergin and Garvey Publishers, Inc.
1982e Bureaucracy and systematic knowledge in Andean civilization. In *The
Inca and Aztec states, 1400–1800*, ed. G. A. Collier, R. I. Rosaldo, and
J. D. Wirth. New York: Academic Press.
1983 Hierarchy and Space in Incaic social organization. *Ethnohistory*
30:49–75.
MS The Royal Game of Government.

Zuidema, R. T., and G. Urton
1976 La constelación de la llama en los Andes peruanos. *Allpanchis Phuturinga* 9:59–119.

Animal Metaphors and the Life Cycle in an Andean Community

Gary Urton

The landscape of the district of Pacariqtambo (Department of Cuzco, Province of Paruro, Peru) is a mosaic of flat pampas; gently rolling grass-covered hills; high, rock-strewn mountains; and steep escarpments forming the gorges of rapidly flowing rivers. Within this immensely varied geological and ecological setting, the *campesinos* of the community of Pacariqtambo and of the numerous small village annexes scattered throughout the district work from day-to-day in a number of agricultural and pastoral pursuits that repeatedly bring them into contact with a variety of nondomesticated animals. During the course of fifteen months of fieldwork in Pacariqtambo, fieldwork that focused on the agricultural and ritual calendars of the community, I became increasingly interested in the animal and bird life of this region.

Prior to living in Pacariqtambo, I had spent some two years in the field, living in highland communities to the north and west of Cuzco, within the drainage of the Urubamba river (Urton 1981). In those communities, I seldom encountered nondomesticated animals beyond the sighting of several different species of birds and the occasional, distant glimpse of a fox. Pacariqtambo, on the other hand, is located along the upper reaches of the Apurimac river valley, some thirty km straight south of Cuzco. The Apurimac valley is not as heavily populated as is the Urubamba valley; in comparison to the Urumbamba valley, the terrain along the Apurimac river is much rougher, more precipitous, and the valley is narrower and less suitable for human habitation and exploitation (Escobar M. 1980). In addition, there appear (on the basis of my own experience) to be more nondomesticated animals in the region of the Apurimac river to the south of Cuzco. Within the district of Pacariqtambo, for instance, the following animals and birds are found fairly commonly: puma, fox, deer, skunk, the ferretlike *unchukulla*, snake, lizard, bat, condor, *qorqenko* (small vulture), hawk, falcon, tinamou, parrot, and many small sparrow-sized birds. The normal habitats of these animals, or the places where encounters with them have occurred, are memorialized in toponyms such as *Puma*wayqo, *Condor*senqa, *Qorqenko*wachana, and Saqsa*waman* (*waman* = falcon), each place accorded a special significance in local lore and mythology with the particular eponymous animal or bird. In addition to nondomesticated animals, there is a great variety of domesticated animals which are, in one way or another, of considerable importance to the economies of the households within the district; these include: cattle, sheep, horses, burros, pigs, llamas (in the north of the district), goats, chickens, guinea pigs (which are kept in the houses), dogs, and cats.

The purpose of this article is to describe and analyze the role of some of the nondomesticated animals mentioned above in the life and thought of the community of Pacariqtambo. More specifically, I will be examining two interrelated problems: The first concerns the conceived relationship between particular animals and different types of human beings; by the phrase, "types of human beings," I refer to people who are at different stages in the human life cycle—from birth to death. The second problem, which involves more interpretation and speculation on my part, turns on a consideration of the social, labor, and ceremonial groups within the community—the *ayllu*s; of how the *ayllu*s are reproduced from one generation to the next; and of how the boundaries of any one *ayllu* are formed (i.e., conceptualized and maintained) with respect not only to other *ayllu*s, but also to other living things, like animals.

Since the aim here is to study the relationship between the life cycle and the *ayllu*s through an examination of animal lore, it will help to clarify the issues from the beginning to provide a description of the connection between the processes of maturation and social formation in Pacariqtambo. This entails a discussion, in the first place, of how "maturity" is defined within the community. Simply stated, in order to be considered an adult in Pacariqtambo, one must be married and, ideally, have at least one child. The normal route to a legal (civil and religious) marriage starts when a young couple begins to sleep together (with the consent of their parents) and gradually begins to accumulate household goods and a store of produce. This period in the relationship is called *servinakuy* (to serve one another). If all goes well, sometime during the first year or two the young woman will become pregnant; soon thereafter, the couple begins formally setting up a household. Depending upon a number of circumstances (e.g., the relative wealth of the couple; the amount of room available in the houses of the parents of the couple; and the ownership by one of the young people of a piece of land suitable for building a new house, etc.), the household will be patrilocal, matrilocal, or neolocal. Upon assuming residence in a household, the young couple is expected to begin contributing to the performance of community-service duties. Some of these duties are performed individually, others are performed as a couple (see below, the *ararihaus*); the majority, however, are undertaken in concert with a certain group of people; these are the groupings called *ayllu*s.

Every mature, land-holding person in Pacariqtambo belongs to one or another of ten *ayllu*s; five of the *ayllu*s belong to the moiety of *Hanansayaq* (of the upper part) five to *Hurinsayaq* (of the lower part). Children (boys and girls) are considered to "belong" to their father's *ayllu*; however, this is only a nominal membership; their father acts as their *ayllu* sponsor, or "guardian," until they reach maturity. In normal practice, young men, upon reaching maturity, become active, participating members of their father's *ayllu*, and their names are added to the roll of male *ayllu* members. Upon marriage, young women "adopt" the *ayllu* of their husbands, and they contribute throughout their lives to the activities of this *ayllu* by performing such duties as preparing corn beer (*chicha*) and food on the occasions of *ayllu* work parties. The duties of the *ayllu*s include such things as cleaning the irrigation canals, repairing the truck road, maintaining public buildings (e.g., the school, town hall, and the walls around the church and cemetery), sponsoring community-wide religious festivals, and sweeping the plazas clean of debris at the time of public festivals (Urton 1984).

Landholding is also an important consideration in the *ayllu* affiliation of a couple. That is, upon marriage, the young man is given the use of parcels of land that have previously "belonged" to his father; a young woman receives land from her mother. Although in practice, land is managed and talked about as though it is privately owned, in fact, most of the land in the community formally belongs to the *ayllu*; individuals only have usufruct rights over individual parcels of land. Although there are other factors in the interrelationship between the life cycle and the *ayllu*, the important points to keep in mind for the purposes of the discussion here are that in order to be considered a fully mature human being in Pacariqtambo one must: be married, have a child, belong to an *ayllu*, contribute to the activities of the *ayllu*, and farm *ayllu* land.

As a final note of introduction, it should be stated from the outset, since I am proposing herein to study, in part, the relationship between animals and human society, that I do not have ethnographic data which would support the suggestion, made as long ago as 1903 in the work of Durkheim and Mauss (1963), that human society is the source of classifications which are projected into an essentially passive natural world to structure the relations of phenomena in various domains of nature, such as animals and plants. Rather, when I discuss the human conceptualization of animals and the "projection" of human characteristics and relationships into the domain of animals, I will be referring to dynamic, dialectical interactions and evocations—ones in which assertions made about animals are generally formulated on the basis of an intimate knowledge of and contact with those same animals; assertions, furthermore, that are predicated equally and simultaneously on the personal, social identity of the speaker as well as on the identity and nature of the object of the utterance: the animal. Therefore, I have no reason to suppose, on the basis of the ethnographic data available to me, that animals are moved about at will, inertly as it were, as a part of an overarching, human strategy of metaphor and classificatory practice; rather, I will argue that animals are active participants in the formulations—the metaphoric syntheses—of which they themselves appear as the predicates. The theoretical position stated here will be elaborated in detail through the presentation of ethnographic data as they pertain to the two problems outlined above. In the conclusions, I will return to a more general theoretical discussion.

In the following section, I begin with a selective, rather than exhaustive, discussion of the animals that are pertinent to the problems posed earlier, moving from one animal to the next according to the associations and assertions made within the ethnographic material. This first section also provides the context for developing more fully the relevance of the human life cycle for a consideration of animals and human/animal relations.

I commence with the puma, the most highly respected and feared animal in the district of Pacariqtambo.

PUMA (FELIS CONCOLOR)

Although elusive and seldom actually seen, pumas are accorded considerable respect and attention in Pacariqtambo. They also provoke a good deal of anxiety, especially during the rainy season (December to February) when, under cover of darkness, rain, and mist, they come into the villages at night and take whatever they want to eat in the way of small, domesticated animals (pigs, chickens, etc.). The silence of the long nights of the rainy season are frequently punctuated by the near-hysterical yelping of dogs that catch the scent of a puma near the village.

Pumas are most commonly referred to in Pacariqtambo as *Machu Compadre* (ancient, male co-parent); they are also sometimes called *Paya Comadre* (ancient, female co-parent). I will discuss these terms more thoroughly in a moment, but first, I wish to mention other terms of reference and lore associated with pumas. The puma is said to be like an *altomisayoq* and a *paqo*; these terms refer to ritual specialists, usually men, who divine the future and cure illness either (respectively) through animal-spirit mediums or by reading coca leaves, corn kernels, or other objects. The puma is also believed to be the *hijo de la tierra* (child of the earth) and, therefore, able to communicate with the spirits and forces within the earth. These spirits inform pumas when someone says bad or derogatory things about them. When pumas learn of this, they go to the offending person's house at night and take an animal. During the time that I was in Pacariqtambo, the family I lived with lost a horse, a dog, and two chickens; the loss of each one of these animals was attributed to pumas. On one occasion, early in the fieldwork, a puma came to the housecompound late at night and carried away two chickens (the puma's paw prints were clearly visible the next day in the mud in front of the house). I swore at the puma and was sternly reprimanded: "Do not say unkind things about *Machu Compadre*," I was told. "When *Machu Compadre* comes for our animals, we say, 'We invite you to these chickens, *Machu Compadre*; we hope you eat well!' "

The principal terms of reference used for pumas, *Machu Compadre* and *Paya Camadre*, both denote ties of ritual co-parenthood. In order to understand the importance of these forms of address in terms of the assertions they make about the nature of the relationship between humans and pumas, it is necessary to explain how these phrases are used in the human institution of ritual co-parenthood, or *compadrazgo*. The forms of *compadrazgo* common throughout the Andes today are an amalgamation of indigenous and Spanish institutions and practices (Skar 1982, 197). In its most straightforward form, *compadrazgo* refers to the "system in which adults contract fictive or spiritual kinship through ritual sponsorship of a child or object" (Isbell 1978, 251). In most cases of the formation of *compadrazgo* ties in Pacariqtambo, the relationships are established essentially in the manner described in the above quotation from Isbell's study of the community of Chuschi (in the south-central Andes). That is, one adult, who is the parent of a child or the owner of an object, contracts with another adult to become the ritual sponsor of that child or object; the adults subsequently refer to each other as *compadre* (male) or *comadre* (female). The ritual sponsor becomes the *Marq'a Papay/Marq'a Mamay* (Quechua; *marq'ay* 'to carry in one's arms') or *padrino/padrina* (Spanish) of the child or object; the reciprocals of these latter terms are *ahijado/ahijada* (godchild).

However, there is in Pacariqtambo another, somewhat special means for contracting ritual sponsorship that is resorted to when a young couple must find ritual sponsors for their firstborn child (*phiwi*). Because it is generally considered that newlyweds are not fully mature and therefore not completely knowledgeable about contracting these important ritual ties, it is deemed best that the ritual sponsors of the firstborn child be selected by the parents of the couple; however, this procedure follows a parallel rule in which, if the child is a boy, his fathers's father selects the ritual sponsor; if a girl, her mother's mother selects the sponsor.[1] The ritual sponsors of subsequent children are selected by the parents. There are also special terms of address that go with this form of *compadrazgo*: *Machu Compadre* and *Paya Comadre* (fig. 1). *Machu Compadre* is the term used by the ritual sponsors of a baby boy for the child's father's father; *Paya Comadre* is used by the sponsors for the mother's mother of a baby girl. A male child is considered actually to "belong to" his father's father, a female child to her mother's mother. The sponsoring couple and the parents of the child call each other *com-*

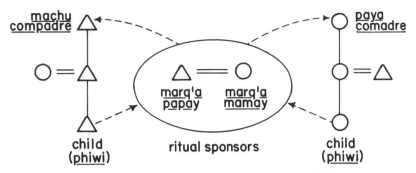

Figure 1. Ritual sponsors for a firstborn child.

padre/comadre. Within the network of relations established in this form of *compadrazgo*, the principal ties are among the grandfather, the ritual sponsors, and the newborn child; the latter is the object of the formation of the set of ritual bonds. The father and mother of the child are, in a very real sense, secondary characters, at least initially, in the formation of these ritual ties; however, as the young couple mature, they gradually assume full responsibility for maintaining this important *compadrazgo* link.

Let us now return to the puma, *Machu Compadre*. When humans use this name in references to pumas, they metaphorically evoke a particular kind of relationship between themselves (as ritual sponsors), pumas (as grandfathers of male *phiwis*), and the "son" and "grandson" of the puma. With this understanding of the social and ritual setting within which metaphorical comparisons between pumas and the grandfathers of newly born babies are situated, it is necessary to consider the remaining positions: the son and the son's son of the puma. The identity of these characters is important if the comparison between pumas and *Machu Compadres* is to have a broader meaning for the people of Pacariqtambo, who consistently make this comparison in their everyday attitudes and discourse about pumas. I will show later how, by analogy with Figure 1, the *fox* occupies the middle position as the "son" of *Machu Compadre* and the father of a newly born baby (*phiwi*); but first, I attend to the baby, the object of the *compadrazgo* relationship described above.

THE CHILDREN OF THE APUS AND THE SPRINGS

As mentioned earlier, the land within the district of Pacariqtambo encompasses considerable extremes of altitude. The central community itself is located at an altitude of 3,580 m above sea level. To the east, the land rises to high mountain puna-land (4,000–4,300 m) that is utilized in the local economies primarily as a source of good pastureland for herding. The highest mountains in the district are referred to, generically, as *apus*. These mountains are considered sacred and are thought to exercise an influence in the affairs of humans, especially through the medium of spirits, called *aukis*, who reside in the summits of the *apus*. People make offerings to these mountains and spirits; the offerings take two principal forms. One is the *despacho* (dispatch, trade), which usually consists of a collection of coca leaves (*k'intu*) that is burned or buried on the mountaintops as a form of propitation to the *apus* to act favorably for the benefit of the community (cf. Dalle 1969); for instance, *despachos* are made at the beginning of the agricultural season in August. Less elaborate but more frequent offerings to the *apus* are made by way of blowing across a glass of corn beer (*chicha*) or a coca *k'intu* and reciting the names of the *apus*.[2] These offerings and signs of respect are important in assuring the continued, benevolent interest of the *apus* and *aukis* in the affairs of the community.

Certain animals are considered to belong to the *apus*, and if humans kill one of these animals it is expected that they will both put the animal to good use and make an offering to the *apus* in exchange for it. One of the most important of these animals is the *taruka*, the deer (*Hippocamelus antisensis*); deer are often called the "cows" of the *apus*. A man once related the following story to me. When he was a young man, he killed a deer one day while in the field. He carried the deer home on his back and presented it to his father; they proceeded to cook and eat the deer. They did this, however, without first making a *despacho* to the *apus* and the *aukis*. Shortly thereafter, three of the man's cattle died, victims (my friend said) of the anger of the *aukis* who had not received payment for the deer.

Therefore, humans may use deer, but they do not own them. In this respect, the relationship between humans and deer is like the relationship between a godparent and godchild; the former is not the parent of the latter, but the godparent often disciplines the child as he is growing up and can press him into service when he needs help in his agricultural and ritual duties. Another dimension is added to this comparison between animals and other people's children when it is recognized that certain of the domesticated animals which humans keep do not actually belong to them; these are the animals that have their origin in springs in the *apus*.

There are innumerable springs in the high mountains around Pacariqtambo, many of which provide water for the extensive network of canals used to irrigate the cornfields in lower altitudinal lands to the west of the community. Mountain springs are generally called *pukiyus*, although they are also often referred to by the term *ñawi*, which means "eye" and "origin" (cf. Isbell, Franquemont, and Franquemont n.d.; Bastien 1978, 47). Several of these high mountain springs are also considered to be the places of origin of domesticated animals, especially cattle and sheep. It is believed that at the time of the new moon during the three rainiest months of the year (December to February), when water gushes forth from the mountain springs, baby cattle and sheep also frequently emerge from the springs. If a person is very fortunate, he or she may happen along the next day and claim the animal and take it home. (A person may also encourage the birth of these animals by placing a *despacho* in or near the spring.) Animals born of the mountain springs are considered to be exceptionally fecund, reproducing at least once a year when fully mature. An individual fortunate enough to acquire one of these animals might therefore build up a large herd that would have had its origin in the mountain springs and the *apus*.[3]

The person who "carries away in his arms" (*marq'ay*) one of these spring-born animals is like the *Marq'a Papay* and *Marq'a Mamay*, the ones who sponsor a firstborn baby, who care for it, and who ultimately are responsible to the grandparents of the baby for its welfare. With human babies, the progenitor/progenitrix is *Machu Compadre/Paya Comadre*; with animals born from the springs, the progenitor/progenitrix is the puma who is, simultaneously, a "child of the earth" and *Machu Compadre*. The puma exercises dominion over these animals and can come at any time to reclaim them, especially if humans speak ill of him or mistreat the animals.

NIÑUCHA—THE YOUNGER BROTHER / CHILD OF THE PUMA

In the *compadrazgo* relationship described earlier, and diagrammed in Figure 1, it is apparent that while the father and mother of a firstborn child are crucial in producing the "raw material" around which a new set of fictive kin ties begins to take shape, the mother and father themselves are, initially at least, somewhat passive members in this process; in effect, they inherit social formations constructed among one parent of the couple, their own child, and an "outsider" couple. Their position clearly epitomizes the stage of life they have reached: a transitional period in the life cycle moving from childhood to adulthood. In most Quechua communities, and certainly this is true in Pacariqtambo, people are not considered to be fully adult until they reproduce.

The transition from childhood to adulthood is a long and arduous period of developing new and different forms of behavior and of receiving from other people in the village confirmation of one's new status through signs of respect, adult terms of address, etc. In Pacariqtambo, one sign of maturity for a young man is when he is no longer addressed publically as "niñucha"; this term combines the Spanish niño (child) with the Quechua diminutive -cha (approximately equivalent to the Spanish -ito). Children are referred to as niñucha if male, niñacha if female, from about the time they begin walking and talking until they reach adolescence (adolescent boys are called maqt'a; girls, sipas); young married people may still be referred to as niñucha/niñacha if they have no children. The father of a firstborn child subsequently undergoes a change of status to one in which he will no longer be addressed as niñucha. I have explained the specific uses and connotations of the term niñucha because when humans speak about the relationship between pumas and foxes, or when they speak to the fox assuming the persona of the puma, the fox (atoq) is addressed as "niñucha."

There is some confusion (perhaps purposeful) in people's statements about the relationship between the fox and the puma. In some accounts, the two animals are brothers (wayqe), the fox being the younger brother of the puma; in other accounts, the fox is in the position of niñucha as seen from the point of view of the puma. In general, the fox is always younger than and subordinate to the puma. Foxes are sometimes also called Pascualito, hijo de la tierra (son of the earth) and perro de los machulas (dog of the ancestor spirits). Foxes, like pumas, are considered to be paqos (diviner-curers). According to one man:

> Fox [atoq] is the brother of the puma; they are both like paqos. The fox
> sleeps at night while the puma hunts; during the daytime, the puma
> often invites the fox to eat with him. In October and November, the fox
> goes to the tops of the apus [sacred mountains] around Pacariqtambo;

he fasts during this time and howls at night. If he howls very loudly and forcefully, people say: "there will be a lot of rain this year and a good harvest." However, if his howling in October and November is weak and faint, people say: "this will be a bad year with little rain."

I will have more to say later about the comparison between foxes and young men as indicated by the use of the term "*niñucha*" in references to both; however, it will be helpful first to elaborate on a point raised in the above quotation concerning the belief that when foxes howl from the mountain tops (*apus*) during the months of October and November they are foretelling the amount of rainfall and the outcome of the harvest for the next agricultural season.

In Pacariqtambo, the planting period begins in mid-August and runs until the end of November; the planting is officially brought to an end with the celebration of the festival of San Andrés, on November 30. The crops then mature throughout the rainy season (December through February), and the approximately two-month-long harvest period begins after the festival of Cruz Velakuy, on May 3 (Urton n.d.). During the planting season people attempt to "read" every available sign that might give them some indication of how good the coming harvest will be; they look at the relative brightness of the Pleiades and at the relative opacity of dark clouds in the Milky Way; they also watch for signs in the behavior of animals and birds (cf. Lira 1946; Orlove 1979; Urton 1981). The belief that the behavior of foxes foretells the abundance of the harvest is not peculiar to Pacariqtambo. The following quotation comes from Tristan Platt's work in the area of Macha, northern Potosi, Bolivia:

> If one sees the fox (*atuj*) make his way towards the high mountains in September (the time of planting), it is thought that the year will be productive in the puna; but if one sees him descending, the year will be good in the valley. Likewise, if the fox excretes the skins of potatoes, the puna will be prosperous; but if he excretes the waste of corn, the harvest will be abundant in the valley. (Platt 1978, 1085; my translation)

In addition to the very important information in the quotation from Platt showing a conceptual relationship between foxes and the crops, these data provide a truly Andean expression of animal lore since the fox is represented as a medium for synthesizing, segregating, and transferring natural products from one ecological zone to another. Although I am not aware of a form of prognostication car-

ried out in Pacariqtambo that centers on the vertical movements of
the fox from one ecozone to another, a similar idea is expressed in the
following myth told to me by different people on three occasions,
which is said to explain the origin of both foxes and cultivated plants:

> One day, there was a banquet in the sky; a condor invited a fox to ac-
> company him to the banquet. When the fox accepted the invitation, the
> condor instructed him to climb onto his back, to close his eyes and not
> to open them until they arrived. The fox did as he was instructed and
> held onto the back of the condor until they reached the sky. The fox
> then took part in the banquet, gorging himself on the good food. When
> the condor was ready to fly back to the earth, the fox was still eating so
> the condor returned without him. When the fox finished eating, he
> looked for the condor but could not find him. The fox then made a rope
> of braided *ichu* grass and began to let himself down from the sky. He
> climbed halfway down and then some *loros* [parrots] came along and
> began to pester him. He shouted at them and made them angry; the
> *loros* cut the *ichu*-grass rope with their beaks and the fox fell to earth,
> splattering his bones, hair, blood, and the food which he had eaten in
> the sky all over the earth. This is why there are now foxes everywhere
> on earth [i.e., they sprang up from the different parts of the fox's
> body].

In addition to accounting for the dispersal of foxes across the
earth, this myth also contains an explanation for the origin of agriculture. That is, while gorging himself at the celestial banquet, the
fox ate corn, quinoa and other plant foods; when he later fell to
earth, cultivated plants sprang up from the food he had eaten in the
sky. In a way similar to the fox lore recorded by Platt, this myth
characterizes the fox as the agent for carrying cultivated plants between different ecological zones. That the myth "glosses" the high
puna land as the sky is indicated by the fact that the fox uses *ichu*
grass which he obtains in the sky in making the rope for his descent
to the earth. As we will see in a moment, *ichu* grass grows only on the
tops of the high mountains, the *apus*.

I want now to follow up on two elements in the preceding material which will bring the discussion back to a consideration of foxes
and the age category subsumed under the label *niñucha*. The first element concerns the question of the vertical distribution of resource
zones in the Andes and, more particularly, of how "verticality," as a
spatial and economic concept (cf. Murra 1972), is of great importance in the ideology of the natural habitats and interrelationships

among different types of humans, plants, and animals in Pacariq-tambo. I relate the following anecdote not only because of its general relevance with regard to this question but also because it, together with the data in the quotation from Tristan Platt and the myth of the fox at the celestial banquet, will help develop a practical understanding of the ecological categories in the thinking of people in Pacariqtambo that will be important throughout the remainder of this article.

During the harvest of potatoes, each family moves itself almost literally lock, stock, and barrel into the puna. While there the family lives in a tiny hut called a *chosita*. The *chositas* are covered with a thick matting of *ichu* grass, the tall, thin grass that grows in clumps only in the very high puna. In Pacariqtambo, the principal source of *ichu* grass is on the 4,300-meter-summit of Apu Cerratachan. A day or two before the beginning of the potato harvest, each man, along with one or two of his sons, goes to the top of Apu Cerratachan and gathers enough *ichu* to construct his *chosita*.

While helping the man with whom I lived cut *ichu* for his *chosita*, we stopped around noon for a rest and had a snack of boiled corn and beans. When a person is eating vegetable produce that has been boiled, it is normally proper to remove the peels and discard them on the ground. Therefore, at the beginning of our lunch on Apu Cerratachan, I began doing as I had been trained and threw my corn and bean peels on the ground. On this occasion, however, my behavior elicited a look of consternation and the following explanation: "Do not throw your peels on the ground; these are shells of things [corn and beans] that do not grow here. If we leave them lying here, Apu Cerratachan will become sad because he does not know [or have] these plants and he will weep." We each kept our own vegetable peels, carried them home in our pockets, and tossed them to the chickens upon arriving at the house.

The similarities between the conceptualization of linked ecological and botanical categories that emerge from a comparison of this anecdote with the fox myth from Pacariqtambo and the fox lore from Macha (Bolivia) are striking. The puna and the valleys are at opposite ends of an ecological continuum; the products from each zone (potatoes and *ichu* grass from the puna; corn and beans from the valleys) are critical factors in representations, evocations, and even prognostications relating to the two zones. These data give an expanded understanding of the "proper" order of objects (e.g., animals and plants) encountered within the environment as well as classifications of the environment itself. The various categories are compounded in regional ideas and representations of the order of things and in symbolic and metaphorical constructions juxtaposing and comparing elements from a variety of domains through the movement of characters (the fox) or products (potatoes and corn) from one zone to another. I turn now to an example in which a particular type of human being—a young man with his family—moves from the settled community into the puna as a part of ritual labor obligations which signal the transformation from the status of child (or adolescent) to that of an adult *ayllu* member. These data provide an analogy between a form of human transformation and the conceptual assimilation of that transformative routine into the animal domain.

ARARIHAUS—THE PROTECTORS OF THE FIELDS

The communal potato fields of Pacariqtambo are located to the east of the community, in the middle and upper reaches of the puna (between ca. 3,600–4,200 m). These fields are usually planted from September to October and harvested in early May. During the long period of maturation, the potato plants are attractive to a number of animals (domesticated and nondomesticated) and birds; since the potato fields are so far away from the community (up to three hours by foot), it is essential that someone stand guard over the crops at all times. Every year community assemblies are held in late November—"when the leaves appear on the potato plants"—in which a few young men are elected to serve as guardians of the crops from December until the beginning of the harvest. These young men are called *ararihua* (public announcer; Lira n.d.), *papa qhawaq* (potato guard) and *mirador* (watcher; cf. Condori M. 1977, 38). Today in Pacariqtambo, the *ararihua*s are young married men who may (but are not required to) have one or two small children. In other words, they are young men who, in their life cycles, are in a position similar to the son of *Machu Compadre* in Figure 1.

One other characteristic of the individuals who fulfill the duties of *ararihua*s should be mentioned in order to understand the broader social and ritual significance of this office in its communal context. In addition to membership in one of the ten social, ceremonial and labor groups—the *ayllus*—everyone in Pacariqtambo belongs to one or the other of two moieties: either Hanansayaq (of the upper part) or Hurinsayaq (of the lower part). The communal potato fields are also divided into moiety sections, and when the time arrives to elect the *ararihuas*, one young man is elected from each moiety; the *ararihuas* are responsible for overseeing the potato fields of their respective moieties. Sometime during the period from late November to the first week of December, men from each of the moieties go to the area where their potatoes have been planted; there, they build huts (*chositas*) in which the *ararihuas* of their respective moieties will live during the growing season.

The post of *ararihua* is one of several "responsibilities" (*cargos*) that young men may assume as an entry into the traditional civil-religious prestige hierarchy, the *cargo* system. In Pacariqtambo, there are separate prestige hierarchies for each of the moieties.[4] The hierarchies consist of a number of ranked positions, each associated with particular duties, that men are elected to fulfill at different stages in their lives; for example: dancer, *ararihua*, headman of an *ayllu*, president, and mayor. The normal course of advancement through the hierarchy of a moiety involves entering the system as a young man through one of the lower-level positions, and progressively accepting more burdensome, hence more prestigious, *cargos* until, around middle to old age, he has served at all levels, and participation is no longer expected. Those who have gone through the prestige hierarchy are often referred to by the honorific "Viracocha" (roughly equivalent to "sir"). Therefore, young men who accept the post of *ararihua* and who, thereby, remove themselves and their families from settled village life in order to go into the puna for several months to oversee the crops are both providing a service to their community and moiety and, in the process, are undergoing a transformation in their own status from adolescents to adult *ayllu* members.

In light of the above description of *ararihuas*, it is important to note that the election (or appointment) of young men to oversee the crops was also a common practice in Incaic and early colonial times in the Andes. In the chronicle of Guaman Poma, there are two especially interesting drawings of *ararihuas*—one in October, the other in March—in which they are shown with fox skins thrown over their heads and shoulders, chasing animals and birds out of the fields with missiles hurled from slings (Guaman Poma 1980, 1159 [1169] and 1138 [1148]; Zuidema, this volume). Here, I want to touch on one aspect of the two drawings (figs. 2 and 3) that I will use as a point of departure for analyzing the ideology of *ararihua*s and their implicit connections with foxes in modern-day Pacariqtambo. This concerns the different familial and social representations of the *ararihua*s in the two drawings (i.e., single as opposed to married with a child). I will suggest that by differentiating between the *ararihua*s of October and March—that is, at the beginning and end of the agricultural season —in this particular feature, Guaman Poma emphasized one important element in the ideology of transformation and transition that is associated with both *ararihua*s and foxes today in Pacariqtambo.

TRANSFORMATIONS OF THE ARARIHUA AND THE FOX

In his drawing of the foxskin-clad *ararihua* in October (fig. 2), at the beginning of the agricultural cycle, Guaman Poma shows a young man standing alone in a field driving birds and an unidentifiable animal away from the newly sprouted plants. In his depiction of the *ararihua* in March (fig. 3), near the harvesttime, the young man chases birds and what is clearly a fox (it is drawn almost identically to the fox skin worn by the *ararihua*) away from the mature corn plants; in the background of the March drawing, a woman with a load of cornstalks or firewood approaches a house, in the doorway of which stands a child. Now, I do not suggest that a literal, sequential reading of these two depictions of *ararihua*s is warranted (i.e., from a young, single man to one with a wife and child), but the drawings do accurately represent the transformations that a young man undergoes today during the period that he (and his wife) resides in the field as guardian of the crops: a process of human maturation linked directly to the maturation of the crops. Guaman Poma has given us one of the most striking representations of a "theory of practice" (Bourdieu 1979) in social formation that one could hope for: the performance of a duty that is part of the process of human maturation, a duty that, itself, is performed within the context of a natural process of growth, transformation, and (re)production.

In light of the fact that the *ararihua* performs his duties in overseeing the crops from December to May, while simultaneously undergoing a change of status that will affect his position and relationships within the village when he returns, it is of particular interest to note that foxes undergo similar transformations at this time of the year as well. The Andean fox (*Dusicyon culpaeus*) begins mating in early spring (August to September), at the beginning of the planting season. The female fox has a gestation period of seven to ten weeks (Ewer 1973, 303); the *Larousse Encyclopedia* (Bertin 1973, 554) gives the period as fifty-six days. According to Walker:

> *Dusicyon* howls when abroad at night, especially during the mating season. From three to six young are born in the spring (October and November), and *the male helps in the feeding of the young*. (Walker 1964, 1160; my emphasis)

The male fox takes on familial responsibilities similar to those the *ararihua* assumes. According to the description of the behavior of foxes by a man in Pacariqtambo that I quoted earlier, the howling of foxes from the mountaintops in October and November is taken to be a prognostication of the harvest during the coming year. With the above quotation from Walker, it is clear that the prognostications of the fox would occur during the period of mating and reproduction. Therefore, the merging of the agricultural cycle with the transformation of the status of the *ararihua* and his wife through reproduction is metaphorically compared to a similar transformation that foxes undergo at this same time; the two are juxtaposed when the *ararihua*, along with his wife and child, move into the puna to oversee the potato plants. In Guaman Poma's drawings, the juxtaposition is carried one step further when the *ararihua* covers himself with the skin of a fox.

We have now followed a chain of associations among a group of animals (puma–fox–deer and domesticated animals born from mountain springs), which took as its point of departure three stages or periods of the human life cycle (grandparent–young parent–baby) expressed within the idiom of ritual co-parenthood. I will add one final animal, the bear, to the above group. The reason for introducing bears (which are not found today in the area of Pacariqtambo) into this discussion is not only because through the comparisons that are made between this animal and a certain "type" of human being —adolescents—we add another stage (and hence a new perspective) to the sequence of life cycle/animal relationships that has been developed up to this point but also because the particular comparison that is made in this instance concerns a form of human being

Figure 2.   *Ararihua* in October. (Guaman Poma 1980, 1159 [1169])

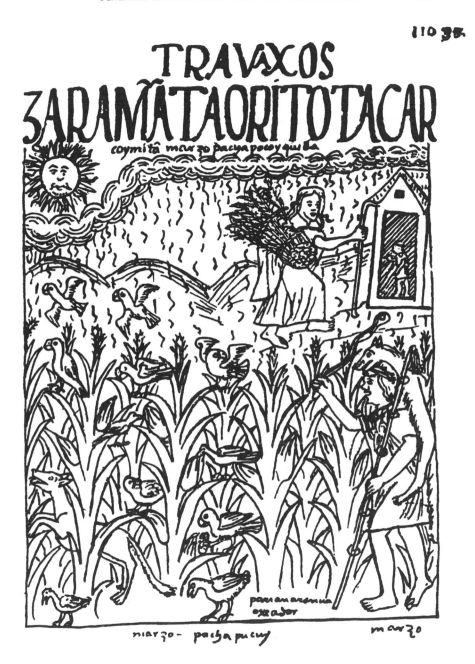

Figure 3. *Ararihua* in March. (Guaman Poma 1980, 1138 [1148])

and an animal which are considered to be on the brink of becoming fully mature human beings: that is, members of *ayllu*s.

BEARS, ADOLESCENTS, AND THE BOUNDARIES OF THE AYLLU

As Catherine Allen has pointed out in a study of bear symbolism and metaphors in Andean folklore, most of the information that people in the Peruvian highlands have about *ukuku*s (spectacled bear, *Tremarctos ornatus*), the real animals, is second or third hand (Allen 1983). *Ukuku*s are still to be found in heavily forested areas in the eastern part of the Department of Cuzco, but, for the most part, few people in communities like Pacariqtambo have ever seen an actual *ukuku*. Given the fact that they exist primarily in people's imaginations, it becomes a matter of great interest to find that *ukuku*s are among the most common animals represented by dancers in Andean villages (cf. Allen 1983; Poole n.d.). The costumes of these *ukuku* dancers are virtually identical from one village to the next in the southern highlands of Peru. They consist of a tubular-shaped garment with arms, which is pulled on over the head; the garment is covered with overlapping layers of black, multicolored or, in some cases, white fringe. A small doll (*paulucha*), which is itself dressed like an *ukuku* dancer, hangs on the front of the costume, usually on the left side of the chest; a bell or whistle hangs on the right side. The dancer wears a knitted "ski" mask that covers his head and face and has white circles around the eyes (like the spectacled bear) and a mirror over his forehead. Each dancer carries a whip of braided leather affixed to a wooden handle that is carved in spiral grooves.

In their local context, *ukuku* dancers are usually young men who begin dancing *ukuku* in festivals soon after entering puberty and continue until they reach maturity. In Pacariqtambo, *ukuku* dancers perform on such occasions as the festivals of the Virgin of the Assumption (August 15) and the Virgin of the Immaculate Conception (December 8); a contingent of *ukuku* and *majeño* dancers is sent to the great regional pilgrimage festival of Qoyllur Rit'i during the week preceding the moveable feast of Corpus Christi (see Wagner 1978; Ramirez 1969; Sallnow 1974; Poole n.d.).

Ukuku dancers are boisterous creatures; they speak in high falsetto voices (like adolescents, whose voices are on the verge of changing), are often sarcastic, and make liberal use of sexual innuendo; all these forms of speech are completely contrary to normal adult dialogue. Their behavior is extraordinary in other ways as well. Their dances are often extremely aggressive; two or three *ukukus* will often hurl themselves at one another, trying to knock each other down. In one dance maneuver, called *yawar mayu* (blood river), two *ukukus* join hands and simultaneously whip each others' calves, sometimes to the point of drawing blood.

The questions I want to address here are the following: Why do *ukuku* dancers behave the way they do? And what do *ukukus*, the animals and the dancers, have to do with mature human beings living in Pacariqtambo?

In approaching these questions, it is important to begin with a brief discussion of the animals in the natural world to which the *ukuku* dancers and stories about *ukukus* refer (for myths about bears, many of which are similar to Spanish myths, see Morote Best 1957–58 and Allen 1983). The mature spectacled bear (*T. ornatus*) ranges in length from 1.5 to 1.8 m and can weigh up to 140 kg. The body is covered with black or blackish brown fur and, in many individuals, there is a ring of white fur around the eyes that extends along the sides of the face down to the upper chest. The spectacled bear is omnivorous, feeding on leaves, roots, and fruit, and they have been reported to prey on deer, guanacos, and vicunas (Walker 1964, 1171). In his very interesting study of *ukuku* mythology, Morote Best gives information about *ukukus* collected in the area of Q'ero where these bears are still found. The *ukukus* are said to kill cows and bulls, and they also eat corn and squash. *Ukukus* will, the people of Q'ero say, run away from men but not from women (Morote Best 1957–58, 136, n. 1). In fact, there are several myths about women being raped by or having sexual intercourse with bears and subsequently giving birth to bear-human children (Morote Best 1957–58, 137–49). Although bears in nature have sexual intercourse in the dorso-ventral position, it is reported that Ecuadorian and Peruvian Quechua speakers believe that bears, like humans, can have sexual intercourse in a ventral-to-ventral position (Allen 1983, 39).

Two aspects of the "*ukuku* complex" seem especially significant. In the first place, almost no one has ever seen an *ukuku*; knowledge about these animals is through hearsay; apparently, a tradition has built up through untold generations about what *ukukus* are and how they act. Second, *ukuku* dancers are ubiquitous in southern Peruvian communities. Furthermore, the type of people who dance as *uku-*

kus—adolescents (young, unmarried men from about nine to eighteen)—is the same from one community to the next. There are two paramount considerations that should be taken into account in order to understand the importance to people in Pacariqtambo of *ukuku* dancing: one is the ideology of adolescence, and the other, the ideology of *ukukus* (those in people's imagination).

Adolescents are people who are emerging from the long period of childhood and immaturity and are about to become mature human beings. As I stated earlier, to be considered a mature human being in Pacariqtambo one must assume the responsibilities of marriage and parenthood, become a contributing member of one's *ayllu*, and farm *ayllu* land. Adolescents are not full members of their *ayllus*; therefore, they are not full human beings; they are people on their way to becoming human beings.

By the same token, it is as though *ukukus*, the bears, are not human beings but rather animals on their way to becoming human beings. Bears can walk on two legs, they perhaps can copulate ventral-to-ventral, and they eat wild and domesticated animals and corn and squash. They do these things like human beings, but they are not human beings. They are unruly, destructive, sexually aggressive, and they do not have language. They are, like adolescents, on the verge of becoming human beings.

Although people do not know a great deal about the real behavior of *ukukus* in nature, they know from tradition enough to be certain that bears are like adolescents. The important thing about *ukukus* is that they are the kind of animals that *should* exist so human society can differentiate itself from the "society" of animals in nature. That is, *ayllu* society can define adolescence as its boundary within the variations of human types, and it can define bears as its boundary at the point of contact between humans and animals. Therefore, *ukuku* dancers do not "symbolize" anything; rather, they *are* that thing. They are a combination of the one human thing (adolescents) and the one animal thing (bears) that best defines the boundary across which one must pass in order to be transformed into a mature human being: a member of an *ayllu*.

HUMAN AND ANIMAL SIMILARITIES AND DIFFERENCES

The discussion has moved from one animal, and stage in the life cycle, to another according to the logic and assertions in the ethnographic material. I now want to restructure the animal/human comparisons according to the natural, hierarchical sequence of the life cycle to which they have been linked and reexamine the implications of the data in terms of their relevance for the formulations of personal and social-group identity within the community of Pacariqtambo. Figure 4 provides a comparison of the types of humans and animals discussed in the foregoing material and juxtaposes the members of each group along the continuum of the life cycle.

HUMAN TYPES	LIFE CYCLE	ANIMAL TYPES
grandparent	elder	puma
young parent	adult	fox
child	adolescent	bear
baby	newly born	deer/spring-born animals

Figure 4. Comparison of types of humans and animals in relationship to the life cycle.

Figure 4 is intended to limit neither the "human types," nor the stages in the life cycle, nor the animals to which these types and stages are compared in the ideology of human-animal relationships in Pacariqtambo.[5] However, for the purposes of this discussion, I will restrict myself to the four categories shown in figure 4 as derived primarily from my field data.

The four "human types" shown in Figure 4 represent the principal age-grade categories into which the people of Pacariqtambo may be grouped. As has become clear through the descriptions thus far of these categories of people, each of the four types has a different set of rights and responsibilities with respect to other people in the household and the community. In general, one's social responsibilities progressively increase from birth through adulthood until, at old age, they begin to diminish. This results in a life-cycle pattern that is truly cyclical, a progression within somewhat a "closed circuit," in terms of social responsibilities, whereby the very young and the very old are merged together; the closeness between old people and first-born children is explicit in the *compadrazgo* formation described earlier. The patterns of social differentiation and group (*ayllu*) identity become increasingly important as a person enters adolescence and moves into adulthood.

When these four types of humans are projected into the animal world through the medium of metaphorical comparison, they are seen afresh in relation to a particular sequence of animals that bears certain resemblances to the hierarchy of human types. That is, the animal types progress from dependents, like deer (who belong to the *apu*s and *auki*s) and spring-born animals (who are kept as herd animals by humans), to the puma (which holds dominion over domesticated and nondomesticated animals). The intermediate stages of the animal hierarchy progresses from the unruly and potentially dangerous bear to the gluttonous fox, who assumes parental responsibilities and is the bearer of cultivated plants. The natural differences among this group of four animals in terms of patterns of dominance/subordinance, independence/dependence, and other factors are used by humans in metaphorical expressions of similar relationships and interactions among various types of humans. However, it is critical to keep in mind that these categories, or types, are not static and separate; rather, they are connected along the dynamic, hierarchical, and transformational axis of the life cycle.

With this summary of the categories of humans which are produced by the hierarchical process of the life cycle and how these categories are compared to particular animals, it is possible now to look more closely at the implications of these processes and categories in relation to human social formations and groupings in Pacariqtambo. In what follows, I will explore these implications as they lead to a clearer understanding of the typologies of humans produced by the life cycle and reproduced, in another dimension, in the *ayllu*s.

At the beginning of this chapter, I stated that the notion of "types of human beings" appears to have some validity as a concept when defined in relation to the stages of the human life cycle. This concept is a crucial one in a consideration of the sources of homogenization and diversification among the people living in a community. However, I would argue that, although the life cycle *naturally* produces an environment of human similarities and differences in which people can be grouped together on the basis of biological characteristics, the groups formed out of the life cycle are not, ultimately, biologically determined, nor are they in the end "natural." Rather, they are socially determined; society breaks the sequence of the life cycle into stages, decides who belongs to any one stage at a particular time, and generally oversees the movement of each individual from one stage to the next with rituals of transition. It seems to me that this process is similar in many respects to the way in which the people of Pacariqtambo are divided into *ayllu*s and to how the *ayllu* are maintained and reproduced from one setting to another and from one generation to the next.

It is important to bear in mind that the moieties and *ayllu*s of Pacariqtambo are hierarchically related; the upper moiety is considered to be superior—in social and ritual terms—to the lower moiety. In addition, the five *ayllu*s of each moiety are conceptualized within a hierarchy; the first *ayllu*s of the moieties have the largest memberships and sponsor the most prestigous festivals within their respective moieties (Urton 1984, n.d.).

Earlier I outlined the set of features by which the *ayllu*s in Pacariqtambo are defined, how they are mobilized, and how their memberships are reproduced from generation to generation. But the crucial, and paradoxical, point these descriptions mask is that underlying the differences between individuals which result from their belonging to different *ayllu*s, all adult people appear on the surface to be the same. By this I do not mean, of course, that all men and women in Pacariqtambo look alike, but rather that most men are equally proficient at speaking Quechua (and some Spanish), farming, making tools, braiding leather, chewing coca, fathering children, dancing, and so forth. Most women, likewise, are equally proficient at speaking Quechua, cooking, spinning, weaving, having children, and dancing. The habits of individuals are, by custom, the habits of the community as a whole. However, amidst this essential and, from the point of view of each family and of the community, desirable sameness (sanctioned by tradition), there are said to exist two major "types" of people—those belonging to the upper moiety and those of the lower moiety; each of which is divided into five "subtypes"—producing the ten *ayllu*s.

My characterization of people from different *ayllu*s being different subtypes should not be taken solely as a figure of speech, referring only or even primarily to the nominal differences indicated by the different names of the *ayllu*s or even by formal differences like the specific plots of land they farm. Rather, belonging to a particular *ayllu* "means" that you behave—or are thought to behave—in a certain way. During my stay in Pacariqtambo, this basic principle of social life was brought home to me in a variety of ways. While in the community, I lived with a family belonging to Nayhua, the first *ayllu* of the upper moiety. On one occasion, I was talking with the people in our household about the upcoming festival of San Juan. This festival, held on June 24, is the responsibility of Waychu, a lower-ranking *ayllu* of the lower moiety. I asked if the festival of *ayllu* Waychu would be a good one; would there be dancing and plenty of corn beer to drink? Would they hire bands from outside the community? These questions provoked a good deal of scornful laughter from my hosts. Of course there would be no bands; the people of *ayllu* Waychu are all old and dull; their festivals are boring. They would be more likely to entertain us with *pututu*s (traditional shell trumpets) than with bands. That's just the way they are; they're boring people. Now, as to the event, Waychu *ayllu did* have a band that year for San Juan; in fact, there were two bands and the festival was quite lively. But the point here is that it is irrelevant whether they had a band or whether the festival was lively; the point, to the contrary, is that people of Nayhua *ayllu* of the upper moiety have ways of thinking about people of Waychu *ayllu* of the lower moiety (and vice versa), and those ways of thinking are *not* constantly re-examined and reformed in the light of the actual behavior of the present-day individuals who make up these two *ayllu*s. Who the members of other *ayllu*s are and what they are like are matters fixed like canons in the mind and reaffirmed through the selective experience of each individual; they are in place because they give access, from ten different points of view, to the recognition of patterns of diversity within the apparent fabric of uniformity. The question then becomes: Is there anywhere the people of Pacariqtambo may look in order to confirm for themselves that this way of thinking about society (in which the individuals of one category are found seemingly randomly distributed among other categories) is a correct or "natural" way of thinking? Two of the principal places where they may look are the homogenizing and diversifying processes of the life cycle and to the domain of animals.

In the case of the life cycle, people, regardless of their *ayllu* and moiety affiliations, may be grouped together as the same kind of human beings on the basis of similarities in the stages of maturation and aging they have attained; each group so formed will undergo transformations in its social identity through time. The members of the same group will interact with each other differently at different stages in the joint life cycle of that group; and, as I have suggested, as each new group reaches maturity, its members become active participants in the processes of social discrimination, which ultimately have their roots in the principles and practices of social identification and group formation.

Similarly, because of processes of evolution, laws of mechanics, regularities between proportions of energy and mass—all matters of little or no interest to the people of Pacariqtambo—there exist innumerable, distinctly different kinds of animals in the environment. But amid the remarkable diversity of animals, all the individuals of each particular type behave the same way. This is merely a fact, and not one that relies upon interpretation for its validation but upon simple, repeated observation. Some animals live high up in the puna and some live low down in the valley; some eat worms and field mice and others eat corn and fruit; some may be kept as domesticated animals, others prey on domesticated animals; some mate and then part ways, and among others the males help raise the young. The redundancies and transformations of form and behavior in the animal world are of crucial importance not because they provide a domain of constancy that remains forever outside the inconstancies and inconsistencies of human society, but rather precisely because it is a realm of dynamic similarities and differences into which people can project those patterns of human and social transformation and interaction that are most essential for their own perceptions of what kinds of people they are, how they relate to each other, and how they change through time.

In the summary of the human/animal correspondences discussed here (see fig. 4), there are a number of examples in which human types are refracted into the animal world through the lens of the life cycle. The resulting human/animal categories are not static; instead, they are articulated through the socially motivated, transforming, and transformational structure of the life cycle. However, the "transformations" along the hierarchy of animal types in Figure 4 are accomplished only indirectly and metaphorically through linkages with human beings. That is, as people progress through the hi-

erarchical sequence from young to old, they are compared with
different types of animals (e.g., from deer to pumas), which, as I
have noted, can be distinguished according to such criteria as domi-
nance/subordinance and independence/dependence. Therefore, although one type of animal is not transformed into another type
(the fox does not become a puma), the hierarchy is nonetheless seen
as progressive and dynamic because it is linked together by a series
of metaphorical comparisons with human beings who are, literally,
transformed throughout life from one type to another.

These observations provide us with the language for discussing
somewhat more precisely the nature of the *ayllu* as a form of hierarchical social organization. Before stating what will amount to a
theory of the *ayllu* that is based upon the life cycle, I want briefly to
mention some of the more general implications of this term with
respect to the issues discussed up to this point.

When one looks at the ethnographic literature on the Andes, the
term *ayllu* appears to cover multitudinous forms of organization and
types of division. *Ayllu*s have generally been described as groupings
of *people* based on kinship, residence, joint rights over land, common
responsibility for labor and ceremonial obligations, and so forth. It is
particularly relevant to note in the present context, however, that
there are suggestions in the literature that the term *ayllu* originally
referred to a more general principle of the formation and recognition
of species, or "types," which (perhaps only recently) has come to be
regarded as relevant solely within the domain of human social
organization. For instance, several people who have discussed the
issue of the *ayllu* have taken as a point of departure the information
in the early seventeenth-century Quechua-Spanish dictionary of
González Holguín (1952). The use of the information in this dictionary has been selective, however; although González Holguín
does give specific uses of the term *ayllu* in relation to Andean social
organization, he also gives applications that have a more general
significance for both social *and* "natural" classifications. For example
(González Holguín 1952, 39–40):

> *Ayllu* – El genero, o especie en las cosas. (The kind [genus], or species
> of things)
> *Huc ayllu hacha* – Los arboles de una especie. (The trees of one species)
> *Huc huc ayllum cama tahuachaquiyoccuna* – Los animales son de diferentes

especies, y generos. (Animals are of different species and genera)
Angel cunam yzcum chacuchacu ayllo – Los angeles son de nueve choros
    distinctos. (Angels are of nine distinct forms [types])
Ayllo pura, o aillo ayllucama hunanacuni – Iuntarse los de un linage, o cosas
    de un genero. (To gather together those of one lineage [class], or
    the things of a genus [kind])

From the above examples, it is clear that the term *ayllu* originally
referred to a general notion of different species, or "types" of things,
and that these things were not restricted to groupings of human beings. In light of my presentation here, that the comparisons which
are consistently made between humans and animals in Pacariqtambo are formulated upon social relationships and processes of
hierarchical group formation merged with the dynamics of the life
cycle, I would argue that this same intersection of processes, relationships, and dynamics underlies the *ayllu*s as a form of hierarchical
social organization. In the one study I have carried out to date on the
*ayllu*s of Pacariqtambo (Urton 1984), I attempted to show, in a pre-
liminary way, some of the major transformations that the *ayllu* organization has undergone since the earliest references (ca. 1569) to
them in the ethnohistorical documents. I will analyze this issue more
thoroughly in a future study. For the moment, I would conclude this
section by stating that there are some indications in the etymologies
of the *ayllu* names in Pacariqtambo that point explicitly to a conceptual similarity between the hierarchical organization of the *ayllu*s and
the hierarchy of the life cycle. For example, the "supreme" or "first"
(*qollana*) *ayllu* of Pacariqtambo is consistently identified as Nayhua,
an *ayllu* of the upper moiety. In the Aymara language, from which
this *ayllu* name is derived, *nayhua*, or *nayra*, is variously glossed as
'first', 'eye', 'seed'; and (most significantly for our interest here) a
"first-born child" was called *hila nayra huahua* (Bertonio 1956).
Therefore, the oldest, supreme *ayllu* in Pacariqtambo can be compared to a firstborn child (*phiwi*). In addition, the lowest-ranking
(fifth) *ayllu* of each moiety is considered the "youngest," having been
added only within the past few decades (Urton 1984).

CONCLUSION

In concluding, I want to emphasize what is, I think, an especially
important point about a theory of the *ayllu* that takes as its point of

departure the processes of the life cycle in concert with principles of
the formation of groups reflected both in the mythology of animals
and metaphorical comparisons made between animals and humans.
Such a theory appears to coincide rather well with both indigenous,
Andean theories of social organization and the *ayllu* (cf. Zuidema
1982) and with the ideology of social and physical maturation. The
best example I can give of the latter is contained in a most remarkable story preserved in a seventeenth-century document commonly
known as *Dioses y Hombres de Huarochirí*. This story contains, I would
argue, all we need to consider in order to build a general theory of
meaning:

> It is related that, in a previous age, deer ate humans. Later, when there
> were already many deer, they were dancing in a circle, saying, "How
> are we going to eat humans?" Then, a baby deer made a mistake and
> said, "How are humans going to eat us?" Upon hearing this, all the
> deer scattered, and it is said that from that time, the deer became food
> for humans. (Urioste 1983, 36–37)

In this initially delightful story that turns decidedly sinister at the
end, the important things to note are, first, the power of assertion
(i.e., things are what they are called) and, second, that there is here
an implicit, urgent moral about why you have to learn to "get it
right." "Getting it right" means learning the proper habits, classifications, and stereotypes and improving on them through practice in
different contexts (e.g., society, animals, and agriculture) until you
no longer have to think about them. In the ironical story of the deer
quoted above, it is significant that the transformation of deer from
consumers of human flesh to human food comes about through a
mistake in language made by an *immature* deer. That is, the explanation for "how things are supposed to be" (as would be known from
the perspective of the people who would have told this story) comes
about through a mistake by an individual who was *expected* to make
mistakes; an individual (like an immature human) who was innocent
of his own nature and who, therefore, could potentially make a fundamental error about his own nature and the nature of the world.

The importance of the story of the deer is that it contains a double
truth, one linked to the other by the motif of the life cycle. The first
truth is that humans, through both the use of language and poorly
learned habits, often make mistakes; the second is that animals, who

do not use language and behave by nature rather than by habit, generally do not make "mistakes." In short, the world of animals forms a backdrop against which humans continually formulate and reformulate, in the language of metaphor, their ideology of themselves, the particular characteristics of their own forms of social interaction, and their personal and social histories.

ACKNOWLEDGMENTS

I would like to thank the following people for their comments on earlier drafts of this study: Billie Jean Isbell, Julia Meyerson, and Tom Zuidema. I am grateful to the National Science Foundation for a postdoctoral research grant (#BNS-8106254) that allowed me to carry out fieldwork in Pacariqtambo from August 1981 to September 1982. I am also grateful to the Research Council of Colgate University for support in preparing the manuscript for publication.

NOTES

1. This form of *compadrazgo* is similar in some respects to the *compadres de ramo* form of ceremonial sponsorship described by Isbell in which, at the wedding of a couple, men and women volunteer to become ritual co-partners of future children of the couple. As Isbell (1978, 114) says, "The relationship is a parallel one, *compadre* to the groom and *comadre* to the bride."

2. There are some ten major *apus* in Pacariqtambo, each having its proper name.

3. For an interesting comparison to this belief, but with regard to llamas and subterranean/spring water, see the seventeenth-century Peruvian myth of "Yacana" in Avila (Urioste 1983, ch. 29) and the discussion of this myth in Zuidema (1982) and Zuidema and Urton (1976).

4. As is true throughout Peru, the *cargo* system in Pacariqtambo has undergone a number of transformations, most of which have resulted in a diminution of the overall importance of this institution, since the time of the Agrarian Reforms of the late 1960s, early 1970s. Many positions and duties within the *cargo* system have been abolished, although the post of *ararihua* persists in Pacariqtambo.

5. For example, Rowe has shown that in traditional Andean (Inca) society, eight to twelve age-grades were recognized among both men and women for the purposes of census taking (Rowe 1958). Zuidema has discussed the role of the ten age-grades and classes in the social and political

organization of Cuzco (Zuidema 1964, 215–18 and 224–27); he has also argued persuasively that in Inca mythology and social organization there are consistent comparisons made between a group of six animals and six sociopolitical groups and marriage classes (Zuidema 1982).

REFERENCES

Allen, Catherine
    1983   Of bear-men and he-men: Bear metaphors and male self-perception in a Peruvian community. *Latin American Indian Literatures* 7(1):38–51.
Bastien, Joseph W.
    1978   *Mountain of the condor: Metaphor and ritual in an Andean ayllu.* American Ethnological Society, Monograph no. 64. St. Paul, Minn.: West Publishing Company.
Bertin, Leon, et al.
    1973   *Larousse encyclopedia of animal life.* London and New York: Hamlyn.
Bertonio, Ludovico
    1956   *Vocabulario de la lengua Aymara* (1612). La Paz: Don Bosco.
Bourdieu, Pierre
    1979   *Outline of a theory of practice.* New York: Cambridge University Press.
Condori Mamani, Gregorio
    1977   *Gregorio Condori Mamani: Autobiografía.* Ed. R. Valderrama Fernández and C. Escalante Gutiérrez. Cuzco: Centro de Estudios Rurales Andinos "Bartolomé de las Casas."
Dalle, Luis
    1969   El despacho. *Allpanchis Phuturinga* 1:139–54.
Durkheim, Emile, and Marcel Mauss
    1963   *Primitive classification* (1903). Chicago: University of Chicago Press.
Escobar Moscoso, Mario
    1980   Estudio comparativo de los valles de Urubamba y el Apurimac. *Actas y Trabajos del III Congreso Peruano "El Hombre y la Cultura andina"* 4:657–74.
Ewer, R. F.
    1973   *The carnivores.* Ithaca: Cornell University Press.
González Holguín, Diego
    1952   *Vocabulario de la lengua general de todo el Perú llamada Qquichua o del Inca* (1608). Lima: Imprenta Santa Maria.
Guaman Poma de Ayala, Felipe
    1980   *El primer nueva coronica y buen gobierna* (1583–1615). Ed. J. V. Murra and R. Adorno. Mexico, D.F.: Siglo XXI.
Isbell, Billie Jean
    1978   *To defend ourselves: Ecology and ritual in an Andean village.* Latin American Monographs. no. 47. Austin: University of Texas Press.
Isbell, Billie Jean, Ed. M. Franquemont, and Christine Franquemont
    n.d.   The unfolding of symmetries: The structuring of Andean cloth. Paper presented at a symposium on "Cloth and the organization of human experience," September 28 to October 5, 1983, Wenner-Gren Foun-

dation for Anthropological Research Symposium no. 93, Troutbeck, Amenia, New York.

Lira, Jorge A.
1946   *Farmacopea tradicional indígena y prácticas rituales.* Lima: Talleres graficos "El condor."

Morote Best, Efraín
1957-   El oso raptor. *Archivos Venezolanos de Folklore* 5:157–58.
1958

Murra, John V.
1972   El "control vertical" de un máximo de pisos ecológicos en la economía de las sociedades andinas. In *Visita de la provincia de León de Huánuco en 1562, Iñigo Ortíz de Zuñíga, Visitador*, vol. 2, ed. John V. Murra. Huanuco: Universidad Nacional Hermilio Valdizan.

Orlove, Benjamin S.
1979   Two rituals and three hypotheses: An examination of solstice divination in southern highland Peru. *Anthropological Quarterly* 52(2):86–98.

Platt, Tristan
1978   Symétries en miroir: Le concept de Yanantin chez les Macha de Bolivie. *Annales Economies, Société, Civilizations* 33:(5/6):1081–107.

Poole, Deborah A.
n.d.   Rituals of movement, rites of transformation: Pilgrimage and dance in the highlands of Cuzco, Peru. In *Latin American Pilgrimage*, ed. N. R. Crumrine and A. Morinis. In press.

Ramiriz, Juan Andres
1969   La novena al Señor de Qoyllur Rit'i. *Allpanchis Phuturinga* 1:61–88.

Rowe, John H.
1958   The age grades of the Inca census. In *Miscellanea Paul Rivet octogenario dicata*, 499–522. XXXI Congreso Internacional de Americanistas. Mexico, D.F.

Sallnow, Michael
1974   Le peregrinación andina. *Allpanchis Phuturinga* 7:101–42.

Skar, Harald
1982   *The warm valley people: Duality and land reform among the Quechua Indians of highland Peru.* New York: Columbia University Press.

Urioste, George L.
1983   *Hijos de Pariya Qaqga: La tradición oral de Waru Chiri* (1606). Foreign and comparative Studies Program, Latin American series, no. 6. 2 vols. Syracuse, New York: Maxwell School of Citizenship and Public Affairs.

Urton, Gary
1981   *At the crossroads of the earth and the sky: An Andean cosmology.* Latin American Monographs, no. 55. Austin: University of Texas Press.

1984   *Chuta*: El espacio de la práctica social en Pacariqtambo, Peru. *Revista Andina* 3:7–56.

n.d.   Calendrical cycles and their projections in Pacariqtambo, Peru. Forthcoming in *Ethnoastronomy: Indigenous astronomical and cosmological traditions of the world*, ed. John B. Carlson and Von del Chamberlain. Washington, D.C.: Smithsonian Institution Press.

Wagner, Catherine A.
1978   Coca, chicha and trago: Private and communal rituals in a Quechua

community. Ph.D. diss., University of Illinois, Urbana-Champaign.

Walker, Ernest P., et al.

1964   *Mammals of the world*. Baltimore: The Johns Hopkins University Press.

Zuidema, R. T.

1964   *The ceque system of Cuzco: The social organization of the capital of the Inca*. Leiden: E. J. Brill.

1982   Myth and history in ancient Peru. In *The logic of culture: Advances in structural theory and methods*, ed. I. Rossi, 150–75. South Hadley, Mass.: Bergin and Garvey Publishers, Inc.

Zuidema, R. T., and Gary Urton

1976   La constelación de la llama en los Andes peruanos. *Allpanchis Phuturinga* 9:59–119.

The Metaphoric Process: "From Culture to Nature and Back Again"

Billie Jean Isbell

Introduction:
From Culture to Nature and Back Again

The subtitle *From Culture to Nature and Back Again*[1] is an attempt to convey an iconic image of what I believe to be the essence of the metaphorical process that becomes constituted through socialization. The use of animal imagery to convey cultural values, as Turner argues, *mis*represents problematic human relationships as natural (e.g., the story of the "mistake" of the baby deer at the end of Urton's article). This "naturalizing" of human relations creates a productive ambiguity between culture and nature; and, much like an expanding and contracting rubber band, the semantic and emotional distance between the two domains are continually reduced or expanded depending upon the contexts and syntagmatic chains created in performance. One result is that conceptually the two domains are constantly undergoing comparative scrutiny as likenesses and differences between cultural and natural domains are elaborated upon. Nature seems to provide culture a negative view of itself, whereby moments of negativity are extremely productive because solutions to life's perplexing problems are presented in metaphorical imagery.

As Urton has argued, the invidual is the recipient of metaphorical messages in myth and ritual. I would add that the emotional components of the metaphorical process enhance the internalization of culturally defined solutions. Therefore, emotional and cognitive dimensions are continually intertwined. In this presentation I take Paul Ricoeur's (1978) perspective on metaphor to South America and expand upon it. The metaphoric process thus *moves* the individual along life's course with imagery that is understood at different points in developmental time on different intellectual and emotional levels. The single coherent image in all of the essays in this volume is movement through life's transitions as a complex metaphorical process whereby both animal and human images are elaborated upon.

At significant points of transition in the life cycle an individual is confronted with new problems, potentials, and new cultural definitions of appropriate behaviors and roles. The guideposts along the path from birth to old age are carved with vivid imagery that depict synthetic cultural stereotypes of one's emerging identity. In the cultures of South America under discussion, cultural stereotypes are embodied in animal forms. As an example let us take a major point of transition: from nonreproductive adolescent to reproductive adult. Young married men become the brothers of macaws among the Bororo, whereas for the Kayapó young adolescent boys are depicted as helpless macaw fledglings who are captive in their nests until they are transformed into adult fire-bearing jaguar/hunters. The Warao on the other hand think of bachelors as robber bees (called honey penises) who are apt to rob the nest of prospective in-laws. For the Desana, the focal problematic relationship is the father-in-law who is compared to a tapir—oversexed and emblematic of excess. The Desana are patrilineal and patrilocal, and therefore the father-in-law relationship is described from the perspective of the family of the in-marrying bride. Among the Quechua of Peru young unmarried men are like unsocialized, sexually unbridled bears who upon becoming reproductive are compared to foxes. True maturity is analogous to the powerful characteristics of the puma.

It is most illustrative to note that the Bororo, the Kayapó, and the Warao share several important features: they are all tropical-forest matrilineal groups who practice uxorilocal postmarital residence, which means that young men are displaced from their natal homes into often hostile environments. Wilbert states, for example, that the Warao groom endures bride service for the lifetime of his spouse. We must ask why these animal images are used for the problematic transition from adolescent to reproductive adult. Why bees and fledgling macaws as metaphors for adolescents? Or pet macaws as young married men? If society were the sole source of classificatory and metaphoric images, might we not expect similar societies to project similar human relations onto similar animals? Rather, we see that animal and human dimensions interact in specific contexts such that culturally coherent bundles of meaning are generated. For example, in the syntagmatic contexts of the Kayapó myth, the adolescent boy/fledgling macaw is transformed into the hunter/ jaguar. In the Bororo case pet macaws are transformed into spirits and young married men are transformed into macaws through ritual performance. Therefore, since similar relationships are communicated by quite diverse complexes of metaphorical meanings, I suggest that we construct an anthropological perspective on metaphor that examines the process whereby problematic human relations are *mis*represented as natural. This metaphorical link between social and natural domains creates a tension and an ambiguity that move the individual in the direction of idealized images or stereotypes of culturally defined transitions. My specific contribution to this collection is to suggest how the metaphoric process moves the individual on both emotional and intellectual levels through the productivity of "Entitlements and Essences" and through "Iconicity and Synesthesia." After discussing these concepts with examples from this volume, I will turn to an old anthropological dilemma: "Totems and Fetishes." Then, I adapt Ricoeur's notion of the metaphoric process to the anthropological enterprise in "Toward an Anthropological Theory of Metaphor." And finally, I close with a few final reflections entitled "Movement and the Metaphoric Process."

ENTITLEMENTS AND ESSENCES

My point of departure adapts Ricoeur's (1978) perspective on metaphor to the anthropological enterprise to argue that we cannot separate intellectual and emotional aspects of the metaphoric process. On the contrary, sounds, smells, shapes, and activities are essential components of that process, and each provides for a particular sensory and/or intellectual suspension of direct reference whereby new connections, comparisons, and distinctions are discovered. I would like to begin with some thoughts about how and why metaphorical complexes or bundles of meaning cohere together. First, let me borrow a term from Kenneth Burke (1966, 359–79) to describe what I think is central to the coherence that underlies the metaphoric process. Burke points out that the title of a novel sums up the vast complexities of elements, giving it its essence or general drift. He coins the term *entitlements* for this sum of complexities brought to mind by a title. We can think of the sum of images, words, sounds, smells, tastes, movements, and activities as entitlements that give the metaphor at hand its essence. Think of all of the figurative associations that come to mind if I invent the following titles for the chapters in this volume:

Men Are Household Pets

Down from the Tree to Manhood

The Stench of the Obese Tapir

The Warao Tale of "The Birds and the Bees"

The Inca Boys Race as the Puma Men Drum

From Bear to Fox to Puma

Now think of the accompanying and contrasting "pictures" of animal images that these titles evoke. Next imagine the iconic and synesthetic codes associated with each animal that is in turn associated with each title. The natural animal emblem (or fetish, to use Turner's term) sums up the "experiential gestalts" (Lakoff and Johnson 1980, 117) associated with key metaphoric chains. Lakoff and Johnson (1980, 44) further argue that the connection between metaphors more often entails coherence rather than consistency. That is, the images that *fit together* in a metaphoric system share a general concept rather than form a consistent image. In Ricoeur's terms, the lack of consistency is vital because ambiguity provides for productivity. I will add to ongoing discussions on metaphor by observing that in all of the essays in this volume the symbolic and metaphoric complexes discussed focus on problematic life experiences. The metaphors for these problematic experiences—sexual conjunction, the displacement of men, and the passage into adulthood—cohere or fit together because they reinforce the culturally defined solutions to life's problems. Metaphorical messages "picture" the solutions to these problems in intellectual and emotional terms. Moreover, the metaphorical answers to life's puzzles keep the individual *moving* through syntagmatic and paradigmatic mazes of mythic and ritual expression. Motion through space is the one code that is shared by all of the figurative expressions in these cultures. The transition from boyhood to manhood for highland Quechua cultures moves or races up and down the topography of mountaintops and valleys (Zuidema). The lowland Kayapó and Bororo utilize the imagery of movement from village to forest and from ground to treetops as a fundamental coherent image; whereas the Desana and the Warao focus on the twirling, entwining, and circling movements associated with the sex act as their primary coherent image. In all cases, the answers to life's problematic experiences are given in complex cultural performances whereby individuals participate in the web of metaphors that can be apprehended on numerous intellectual and emotional levels. The metaphoric process propels the individual along the path of maturation with images that bounce "from culture to nature and back again," establishing analogies between the human and animal worlds and thereby transforming them.

Fernandez (1972, 43) has suggested that we view metaphor as "a strategic prediction upon an inchoate pronoun (an I, a you, a we, a they) which makes a movement and leads to performance." He views culture as a quality space and society as a movement of pronouns within this space. Metaphors, he argues, operate on continua: up-down, hard-soft, light-dark, and so forth. Metaphoric processes move their subjects along a dimension or set of dimensions. The destinations of the metaphoric movement along the life cycle are the ideal types, the models, that culture values: the quality of the hunter/jaguar for the Kayapó or the beauty of the macaw/spirit for the Bororo. The movement of metaphor is best seen in Urton's paper where the inchoate male individual is first modeled after a bear. He *becomes* the bear in ritual performances. Then, when he is initially reproductive with one or two children, he is compared to the fox; and as the fox he guards the planted fields. After assuming adult responsibilities such as performing the duties of godfather, sponsoring rituals for his *ayllu*, and serving in various communal offices, he becomes like the puma. The continua upon which these metaphoric animal images move are from sexually unbridled to socially reproductive, from self-gratifying to self-sacrificing for communal interests, from irresponsible to responsible. In ritual settings the bear is performed as a silly, chattering creature who is the emblem of the unsocialized male. Note that the bear comes from below in the tropical forest and invades Andean villages to impregnate women and wreak havoc on civilized life. The puma is the model of strength, wisdom, and maturity who is the older brother of the fox. Both are associated with the earth and fertility of domesticated animals. The howl of the fox prognosticates the fecundity of the herds as well as the amount of rain and the quality of the harvest.

The fox figure is interesting. He, like the puma, is "a son of the earth," a diviner-curer; he is clearly associated with agriculture as well as with herds. But the fox is the model of the unreliability of young adulthood. During early adulthood a man is probably reproducing society as the father of one or two children, but there is a 50 percent chance that his children will die. He is the guardian of the fields, but agriculture is precarious. It is thus understandable that the fox is the trickster figure in Andean culture. Likewise, young in-marrying men perform trickster-affine roles in the rituals of their wives' families. Their inclusion in weddings and funerals, for example, is considered essential. Young adulthood is the major life-cycle transition and, by the young husband's actualizing the character of the fox, both the problems and potentialities are emphasized.

The theme of movement is central in Zuidema's chapter. Consider the iconic imagery of the Inca puma-men who wait for the young noblemen to race to the mountaintops and back to the center of Cuzco to become initiated as adult men. The tokens (to use Turner's term) of their adulthood included a shield, club, and sling for warfare. The puma-men pierced the ears of the initiates in cultivated fields near sources of water; and the initiation rite occurred during the December solstice, which is the point of time when the sun makes a visible turn from its extreme southern point on the horizon and begins its march to its northernmost extreme, which marks the June solstice. The sun, states Zuidema, was believed to be at its strongest in December. The boys' initiation culminated with a ritual bath, after which they donned adult dress. Other aspects of transition during this time concerned the agricultural cycle: planting stopped, heavy rains commenced, and the young initiates were transformed into warrior/fox-boys who battled snow, hail, and predators and sang victory songs to ensure the harvest. Again, we see the theme of transition and movement in the social, natural, and domesticated world "entitled" in the images of pumas and foxes. One of the major transitions of the life cycle for Inca youths was coordinated with the movement of the sun, the flowering of domesticates, and the return of irrigation water to the rivers. The puma priests played drums (in imitation of thunderclaps of the oncoming torrential rains) continually for six days before piercing the ears of the initiates. We can imagine the emotionally highly charged experiential gestalt the Inca boys must have felt as they "raced toward manhood."

CONNECTING THE INTELLECTUAL AND THE EMOTIONAL
THROUGH ICONICITY AND SYNESTHESIA

An often raised issue is the place of emotion or feeling in symbolic and metaphoric processes (see Fernandez 1974). Many authors object to the so-called excessive intellectualism of Lévi-Straussian structuralism. Others object to many theories of metaphor that exclude emotion from their considerations (for example Richards 1936; Black 1962, 1979). I agree with Ricoeur (1978) that there is a structural analogy between the cognitive, the imaginative, and the emotional components of the metaphorical process.

As Charles Osgood (1975, 396) has pointed out, a fundamental characteristic of human thinking involves the lawful translation from one sensory modality to another (synesthesia) along dimensions made parallel in perceiving. Although Osgood limits his discussion to auditory-visual synesthesia, this collection of essays provides us with abundant evidence for multiple sensory modality translations. It appears to me that in cultural contexts, synesthesia is the means of establishing basic similarities between disparate domains in addition to providing the necessary sensory data for the structured coherence essential to the emotional base found in metaphor production. The more numerous the sensory modalities that are translated, the more powerful the "interiorization of thoughts" (Ricoeur's notion of feeling). Synesthesia is one of the cognitive processes by which iconicity is achieved. Often the translation of one sensory modality into another is accomplished in the syntagmatic chains of ritual or myth. Metaphor and synesthesia both translate experience from one domain into another by operating on a commonality that can be generalized (Fernandez 1972, 47).

Consider the example of the Inca puma-men discussed above. By making the sounds of thunder while presenting the visual image of pumas, they become the generalized icon for rain/fertility of the earth/makers of men. The synesthetic bundles acquire new meanings when they pierce the ears of the initiates, who thereby are symbolically fertilized as well. A new chain is created, and blood/rain fertilizes the planted fields. By including numerous sensory experiences—visual images, auditory representations, bodily pain, the race up and down the mountains, not to mention the feasting and drinking that accompanied the rite—the interiorization of meaning produces the desired emotional response. The initiates *experience* emotionally and intellectually the model of the social stereotype that is the goal of their social transformation. They become foxes soon to be pumas themselves.

Salient examples of synesthesia are provided in Reichel-Dolmatoff's chapter. As ancestors, the mythical tapir people provided women to the Desana and thus became the Desana's first exchange partners. The tapir plays other significant mythical roles as well. The tapir's voice was stolen by the earlier Desana and transformed into the sound of the sacred trumpets, leaving the tapir with a pitifully weak and squeaky voice. When the large sacred trumpets are played, the ripe pollen on the palms and other fruit-bearing trees "vibrates" and falls down, fertilizing the trees. The Desana shamans equate this process with human sexuality; thus, the sound becomes a generalized icon.

The Desana have elaborated a complex symbolic system centering upon the perceived qualities of the tapir, the largest mammal of the tropical rain forest. In his exploration of the avoidances that surround the tapir, Reichel-Dolmatoff discovers that various sensory modalities are associated with the metaphoric complex. The following synesthetic translations are attributed to the tapir: *shapes*—forked objects that refer to copulation; twisted threads that refer to a line of descent; hourglass designs worn by women married to Desana men. *Smells*—humanlike body odor. *Tastes*—too strong, too fat, too tough. *Sounds*—the sacred trumpets are the stolen voice of the tapir. These various sensory experiences are structured into a *gestalt*, an image, a complex of depicted relations upon which the metaphoric process operates. This gestalt is now imbued with feeling because it is interiorized through various senses.

This sensory experience of the tapir centers on unbridled sexuality. The male tapir is believed to have oversized testicles; moreover, the animal's diet is said to consist of foods that are aprodisiacs. Supporting linguistic evidence adds to our growing picture of coherence. The term that is used to refer to the tapir is used also to refer to fathers-in-law; the same lexical term also means "saturated" or "satisfied." The compounded images communicate excesses of all types: too large, too tough, too fat, too sexual, and so forth. Excess is the cultural coherence that underlies the various images.

The Desana have utilized sensory modalities to classify phenomena. One classificatory scheme is organized by attributed "color energies" (Reichel-Dolmatoff 1978); another classificatory scheme links animals and humans by olfactory qualities (Reichel-Dolmatoff, this volume). The dichotomy between moderation and excess appears to be a primary organizing principle in these classificatory schemes. The Desana eschew all forms of excess and value moderation as a behavioral goal; therefore, the coherent images of excess communicate a value that is *in*consistent with the cultural value of moderation. Moreover, the category of foreign, which is tantamount to exaggerated excess, is expressed metaphorically through the tapir/father-in-law analogy. Thus, although the foreign father-in-law assumes the qualities of the tapir—over-sexed, gluttonous, and unsavory—conversely, the tapir becomes an old man, impotent, and forbidden. The semantic distance between the two domains is reduced by the coherent sensory structure expressing the Desana notion of excess. In addition, this sensory structure is the basis for iconicity through which the intellectual and the emotional are united.

Wilbert's chapter on the Warao provides other examples of the importance of synesthesia and iconicity in the construction of metaphors. Wilbert analyzes the Warao origin myth of the primordial House of Smoke with its original mythical inhabitants: the red wasp, the black bee, the blue bee, the yellow termite, the blind snake, and the swallow-tailed kite. The latter is the creator-youth in the myth. Wilbert argues that the House of Smoke represents a replica of the ecological food chain of these creatures, who, in real life, are engaged in a compelling struggle for survival. Conversely, in the House of Smoke, they coexist peaceably because their aggressive natures are contained by the powerful insecticide, nicotine. In this wispy but potent container in the Upper World, the insects are obligated to continuously play a game of chance.

In the game/dance that takes place in the mythical House of Smoke, the players continually invade each other's space according to the throw of the dice by the swallow-tailed kite/mythic hero. The

winner/invader is given renewed life by the serpent, who has a luminous ball on the tip of her(his) tongue.[2] The name of the game also
means "to take excessive sexual liberties with someone's wife."
Only the power of tobacco constrains the destructive potential of the
natural animosity of the game/dance/sex. The iconic images ration-
alize the *naturalness* of animosity between the sexes and the necessity
to overcome their natural aggression in order for society to reproduce itself.

Iconicity and synesthesia abound in Wilbert's rich analysis. The
iconicity of shapes and motion are especially striking: the dance
rattle/phallus and the calabash gourd/uterus connote sexual conjunction; the movements of men during copulation are compared to fire
drilling and spinning toy tops. These latter images are so obviously
sexual that the Warao prohibit women from engaging in either of
these activities. Activities and motor patterns appear to provide
another avenue for the interiorization of feelings and thereby give an
emotional "punch" to the imaginative level of figuration. The
translation of these sexual images to auditory sensations further
enhances the affective dimension of Warao metaphors. The buzzing
sound of termites is compared to the sound of the dance rattle, which
is the key conjunctive symbol for sex. One last example will suffice to
illustrate the importance of iconicity and synesthesia to the metaphoric process. For many tropical forest cultures, the sweetness of
honey is explicitly equated with sexual orgasm. Only deities and
shamans eat honey undiluted; however, the Warao say that honey
and tobacco are their original and true foods. Remember that the
mother-of-honey/bee wife/frigate releases the kite/hero shaman/
master of tobacco from his seizurelike state. Again, another sensory
experience participates in the construction of the metaphors through
which the Warao understand the complexities, pleasures, and problems of human sexual relations. The sensory experiences discussed
above provide the essential link between synesthetic levels of feeling,
cognitive levels of perceiving and organizing, and imaginative levels
of figuration. Synesthesia and iconicity provide the means to unite
the emotional with the intellectual in such a way as to provide
powerful but diverse messages to an individual at different points in
her(his) life. The polysemous bundles of meanings that communicate the cultural norms and attitudes about sex are complex
and varied enough to provide guideposts along the way as an in-

dividual Warao unravels the mysteries of sex for herself or himself. What makes the metaphoric messages in myth and ritual meaningful throughout life is that different levels of intellectual and emotional understanding are achieved and tested by experience. The metaphors are kept alive though developmental praxis. Changing experiences are interpretable through the metaphoric process which is sustained by an underlying system of cultural coherence. Metaphoric "picturings" involving shapes, colors, movements, sounds, smells, and even tastes cohere around a focal cultural value. Thus, the metaphors that are kept alive generation after generation are those which express the *essence* of a cultural value. The *essences* that move throughout a lifetime are necessarily contradictory. For example, the Bororo man overcomes the apparent contradictions in the cultural value of reproducing a society that subjugates him to a domesticated petlike existence in his wife's house when he metaphorically transcends those dilemmas by becoming the other configuration of the macaw as a beautiful vehicle for a spirit of the dead. The synesthetic entitlements of the spirit/macaw include extended chants that describe the various activities of the spirits of the dead referred to metaphorically as "a multicolored cloth which stretches just as a trail along which singers and the song progress." The multicolored cloth is an image of the multicolored *essence* of spirit, which in turn is manifest in the multicolored plumage of the macaw. The Bororo man adorned in macaw feathers, therefore, becomes the metaphor through synecdochic or syntagmatic associations (as does the *ararihua* in Zuidema's article who dons the skin of a fox).

TOTEMS, FETISHES, AND CLASSIFICATION

In the late 1960s and early 1970s, a series of influential articles appeared focusing on the questions of totems, taboos, and anomalous animals (Beidelman 1975; Bulmer 1967; Douglas 1966, 1972, 1973, 1975; Leach 1964; Tambiah 1969). Bulmer (1967, 25) responded to Douglas's 1966 theory of pollution with the observation that pollution is indeed associated with things that are out of place; "but the problem is that things can be out of place in so many different ways, in terms of so many different, even if linked dimensions." That statement holds true today, and we can add that things can be *ordered* and *classified* in so many different ways as well. Tambiah (1969) concluded that the answer to why humans have ritual attitudes toward animals is still a haunting question. He argues that the answer will demonstrate that intellectuality and emotionality cannot be rigidly separated. His discussion is just as pertinent today as it was in 1969. The same point has been made by Fernandez (1972, 1974, 1977). Moreover, classifications and cognitive schema function on intellectual, functional, and emotional levels of experience.

Two of the authors in this volume (Crocker and Turner) directly address the question of totems and taboos. The relationship of prohibitions to classificatory systems, however, is either explicit or implicit in all of the essays. Both Crocker and Turner explicitly discuss the applicability of the concept of totem to their analyses. Crocker argues that there are general difficulties with Lévi-Strauss's absolute division between natural and cultural realms, and instead of division he focuses on the bases of comparisons and connections between cultural and natural realms. This is a perspective shared by all the authors; whether they share Crocker's reading of Lévi-Strauss is not clear. Crocker concludes that certain Bororo "ritual attitudes" toward macaws as "brothers" involve cultural and natural synecdoches. That is to say, a part of the whole, or vice versa, operates between cultural and natural domains—between men's ambiguous position in a matrilineal, uxorilocal society and macaws' ambiguous position as pets, which places them between nature and culture. Other comparisons he argues involve syntagmatic contiguity, but he would hesitate to label macaws "totems." What is clear is that the Bororo connect their paradigm of the essence of "macawness" with their paradigm of the essence of "maleness." The macaws' ambiguous position between nature and culture serves as a way of picturing men's ambiguous position in society when the Bororo claim that "men are macaws."

In Turner's terms this *mis*representation of men's position in the social structure as "natural" is an instance of fetishism on the hoof. He argues that animals (such as macaws and jaguars) are so heavily used as symbols because "they are the most suitable symbolic vehicles for the alienation of human (social) consciousness of the social nature of social phenomena through the *mis*representation of those phenomena as 'natural.'" Thus the ambiguous positions of men in Bororo, Kayapó, and Warao societies are *mis*represented as "natural." I would like to add that underlying this "natural" *mis*representation is a cultural system of coherence that embodies their notion of displacement. As already noted, men in these matrilineal societies are displaced from their natal homes into the domain of their wife's household; macaws are displaced as fledglings from their nests into the households of women as their pets. "Robber bees" potentially displace the brood of other species of bees just as sons-in-law displace their wives' parents.

Now let's return to the issue of taboo and anomalous classificatory status. As Crocker has summarized, various anthropologists have pointed out that pets are excellent vehicles for complex symbolism because they are structurally anomalous (neither human nor animal). But as Bulmer (1967, 25) has observed, there are so many ways that animals can be seen as out of place. My point is that conversely, there are so many ways in which animals can be considered *in place*. I suggest that a systematic relationship may pertain in many cases in which animals are considered "out of place" (anomalous in nature and *in place* in culture). For example, in several cases from this collection, the "out of place" animals become exemplar figures for defining metaphorically desirable human qualities. For Andean cultures past and present (Zuidema, Urton) the puma epitomizes the qualities of adult male status. For the Kayapó and Bororo, the jaguar is the model of the hunter, and the pet macaw is the model of the displaced male. For Andean peoples, however, the jaguar is the epitome of the savagery that they believe characterizes everything about the tropical forest. One culture's anomaly may be another culture's exemplar or prototype. Moreover, anomalies attributed to natural categories may become cultural prototypes. The peripheral animal in nature may become transformed into the exemplar "essence" or focus of a category in culture (fathers-in-law, fathers, hunters, shamans, etc.). These transformations should be a part of symbolic analysis.

Classificatory systems are complex cultural constructs that address many human activities. Some function simply as identification procedures for perceptual phenomena (Anderson et al., in press) and others function to identify exemplariness or prototypes (Rosch 1975, 1978a, 1978b).[3] In addition, even motor patterns (Rosch 1978a, b) or "activity signatures of taxa" (Hunn 1982) may be the organizing principles for classificatory schemes. Over the past two decades, anthropologists and psychologists have been searching for

the key to organizational principles of conceptual domains and classificatory systems. It is now clear that peoples' responses do not
reflect the organizational principles of their cognitive categories (Anderson et al., in press) or classificatory schema (Randall 1976).

Rather, cognitive schema must be studied in use and in context.
Even though subjects cannot describe what it is to be a tapir, a
puma, a macaw, or a swallow-tailed kite, they still maintain the idea
that there are *essences*[4] of these animals. The qualities attributed to
animals become potential key elements in activating cognitive
schema in specific contexts.

For example, the anomalous qualities of the tapir provide a
bundle of meanings that surround the image of the animal. The
essence of the animal is wrapped up in the bundle of meanings that
constitute the metaphorical connection between the tapir as father-
in-law and the tapir as animal. He (father-in-law *cum* tapir) is considered sexually overactive with genitalia that are too large. He is
considered a glutton and a rank-smelling male. But at the same time
he is thought to be a powerful ally, a swift but clumsy runner, and a
graceful dancer. Among the Desana, these qualities are attributed to
foreigners in general and to fathers-in-law in particular. The statement, "my father-in-law, the tapir," or calling the tapir "the old
man," translates both natural and cultural idioms into one another.

In classificatory terms, the tapir is grouped with two other large
mammals of the Amazonian rain forest, the deer and the peccary.
The three are the largest mammals of the tropical rain forest; they
are fairly abundant, especially the deer and the peccary. Among the
animals of the tropical rain forest, the tapir is called "old club-foot,"
referring to its status as the only ungulate in the Desana category of
large mammal; this further contributes to its anomalous status in the
classificatory system. The Desana classify game animals into larger
animals that are prohibited as food and smaller animals that are
preferred as food. The preferred animals include the paca, the
agouti, the armadillo, and the tinamou. Reichel-Dolmatoff gives a
number of practical reasons for this preference: the deer and the peccary must be tracked into the depths of the forest, whereas the
smaller animals can be found near household compounds; in addition, even though the tapir responds to the hunter's call, it is a
solitary animal and therefore more difficult to hunt. The Desana

claim that the deer, the peccary, and especially the tapir are repugnant; they have strong body odors and their meat tastes too strong. In combination, these qualities render the meat of these animals indigestable. The taste and smell of the tapir's flesh is attributed to its preference for foods that increase sexual appetite and fertility. Even with these characteristics, the tapir is considered to be a clean animal because it spends so much time in the water.

Within the Desana system of animal classification, the tapir is anomalous; within their system of kin classification, the tapir becomes an exemplar of problematic human relations. The tension between these two contradictory paradigms gives the tapir metaphor its special power.

Reichel-Dolmatoff's analysis recalls many of the objections made to Douglas's (1975) argument that the human body symbolically functions as an image of society or, as Leach (1964) claims, that systems of classification must be able to produce a graduated scale on the continuum of "more like me to less like me with the self as the focus." The authors in this volume do not take the human body, the self, or society as the loci for the direct motivation of symbolic systems. Rather, the *mis*representation of the cultural as the natural, as Turner has so aptly argued, is the motivating force that transforms problematic relations and experiences into models and emblems. To rephrase the famous phrase of Lévi-Strauss: are some animals better to think with than others? The essences attributed to animals are realized in cultural domains through the metaphoric process, and some animals do seem better to think with than others.

Sapir (1981, 539) in "Leper, Hyena and Blacksmith," concludes that lepers and hyenas are "natural symbols" and are therefore susceptible to symbolic elaboration because they are a priori marked in nature. If we look at the animal species discussed in this volume it becomes clear that many of them are somehow salient and amenable to symbolic elaboration. The salient features of the tapir, the macaw, various insects, and the great cats have been discussed. Let us take another example: in Wilbert's chapter, the blind snake is the paragon of aggressive behavior; she bores her way into the wasp's nest and deposits an egg from the tip of her tongue. Her offspring feed upon the wasp's brood. For a Warao observer, the blind snake's behavior may be interpreted as marked, or somehow aberrant to normal expectations of a category or class of snakes. The salient features of the blind snake are elaborated upon symbolically, and for the Warao she becomes the axis of the House of Smoke.

If markedness in nature does function to isolate those species whose behaviors and characteristics are somehow different from what is expected, then markedness can only function as a concept in contrast to *un*markedness, the lack of additional or unusual information. I would not state that certain species are a priori marked in nature because I think those species selected for the most elaboration due to their saliency contrast to other species selected due to their *lack* of saliency. The latter may function as best examples of categories that the marked species help to define. Perhaps the blind snake as a marked and peripheral member of the category of snakes helps define the category as well as provide the salient features for symbolic elaboration. But in other contexts or syntagmatic chains, snakes may function as the elaborated-upon concept in contrast to something else. It becomes an ethnographic question as to which species are placed on which polar extreme in the contrast between markedness and *un*markedness. Animals selected for markedness and symbolic elaboration will be those animals *experienced* as anomalous. Another problem with a priori designations of natural symbols is that an anomaly in one culture may not be so in another. The tapir is an important food animal for a number of South American tropical forest cultures.[5] Whether an animal is considered anomalous appears to depend largely on cultural perception of its attributes.

In many contexts where metaphor prevails, the contrast between marked members and exemplars may be systematic. What is more, when a marked species (i.e., the tapir) functions as a metaphor for a cultural concept (i.e., the father-in-law), it is transformed into a cultural stereotype or exemplar. With this perspective in mind, it would be interesting to ask the Desana to name the best example or prototype of affines. If they were to name father-in-law we could then investigate how the metaphorical link to "tapirness" is central to exemplar designation. In other words, do the attributed marked qualities in nature become the stereotypic qualities in culture? Are there systematic transformations in the passage "from culture to nature"? Does the boundary member of a natural realm become the focal or central member of a cultural realm?

We *Homo sapiens*, as the symbol-using, symbol-making, and symbol-misusing animal (Burke 1966, 6), are fortunate that nature provides so many "good" animals with which to construct our symbolic complexes. As Burke also observed, there are no negatives in nature—culture constructs them. The perceived relationships between marked and unmarked entities or between anomalies and exemplars provide the symbolic material for constructing positive and negative images that keep alive a culture's expression of the problematic relationships and experiences that each generation will face. The *mis*representation of nature provides effective (and affective) means of transmitting these images whereby culturally defined solutions and stereotypes thus continue to be considered "natural."

Toward an Anthropological Theory of Metaphor

During the past decade, anthropology has addressed the question of the role of metaphor in symbolic systems.[6] Ethnographic research is, in large part, a confrontation with the metaphorical processes that occur in a culture (Fernandez 1972). As we search for the underlying structure and meaning of the paradoxes and inconsistencies that we find in all cultures, we are provided the images and contexts with which to build a powerful theory of metaphor. Unlike the literary and philosophical traditions, we are compelled to confront metaphor in diverse cultural contexts: in myths, in rituals, in discourse, and in art. Our texts are performances and activities as well as words.

As mentioned in my introduction, the view of metaphor I find most amenable to the anthropological task is that of Paul Ricoeur (1978). Ricoeur advocates a theory of metaphor that sits on the boundary between a semantic theory of metaphor and a psychological theory of imagination. Theories of metaphor, he states, must take into account imagining and feeling. Imagining, Ricoeur (1978, 148) claims, is *not* to have a mental picture of something but rather to *display relations* in a depicting mode (emphasis mine). Imagination is understood by Ricoeur as the "seeing" that affects the logical distance between entities or categories being connected by the metaphorical process. When a connection is made the semantic distance is reduced. Again, we find movement the key to the metaphorical process.

This new rapprochement runs against previous categorization that resists but, at the same time, yields to the new insight into likeness. What is created, according to Ricoeur, is a kind of semantic proximity in spite of categorical distance. The rapprochement of the two domains is achieved by creating a flow of images that present the new connection. Ricoeur calls this predicative assimilation; things or ideas that were remote now appear close. Ricoeur goes on to say that a specific kind of tension is created by predicative assimilation which retains the previous categorical incompatibility while establishing new compatibility. Thus two images are presented at once; one is intended, and the other is the concrete aspect under which the first is presented.

Ricoeur calls this the *picturing* function of metaphor. The statement "my father-in-law is the tapir" is a good example: fathers-in-law are presented in the concrete imagery of the tapir, and all of the cultural beliefs that surround the animal are projected into the domain of affines and foreigners. A level of tension is retained, however, between the two domains by constantly reaffirming the similarities and differences between them. In all of the examples set forth in this volume we see that this is the case. The two domains, animal and human, preserve their remoteness while establishing proximity through the establishment of new connections. The metaphorical process moves the natural and the cultural closer semantically while retaining categorical distance. Depending on the contexts or on the syntagmatic chains constructed in the performance of myths or rituals, either proximity or distance between nature and culture can be emphasized; hence my image of movement "From Culture to Nature and Back Again."

Several models of tropes consider interactive metaphors as the most productive (see Black 1979). These models generally follow the work of Richards (1936), who developed the terms *tenor* and *vehicle* for the two participating terms in metaphors. Psychologists Pavio (1979, 167) and Ortony (1979, 193) have suggested that concrete vehicles provide rapid access to information-rich images. Ortony goes even further and suggests that concrete vehicles have more salient "features" associated with them than abstract tenors. For example, tapirs are more salient than fathers-in-law, jaguars more so than fathers, and bears more so than adolescent boys. But, if we take an anthropological perspective on the issue we see that in many contexts the more abstract entity—the tenor—provides images that affect our concepts of the more concrete vehicle. When the metaphorical link is established between tapirs and fathers-in-law, then the tapir takes on some "father-in-lawness" as well. Tapirs are referred to as the "old man of the forest." Likewise, Bororo men are macaws and Inca men are pumas. Courting bachelors are robber bees. Which is the tenor and which is the vehicle? The myths and rituals of the South American cultures discussed in this volume illustrate what Ricoeur calls the metaphoric process. They also illustrate Ricoeur's notion of imagining in a depicting mode as a set of relations. They have depicted these relations in a reversible fashion. The notion of vehicle and tenor does not apply.

The final step of the metaphorical process as described by Ricoeur is on the level of feeling or "internalized thoughts." When the new connections are grasped, a moment of negativity prevails, and the new connection is accompanied by ideas of what the entity being metaphorically imagined is *not*. In other words, tapirs (and fathers-in-law) are contrasted to what they are not: boys to men, macaws to jaguars, pumas to bears, and so forth. Thus the power of "world-making," which is so important to the metaphorical process, opens the doors to strings of images of likes and unlikes made possible by the suspension (*epoché*) of direct references (Ricoeur 1978). Inasmuch as the metaphorical process that we are considering concerns those animal images that depict transitions along the life cycle, we find that the level of feeling is enhanced even more so by direct emotional experiences generated through ritual participation or identification with the experiences of a mythic character. For examples, think of the ear-piercing initiation of young Inca boys accompanied by six days of constant drumming, or the Kayapó boy stranded in his treetop nest unable to descend to the ground and adult status. Moreover, I would argue that the translation of sensory codes across modalities converge on the individual and cause heightened emotional responses. Fernandez (1972, 43), noting that emotion and feeling are important to metaphor, asks whether there might not be a structure to sentiment. I would answer that most certainly there must be a structure to sentiment which is articulated with cognitive aspects of the metaphoric process through the production of iconicity and synesthesia.

As Boon (1982, 230) observes, "cultures are more than just empirically comparable: they are intrinsically comparative." The most powerful moments of internal comparisons are those moments of negativity when a new connection is accompanied by images or "picturings" of what a concept is not; pumas/bears, adult men/adolescent boys, macaws/jaguars, frigate bird/swallow-tailed kite, and mother-of-honey/Bahana shaman all conjure up chains of images that are sustained by the suspension (*epoché*) of direct reference. As Boon further observes, all cultures have their own comparative and contrastive operations built in (their own "/" built in). The productivity of ambiguity is realized as the rituals and myths are performed because of the polysemous and multileveled nature of the performances. Visual metaphors can contradict or reinforce auditory ones; the sound of Desana sacred trumpets, the stolen voice of the tapir, iconically represents the prowess of the sexually excessive animal/father-in-law. By stealing his voice/trumpet, the Desana culturally channel sexual excess to productive means, the trumpets cause pollen to fall and thus fertilize plants. The tapir/father-in-law is left with a weak voice; his unbridled sexual prowess is not only constrained, it is culturally appropriated.

Iconicity (see Becker and Becker 1981)[7] of expressive forms can be found in all of the essays. I will use the more graphic examples from Wilbert's analysis to illustrate further how the metaphorical process facilitates internal comparisons in Warao culture. The frigate and the swallow-tailed kite embody the *essence* of sexual symbolism in the culture. As I discuss the specific chain of metaphorical links, I hope the reader is struck as I am by how much easier it is to think about the bundle of meanings basic to the Warao's conceptualization of sex and reproduction if we think and talk the metaphorical language of raptorial "birdiness" that expresses the *essence* of the frigate and the kite, which in turn maintains a tension with the *essence* of sexual conjunction for humans. *Epoché* suspends direct reference.

In the myth the swallow-tailed kite's/hunter's/shaman's seizure-like state/copulatory excitment is cured by the frigate/mother-of-seizures/mother-of-honey. The frigate's mating behavior is accompanied by clamorous rattling as the male clacks his long beak and puffs out his "chest." These composite images are the Warao notion of the "essence" of maleness which is compared to the "essence" of femaleness: the frigate, who is also a competitive raptor, but who has the power to release males from their seizurelike state with the gift of honey/sex.

It should be clear that evoking the image of the two birds, kite/ male and frigate/female, with their bundles of associative images is more productive cognitively and, most important, more productive symbolically because the ambiguity is left intact. The tension between the two raptorial birds iconically presented as metaphors for the problematic relations between men and women is easy to think about in animal imagery. Many other examples could be given from Wilbert's analysis: the world axis with its scrotal appendage of the Cosmic Egg as visually iconic with the honey-wasp nest and the testis (both referred to as *ono*), the calabash, and the ceremonial rattle are only a few of the visual icon forms found in Warao symbolism. All of these reinforce the point that Worth (1979) made about visual metaphors as caricatures for systemic analogies. Moreover, these analogies across domains promote a heightened sense of emotion. The emotional and the intellectual operate together to allow the individual to "see" new connections imaginatively and to "feel" these connections between the cultural and natural worlds poetically.[8] Thus, the metaphoric process moves the individual along the path of the life cycle pausing in a state of suspended direct reference or *epoché* as each point of transition is "pictured and internalized as natural." The process is enhanced by iconicity and synesthesia whereby analogies or synthetic essences are created across sensory domains; visual experiences are linked to auditory, tactile, and even olfactory experiences to create stereotypes and emblems that provide models for the individual's journey.

FINAL REFLECTIONS: MOVEMENT AND THE METAPHORIC PROCESS

I have drawn on the essays in this volume to call attention to the relationship between the movement of the individual through life and the metaphoric process. This is a perspective similar to that taken by Fernandez (1972). I have also drawn on Burke (1966) and Ricoeur (1978) and others in philosophy and literary criticism as well as such diverse disciplines as ethnomusicology and developmental psychology in order to capture a glimpse of the complexity that the individual experiences in moving through the major transitions of life. Fernandez, in a moment of reflection states that: "In the privacy of our experience we are usually not sure who we really are. A metaphor thrust upon us often enough as a model can become compelling" (1972, 54).

In the South American cultures we have before us, a number of compelling metaphors have been discussed. I have described them as images carved in the guideposts along the journey of the life cycle. I see these metaphoric models of culturally valued stereotypes as being especially salient at the transition points along the path from birth to childhood, then the transition into adolescence, next the move into adulthood, and finally old age and death. I have drawn on materials in this volume to illustrate the metaphoric process and the use of animal imagery at the transition from adolescence to adulthood. It would be informative to examine the various metaphoric images used to move males and females along the life course in any given culture. Doing so would lay bare the culture's values and systems of coherence that directly motivate the metaphoric process. Looking at the moments of suspended direct reference and suspended sentiment would allow a window onto the inner mechanisms of the movement through life stages defined by metaphoric imagery.

The brief comparative examination of the moments of transition from adolesence to adulthood in the South American cultures under discussion lead me to offer the following concluding reflections. Even though several differences are striking, two similarities are even more salient. I will first discuss a few of the differences. The most obvious is the diversity of animal images for the same life experience: moving from the status of adolescent to that of socially recognized adult male. In addition, transition is symbolized in the tropical forest cultures by the acquisition of the tokens and emblems of adult status. In the Kayapó myth, for example, adult male tokens (fire, bow and arrows) are augmented by the acquisition of the symbol of female reproductivity (cotton string). For the Quechua agriculturalists the transition is more gradual and less secure. The passage from unsocialized (bear) to reproductive male (fox) remains fraught with the paradoxes of life's realities during that stage of social development. It seems as if uncertainties predominate and the dilemma of young adulthood is embodied in the metaphoric model of the fox. Adulthood is not achieved until reproductive and productive success is assured. For the highland cultures the movement along a temporal dimension appears to be socially defined by the concerns of the society or the state and, therefore, the caution in deferring adult status may be understandable on those grounds. For the forest cultures, the temporal dimension can be called "household time": the individual moves along the life cycle in regard to the developmental cycle of the household. Nevertheless, two similarities loom large. For both types of cultures, the fundamental by-products of the movement of the individual (always male in the examples discussed) along the life cycle by the metaphoric process are (a) the reproduction of society and (b) productivity (agriculture and/or hunting). The ideal "naturalized" models of newly defined adulthood ensure that reproduction and production continue. Ironically, the human is thereby "domesticated" by culturally constructed animal metaphors. As generation after generation experience the moving forces of the metaphoric process, the tension between culture and nature expands and contracts allowing the negative reflection of culture that is afforded by nature to be realized. This dynamic process is the key to the promise of social (re)production.

NOTES

1. I have profited greatly from the comments and criticisms of a number of my colleagues who have read this manuscript in its numerous manifestations. I wish to thank the following: Catherine Allen, James Boon, David Holmberg, Kathryn March, Jenny Robertson, and Andraŝ Sandor for their comments. Of course, none of these individuals is responsible for the interpretations presented here; in point of fact, we have had lively discussions and thus the dialogue has already begun. Members of my graduate seminar on Cognition and Classification have been especially helpful. I thank Chris Franquemont, Sharon McCoy, Jorge Recharte, Roy Reese, and Mike Thomas. I would like to thank Bruce Mannheim for suggesting the various articles in ethnomusicology that have provided key insights. Barbara Koslowski brought to my attention the Armstrong, Gleitman, and Gleitman article while it was in press. I must thank Terry Turner for his careful reading of an earlier draft. Finally, I want to thank Gary Urton for his comments, suggestions, and patience in seeing this volume to completion.

2. The gender of the primordial snake in the House of Smoke is somewhat problematic. One solution would be to entertain the possibility of dual-gender symbolism as the snake *moves* from the underworld to the upperworld. In fact, one notices the relative lack of sensitivity to the analysis of gender in animal metaphors. Turner notes that the myth he analyzes is directed toward young males. Zuidema and Urton mention scant hints of female animal imagery. Zuidema says that during the harvest rituals young women wore the puma skins impersonating *pachamama suyrumama*. Urton mentions the female puma who is equated with the social position of grand-

mother and *comadre*. Only Reichel-Dolmatoff and Wilbert include numerous images for native metaphors of copulation and activities associated with sex. And only Wilbert carries his analyses to considerations of gender in his conclusion. One wonders if the omission of gender rests with the authors or with the native South American cultures under discussion.

3. Recent investigations in psychology, especially the work of Eleanor Rosch and her associate (1975, 1978a, 1978b, 1975 with Mervis), have argued that human beings categorize objects in the world in terms of prototypes and family resemblances. Prototypes are those members of a category that most reflect the redundancy structure of the category as a whole (Rosch et al. 1975, 105–6). Prototypes maximize the clusters constituting a category, such as size, shape, color and such behavioral characteristics as mating and eating habits. Prototypes have the least amount of overlap with other categories and, therefore, serve as the standard, or best examples, with which to compare potential members. Rosch (1978a, 33) has argued that inseparable from the attributes of natural objects are the motor patterns and functions that characterize the ways in which humans habitually use or interact with them. In similar fashion, Hunn (1982) proposes that taxa have "activity signatures" defined by the uses, actions, and activities that humans engage in when interacting with the taxa. Hunn has demonstrated empirically the validity of the notion of "activity signatures" for taxa. He has developed the concept of the "natural core model" of folk taxonomy based on the practically motivated reasoning developed through use, interaction, and intimate knowledge of the natural world. His concept of "natural core model" is very similar to Rosch's notion of prototype and basic categories. Hunn's functionalist argument was anticipated by Firth (1966).

Rosch claims that the concept of prototype is a convenient grammatical fiction. In natural language categories there are *degrees* of prototypicality. We might think of categories as perceptual spaces with the best examples of the members of the category clustered in the center. For example, taken together, the average shapes of these members, the average size and so forth, along with the motor patterns and activities humans engage in when interacting with them, define prototypicality. Excellent criticisms of prototypicality theory can be found in Armstrong, Gleitman, and Gleitman (in press).

4. In a recent public lecture entitled "Seeing and Knowing" (Cornell University, October 24, 1984), Ullric Neisser argued that young children begin sorting out their perceptual world assuming that *inner essences* and intrinsic qualities of living things are permanent and form the bases for categorization. As the child grows older she/he must shift her/his bases for categorization in order to partake of scientific knowledge. It is interesting to contemplate the role of the metaphoric process in establishing the child's concepts of inner essences. Might not emotionally charged, complex images of animal metaphors experienced in ritual and mythic performances contribute to the child's notion of intrinsic qualities?

5. For contrasting views on the tapir among tropical forest cultures of South America, see Murphy and Murphy (1974) and the two Hugh-Joneses books (1979).

6. As mentioned in the section on "Totems, Fetishes, and Classification," the debate over the relationship between taboos and classificatory systems has a long history in anthropology. See Douglas (1966, 1972, 1973, 1975), Leach (1964), Bulmer (1967), Tambiah (1969), Beidelman (1975), Levy-Bruhl (1966), and, of course, Lévi-Strauss (1966). See Sapir and Crocker (1977) for a good representation of the current issues in the anthropology of rhetoric. Fernandez (1972, 1974, 1977) has been innovative in exploring the relationship among feelings, experiences, and metaphor. Lakoff and Johnson (1980) have developed the concept of coherence that I apply in this article. The concern for metaphor has a long tradition in anthropology. Consult Sapir's "The Anatomy of Metaphor" in his and Crocker's *The Social Use of Metaphor* (1977) for background reading. Keith Basso (1976) has admirably summarized many of the issues and has provided a dialogical (D. Tedlock 1983) perspective on how to study metaphor production and comprehension.

7. Ethnomusicology has recently developed methods and theories that provide models, other than linguistic ones, to explain metaphor and symbolism. Becker and Becker's (1981) illustration of iconicity of form between Balinese music and time is one such model. Feld (1981, 1982), Roseman (1984), and Seeger (1979) are excellent examples. B. Tedlock's (1982) discussion of sound texture and metaphor is especially exciting.

8. The surrealist painter-philosopher Magritte explored the world of poetic analogies in form and in language and along with many artists of the vanguard movement in Europe in the 1920s and 1930s concluded that ambiguity allows one to discover what Magritte called "unborn realities." See Noel (1977) and Foucault (1982) for further discussion. I would like to acknowledge Mercedez Lopez-Baralt and Jorge Recharte for independently making the connection between the productivity of metaphor and ambiguity in modern art and the metaphoric process in native cultures. The suspension of direct reference (*epoché*) of Ricoeur seems to apply neatly to Magritte's notion of the discovery of "unborn realities." Both the metaphoric process and the artistic discovery operate on cognitive and emotional levels for the perceiving individual; that is what gives both their power.

REFERENCES

Armstrong, Sharon Lee, L. R. Gleitman, and H. Gleitman
    n.d.   What some concepts might not be. *Cognition*. In press.
Basso, Keith
    1976   "Wise words" of the Western Apache: Metaphor and semantic theory. In *Meaning in anthropology*, ed. K. Basso and N. Selby, 93–121. Albuquerque: University of New Mexico Press.

Becker, Judith, and Alton Becker
    1981   A musical icon: Power and meaning in Javanese gamelan music. In *The sign in music and literature*, ed. W. Steiner. Austin: University of Texas Press.
Beidelman, T. O.
    1975   Ambiguous animals: Two theriomorphic metaphors in Kaguru folklore. *Africa* 45(2):183–200.
Black, Max
    1962   *Models and metaphors*. Ithaca: Cornell University Press.
    1979   More about metaphors. In *Metaphor and thought*, ed. Andrew Ortony, 19–45. Cambridge: Cambridge University Press.
Bulmer, Ralph
    1967   Why is the cassowary not a bird? A problem of zoological taxonomy among the Karam of the New Guinea highlands. *Man* (n.s.) 2:5–25.
Boon, James A.
    1972   *From symbolism to structuralism: Lévi-Strauss in a literary tradition*. New York: Harper Torchbook.
    1982   *Other tribes, other scribes: Symbolic anthropology in the comparative study of cultures, histories, religions, and texts*. Cambridge: University of Cambridge Press.
Burke, Kenneth
    1966   *Language as symbolic action*. Berkeley: University of California Press.
Dougherty, J. W. D., and James W. Fernandez
    1981   Introduction. In *Symbolism and cognition*. Special issue of *American Ethnologist* 8(3):413–21.
Douglas, Mary
    1966   *Purity and danger*. London: Routledge and Kegan Paul.
    1972   Deciphering a meal. *Daedalus: Journal of the American Academy of Arts and Sciences* 101(1):61–81.
    1973   *Natural symbols: Exploration in cosmology*. New York: Vintage Books.
    1975   Do dogs laugh? In *Implicit meanings: A cross-cultural approach to body symbolism*. London and Boston: Routledge and Kegan Paul.
Feld, Steven
    1981   Flow like a waterfall: Metaphors of Kaluli musical theory. *Yearbook of traditional music* 13:22–47.
    1982   In the form of a bird: Kaluli aesthetics. In *Sound and sentiment*, 217–38. Philadelphia: University of Pennsylvania Press.
Fernandez, James W.
    1972   Persuasions and performance: Of the beast in every body and metaphors of every man. *Daedalus: Journal of the American Academy of Arts and Sciences* 101(1):39–60.
    1974   The mission of metaphor in expressive culture. *Current anthropology* 15(2):119–45.
    1977   The performance of ritual metaphors. In *The social use of metaphor*, ed. J. D. Sapir and J. C. Crocker, 100–31. Philadelphia: University of Pennsylvania Press.
Firth, Raymond
    1966   Twins, birds and vegetables: Problems of identification in primitive religious thought. *Man* (n.s.) 1:1–17.

Foucault, Michel
    1982   *This is not a pipe*. Berkeley: University of California Books.
Hugh-Jones, Christine
    1979   *From the Milk River: Spatial and temporal processes in northwest Amazonia*. Cambridge: Cambridge University Press.
Hugh-Jones, Steven
    1979   *The palm and the Pleiades: Initiation and cosmology in northwest Amazonia*. Cambridge: Cambridge University Press.
Hunn, Eugene
    1982   The utilization factor in folk biological classification. *American Anthropologist* 84(4):830–47.
Lakoff, George, and Mark Johnson
    1980   *Metaphors we live by*. Chicago: University of Chicago Press.
Leach, Edmund R.
    1964   Anthropological aspects of language: Animal categories and verbal abuse. In *New directions in the study of language*, ed. Eric H. Lenneberg, 23–63. Cambridge: MIT Press.
Lévi-Strauss, Claude
    1963   *Totemism*. Boston: Beacon Press.
    1966   *The savage mind* (1962). Chicago: University of Chicago Press.
    1969   *The raw and the cooked* (1964). New York: Harper and Row.
    1974   *From honey to ashes* (1966). New York: Harper and Row.
Levy-Bruhl, Lucien
    1966   *How natives think*. New York: Washington Square Press.
Lounsbury, Floyd G.
    1959   Similarity and contiguity relations in language and culture. In *Report of the Tenth Annual Round Table Meeting on Linguistics and Language Studies*, ed. Richard Harrell, 123–38. Georgetown University Institute of Languages and Linguistics, Monograph no. 12. Washington, D.C.
Murphy, Yolanda, and Robert F. Murphy
    1974   *Women of the forest*. New York: Columbia University Press.
Nocl, Bernard
    1977   *Magritte*. New York: Crown Publishers.
Ortony, Andrew
    1979   The role of similarity in similes and metaphors. In *Metaphor and thought*, ed. Andrew Ortony, 186–201. Cambridge: Cambridge University Press.
Ortner, Sherry B.
    1973   On key symbols. *American Anthropologist* 75:1338–46.
Osgood, Charles, W. H. May, and M. S. Miron
    1975   *Cross-cultural universals of affective meaning*. Urbana: University of Illinois Press.
Pavio, Allan
    1979   Psychological processes in the comprehension of metaphor. In *Metaphor and thought*, ed. Andrew Ortony, 150–71. Cambridge: Cambridge University Press.
Randall, Robert A.
    1976   How tall is a taxonomic tree? Some evidence for dwarfism. *American Ethnologist* 3(3):543–53.

Reichel-Dolmatoff, Gerardo
  1971   *Amazonian cosmos: The sexual and religious symbolism of the Tukano Indians.*
          Chicago: University of Chicago Press.
  1975   *The Shaman and the jaguar: A study of narcotic drugs among the Indians of
          Colombia.* Philadelphia: Temple University Press.
  1978   Desana animal categories, food restrictions, and the concept of color
          energies. *Journal of Latin American Lore* 4(2):243–91.
Richards, I. A.
  1936   *The philosophy of rhetoric.* London: Oxford University Press.
Ricoeur, Paul
  1978   The metaphorical process as cognition, imagination, and feeling. In
          On metaphor, ed. Sheldon Sacks, 141–58. Chicago: University of
          Chicago Press.
Rosch, Eleanor
  1975   Cognitive representations of semantic categories. *Journal of Experimen-
          tal Psychology* 104(3):192–233.
  1978a   Human categorization. In *Studies in cross-cultural psychology,* ed. N.
          Warren, 1:1–49. New York: Academic Press.
  1978b   Principles of categorization. In *Cognition and Categorization,* ed. E.
          Rosch and B. B. Lloyd. Hillsdale, N.J.: Laurence Erlbaum Assoc.
Rosch, Eleanor, and Carolyn B. Mervis
  1975   Family resemblance: Studies in the internal structure of categories.
          Cognitive Psychology 7:573–605.
Rosch, Eleanor, C. B. Mervis, W. Gray, D. Johnson, and P. Boyes-Braem
  1975   *Basic objects in natural categories.* Working Paper, no. 43. Berkeley:
          University of California Language Behavior Research Laboratory.
Roseman, Marina
  1984   The social structuring of sound: An example from the Temiar of
          peninsular Malaysia. *Ethnomusicology* 28(3):411–45.
Sapir, J. David
  1981   Leper, hyena and blacksmith in Kujamaat Diola thought. *American
          Anthropologist* 8(3):526–43.
Sapir, J. D., and J. C. Crocker
  1977   *The social use of metaphor.* Philadelphia: University of Pennsylvania
          Press.
Searl, John R.
  1979   Metaphor. In *Metaphor and thought,* ed. Andrew Ortony, 19–45. Cam-
          bridge: Cambridge University Press.
Seeger, Anthony
  1979   What can we learn when they sing? Vocal games of Suya Indians of
          central Brazil. *Ethnomusicology* 23(3):373–94.
Tambiah, S. J.
  1969   Animals are good to think about and good to prohibit. *Ethnology*
          8:423–59.
Tedlock, Barbara
  1982   Sound texture and metaphor in Quiche Maya ritual language. *Current
          Anthropology* 23(3):269–72.
Tedlock, Dennis
  1983   *The spoken word and the work of interpretation.* Philadelphia: University of
          Pennsylvania Press.

Turner, Terence S.
   1977   Narrative structure and mythopoesis: A critique and reformulation of
             structuralist concepts of myth, narrative and poetics. *Arethusa* 10(1):
             103–63.
Worth, Sol
   1979   Seeing metaphor as caricature. *New Literary History* 6:195–209.

INDEX

Abduction: of women, 109, 113, 131, 139; of women and children, 146

Acapana, 217

Adolescence, 76, 260, 264, 265, 267, 270, 272, 273, 286, 287, 302, 306

Adolescent, 82

Adoption, 72, 73

Adultery, 132

Adulthood: and *ayllu* membership, 264, 265; identified by role of "hunting companion," 77, 104; and reproduction, 252, 286; role of membership in men's association in, 90; as stage of life cycle, 273, 306; symbolized by weapons, 84; transition to (Quechua), 260, 289; transition to, represented in Kayapó myth, 59, 64, 65, 67, 71, 81, 84, 89, 90, 91, 105

Affine, 40, 67, 104, 115, 158, 162, 169, 300, 302. *See also* Brother-in-law; Daughter-in-law; Father-in-law; Mother-in-law; Sister's husband; Son-in-law; Wife's brother

Age class, 60. *See also* Age grade

Age grade, 262, 273, 281n.5. *See also* Age class

Aging, 37

Agouti, 110, 136, 137

Agouti People, 137

Agriculture, 196, 274, 290; origin of, 262

Altomisayoq, 255

Amaru, 183, 228, 230, 231

Ambiguity, 94, 304

Anaconda, 63, 131, 179

Anaconda People, 131

Anahuarque, 194

Ancestor: Bororo beliefs about, 20, 25, 26; in Inca ritual, 194, 201, 204, 209, 214, 220; Tukano beliefs about, 108, 115, 135, 137, 139

Animal, 9, 70, 94, 104, 122, 138, 139, 274, 276, 281; ancestral, 139; anomalous, 295, 297; domesticated, 32, 252, 255; killing of, 83; nondomesticated, 252; odor classification of, 125; symbolic value of, 109

Anomaly, 26, 295, 297, 300, 301

Antler, 130, 131

Apaporis, 110

Aphrodisiac, 111

Apiary, 122, 155

Apu, 258, 259, 260, 261, 262, 263, 274

Apu Cañachuay, 228, 242

Apu Cerratachan, 263

Apurimac River, 221, 251

Apu Tinya, 230

Arara, 14. *See also* Macaw; Parakeet; Parrot

Ararihua, 187, 193, 199, 241, 264, 265, 266, 267, 281n.4

Arawak, 124, 130, 131, 132, 134, 136, 138, 140

Archer, 153, 154

Armadillo, 20, 21, 22, 25, 26, 110, 136, 137

Armadillo People, 137

Armadillo Spirit, 20, 21

Armadillo Women, 137

Aroe, 19, 20, 28, 37, 38, 39; characteris-

Puna, 258, 263
Pururauca, 204, 211, 212, 217, 240, 244n.22
Pututu, 276. *See also* Trumpet
Pyramid. *See* Quartz pyramid

Quartz pebble, 148, 150, 154
Quartz pyramid, 148, 174–77
Quechua, 251, 288, 306
Quero. See Beaker

Rain, 37, 187, 193, 199, 209, 214, 222, 228, 241, 261, 291
Rainbow, 29, 183, 192
Rainy season, 37, 231, 255, 261
Rape, 132, 139, 140
Rat, 231
Rattle: Bororo, 21, 34; Tukano deer-hoof, 142n.14; Inca 187, 216; Warao, 156 fig.2; in Warao mythology, 150, 153, 155, 158; Warao symbolism of, 167, 172, 173, 174, 179, 304
Raw, 74, 86, 91, 95, 96, 193
Reciprocity, 88, 115
Red, 29
Red Faces, 146
Red Macaw Spirit, 20
Reincarnation, 31
Replica, 82, 84, 91, 92, 93, 101, 103
Reproduction, 37, 167, 259, 267, 304, 306
Residence, 61, 253; matri-uxorilocal, 60; uxorilocal, 18, 38, 39, 71, 115, 135, 145, 162, 169; virilocal, 107, 131, 137, 169
Resin, 86
Rhea, 30
Río Negro, 110
Rite of passage, 34, 81, 197, 227, 240
Ritual, 34, 52, 147, 184, 218, 219, 240, 304
River, 28, 241; of blood, 271; conflu-ence of, 185, 220; in Inca ritual, 214, 219, 220, 221, 222, 223, 227; in Kayapó myth, 58, 81
River Crab People, 150
Rodent, 136, 140
Rope-bridge, 147, 160, 165

Sacrifice, 195, 207, 211, 219, 220, 222
Sacsayhuaman, 185, 234, 236
Sahuasiray Pitusiray, 209, 230
Salt, 223
Salt lick, 118
San Andrés, 261
San Juan, 276
Sapi, 215, 236, 237
Sayhuite, 226
Season, 37; dry, 231; rainy, 231, 255, 261
Seed, 279
Seizure, 150, 169–70
Seizures, Mother of, 167
Serpent, 148, 149, 178, 179, 183, 187, 215, 225, 228, 230, 234, 294; four-headed, 164. *See also* Plumed ser-pent; Snake
Servant, 108
Servinakuy, 253
Sex, 112, 158, 170
Sexuality, 292, 294, 295, 298
Shadow, 56, 70
Shaman: Bororo, 29; *bahana* (Warao), 154, 164, 166; Tukano, 114, 118, 140; in Tukano myth, 108; relation-ship of Tukano, with animals, 119–23, 140
Shape, 292
Sib, 107, 134, 136, 137, 138
Sibling, 40, 113
Sickness, 221. *See also* Illness
Sign, 52
Silver, 196
Sin, 193, 207
Singer, 108
Sister, 5, 59, 88, 130, 135
Sister exchange, 107, 109, 114
Sister's husband, 55, 56, 61, 63, 67, 68, 69, 70, 73, 80, 104
Sister's son, 22
Situa, 221
Skin, 35; of fox, 186, 193, 241, 265, 266, 267; of lion, 204; of potato, 261; of puma, 184, 185, 187, 192, 194, 201, 212, 218, 224, 225, 231, 241, 242; of tapir, 116
"Skin payment," 158
Skunk, 192
Sky, 65, 262
Slavery, 146